Bacchylides: The Victory Poems

BACCHYLIDES

The Victory Poems

Translated with Introduction
and Commentary by

Arthur McDevitt

Bristol Classical Press

First published in 2009 by
Bristol Classical Press, an imprint of
Gerald Duckworth & Co. Ltd.
90-93 Cowcross Street, London EC1M 6BF
Tel: 020 7490 7300
Fax: 020 7490 0080
info@duckworth-publishers.co.uk
www.ducknet.co.uk

A catalogue record for this book is available
from the British Library

ISBN 978 1 85399 721 1

Illustration sources

Fig. 1: Kapon Editions, Athens, and Ms Maria Kataga;
Fig. 2: Alison Frantz; Figs 3 and 4: Kapon Editions, Athens;
Figs 5, 9 and 10: Arthur McDevitt; Fig. 6: Archaeological Museum,
Delphi; Fig. 7: British Museum, London; Fig. 8: James Renshaw,
www.thesewerethegreeks.com

Typeset by Ray Davies

Contents

Preface

This book was born of the belief that the large, and growing, number of students whose contact with ancient Greek culture is made through translations, come to the subject with very little prior knowledge of the world of ancient Greece, and frequently do not have easy access to the kind of information that they might want or need to appreciate the literature more fully. There are many excellent translations available, but full and extensive commentaries accessible to these non-language students are much fewer. I have therefore tried to fill this gap, at least for Bacchylides, by providing a detailed commentary, with as much background and explanatory information as possible, in the hope of enhancing the student's understanding and appreciation of these charming poems. At the same time, 'nothing arises from nothing', as Lucretius said, and I have therefore tried also to contextualize the work of Bacchylides within the spectrum of Greek literary history. In particular, I have frequently pointed out Bacchylides' debt to, as well as his independence from, Homer, especially in regard to his creative treatment of the mythological material.

The translation is based on the text established by Prof. Herwig Maehler and published by him in volume 1 of his two-volume edition of the victory poems: *Die Lieder des Bakchylides: Die Siegeslieder* (Leiden, E.J. Brill, 1982). Although the book is aimed primarily at non-language students, my own interest in the language will be evident throughout, and I have thought it worthwhile to include discussion of linguistic matters from time to time, where I believe that this can enhance appreciation of the poem, and, perhaps, stimulate further interest in the language. Here again I have frequently drawn attention to Bacchylides' debt to Homer (a debt shared by all ancient Greek writers) as well as to his originality in the creation and use of poetic vocabulary.

Finally, I would like to offer my sincere thanks to Professor Pat Easterling, of Newnham College, Cambridge, for her unfailing encouragement, help and support. Professor Easterling was kind enough to read a first draft of the book, which has been much improved by her helpful comments. She is not, of course, to be held responsible for the faults which remain.

Introduction

In 452 BC, almost two and a half thousand years ago, a young man called Lachon, from the little island of Ceos just off the east coast of Greece, won the under-eighteen 200-metre race at the Olympic Games. And who today would know the name of Lachon if he had not won this splendid victory? Some of those whose names we know as winners at the Olympic and other ancient Games were, it is true, kings and aristocrats, princes and politicians – people like Hieron, king of Syracuse, Theron of Akragas and Megakles from Athens – their names known to us already from the broad sweep of history. But the great majority were not. They were 'ordinary' people, men and boys from families often without any particular distinction of wealth or position, often living in undistinguished communities which played no great part in the affairs of Greece. But they had one thing in common – the drive to achieve undying fame, and with their victory in the great Games they achieved it.

The Games in ancient Greece were associated from the beginning with religious festivals, and remained so throughout their history. The first athletic competition was introduced into the festival of Zeus at Olympia – the traditional date is 776 BC – and over the following centuries the Olympic Games grew in scope and significance, attracting competitors from all over the Greek world. Similarly, the other great festivals – the Pythia, held every four years at Delphi, on the slopes of Mt Parnassos, in honour of Apollo, the Isthmia, in honour of Poseidon, held every second year in the sanctuary of that god close to the isthmus of Corinth, and the Nemea, honouring Zeus, originally at Nemea in the north-east corner of the Peloponnese, but for most of its history held at Argos – included a variety of athletic, equestrian and musical competitions from their inception. In addition, there were countless local festivals held in small communities all over Greece, and these too, no doubt in imitation of the Olympic and the other major festivals, regularly included Games in their programme. But even as the Games grew in importance, to become the central and most significant feature of the festivals, even when, for example, the Echo Stoa was built in the fourth century BC along the eastern side of the sanctuary at Olympia, thus effectively cutting off the stadium from the sacred enclosure, the close connection between religion and competition was not lost.

Thus the Games were always part of a religious occasion, and participation was a way of honouring the god. No doubt there were many reasons why an individual might decide to compete. The competitive spirit seems to have been central to the Greek national character from the beginning of its recorded history; already in Homer we hear of two fathers who advised their sons 'always to be the best and to surpass the others' (*Iliad* 6.208, 11.782), and the athletes were, on one level at least, giving expression to this impulse. No doubt also many were motivated by the desire to win personal glory, as well as to bring honour and renown to their families and to their native cities. There was also the financial incentive. Many of the regional Games offered prizes of sometimes considerable monetary value (so much so that a class of professional athletes grew up, who spent their time travelling around the festivals), while the winners at the great panhellenic Games, where the prize was a simple wreath to crown the head, were often handsomely rewarded by their home towns on their return, and enjoyed extensive civic privileges. Politics too sometimes played a part. For example, a usurper or tyrant might seek to legitimize his rule by lavish displays of generosity to the gods in their sanctuaries and by taking part in the Games. But underlying all of this, there was the desire to achieve and display that perfection of mind and body which lay at the heart of the Greek ideal. The Greeks did not separate physical training from intellectual activity in their education; each area complemented the other, and the two together constituted the whole man. The Greek gods were conceived and created in the image of man, and in their perfection they represented the ideal to which mortal men might aspire.[1] Thus the quest for physical perfection, in the gymnasia and elsewhere, can be seen as an attempt to approximate to the divine, and it is not too fanciful, I believe, to say that the drive to success in the Games represented, in a sense, the drive to achieve immortality, the drive to become a god.

And that is where the poet comes in. For it was common for the successful athlete to commission a poet to compose a song (sometimes more than one) in praise of his victory. For the victory alone was not enough, and the question with which we began should rather be: who today would know the name of Lachon if Bacchylides had not written a poem in honour of his great success? The victor commissioned the poem, and the poet immortalized the achievement. There was thus a kind of symbiotic relationship between victor and poet, between victory and poem. The victory was always seen as the gift of the god to the victor; it elevated the successful athlete to the realm of the divine, while the poet, servant of the Muses, was the intermediary between god and man, serving to spread abroad the victor's fame among men. The poets themselves were well aware of this crucial aspect of their role and the poems are replete with allusions to it: 'splendid success, when it wins real praise, is treasured on high among the gods' (Bacchylides 9.82-4); 'far-shining Excellence ... rich in renown enduring, spreads unfailing, over the earth and the restless sea' (Bacchylides 13.175-81). At the end of Ode 1 Bacchylides claimed: 'Excel-

Fig. 1. Head of Apollo, detail from the west pediment of
the temple of Zeus, Olympia.

lence ... when brought to its proper end, leaves for a man, even when he is
dead, an enviable monument of renown' (1.181-4). And he was right. Had
Lachon not won, his name would certainly have perished with his body,
'hidden in the lightless veil of night' (Bacchylides 13.176-7), but as it is, his
fame lives on forever.

Competition and the Greeks

The ancient Greeks, as is well known, were a very competitive people;
indeed competition was one of the most significant and pervasive aspects
of the society and culture as a whole. Probably the best-known illustration
of this, apart from the athletic competition of the Games themselves, is to
be seen in the Greek drama. Every year in Athens, at the festivals of the
Great, or City, Dionysia, and the Lenaia, tragedies and comedies were

presented by selected authors in competition for a prize; similar contests were held at the Rural Dionysia, and very probably at the lesser regional and local festivals also. At the other major festival in Athens, the Great Panathenaia, established by the tyrant Peisistratos in 566 BC and held every four years in honour of the city's patron goddess Athena, there was a competition for the rhapsodic recitation of Homer. (Indeed it was once orthodoxy in Homeric scholarship to credit Peisistratos with the establishment of a coherent text of the Homeric poems.) The Panathenaia also included competitions for dancing, as well as musical events for kithara and aulos, both as solo instruments and as accompaniment for song. (The kithara was a type of lyre; for the aulos – a woodwind instrument often misleadingly translated 'flute' – see the commentary on Ode 2.12). So too the great Pythian Games at Delphi in honour of Apollo had included musical contests from the beginning, while events for trumpeters and heralds were added to the programme for the Olympic Games in 396 BC. Elsewhere, and from various periods, there is inscriptional and other evidence for a wide variety of competition.[2]

This competitive spirit, as far as we can tell, seems to have been unique to the Greeks among contemporary cultures in the Mediterranean. There is, for example, no compelling evidence to suggest that the Phoenicians engaged in athletics early enough to have influenced the Greeks, nor that the sporting or athletic activities evident on Egyptian wall-paintings and tomb reliefs were competitive in the Greek manner.[3] Even the Minoans in Crete, whose culture was overtaken by the Mycenean Greeks from the mainland, do not seem to have had much influence on the nature or practice of Greek sport. It is well known, for example, that the Minoans engaged in boxing, but on the famous fresco from Akrotiri on the island of Thera (Santorini) which depicts two boys boxing, the combatants are each wearing a protective glove on the right hand, which is foreign to later Greek practice. Similarly, there is a rhyton (a stone vessel of inverted conical shape, perhaps for sacrificial or ritual use) from Agia Triada in Crete, decorated with several bands of low relief. The rhyton is much restored, but according to Golden[4] two of these bands depict boxers; those shown on the higher of these two bands are wearing protective gear, while those on the lower band are not. If this does indeed relate to competitive sport, it might be thought that the two bands depict, respectively, boxers in training and boxers in competition, but this is mere conjecture. Golden quotes a suggestion that the two bands of relief show two stages in the initiation of young Minoan men.

Perhaps the best-known activity among the Minoans which might be indicative of competitive sport is the spectacular (and, no doubt, highly dangerous) practice of bull-leaping. Frescoes from Knossos, as well as signet rings and other material, show young men grasping a charging bull by the horns and vaulting, with great skill and athleticism, over its back. But the context of this amazing practice is completely unknown. There is

Fig. 2. Statue of Nike, goddess of victory, by Paionios. Olympia, Archaeological Museum.

nothing to suggest that it was indeed a sporting competition; if it was, one might well wonder how the winner was determined. Perhaps, like the boxing, it had some sort of ritual function, but this too remains purely speculative, and we have no clue as to the nature or meaning of any such ritual. It may be, finally, that the bull-leaping was presented simply as a form of public entertainment. (The legend of Theseus and the Minotaur is worth noting in this context. Every year the Athenians were obliged to send seven youths and seven maidens to the palace of Minos in Knossos, to be sacrificed to the Minotaur, a monstrous creature, half-human, half-bull, which lurked at the centre of the labyrinth. This continued until Theseus volunteered to be one of the seven youths; with the help of Ariadne he killed the Minotaur and escaped, thus freeing the Athenians from the payment of this tribute. It seems very likely, on the face of it, that this story is related in some way to the bull-leaping. Perhaps the Minoans began to find it difficult to find volunteers for this entertainment, and were obliged to look further afield. The Athenians may have been sent to Knossos, then, not to be sacrificed to the Mino-taur, but to take part in the bull-leaping – which from their point of view probably amounted to the same thing). There is evidence (e.g. a painted funerary chest from Tanagra in Boeotia of the thirteenth century BC) that the practice of bull-leaping was taken over by the Myceneans on the mainland (along with much else) after their conquest of the Cretan palaces in the mid-fifteenth century, but in any case, bull-leaping, whether as competition or entertainment, did not survive the downfall of Bronze Age culture, and there is no substantial evidence to suggest that later Greek sport owed anything to the Minoans. Chariot-racing, for example, so popular among the Myceneans and later Greeks, was unknown to the Minoans.

On the other hand, if we can believe Homer, the competitive spirit was already alive and well in the aristocratic society of Mycenean Greece. In the two passages from Homer referred to earlier, Glaukos tells how his father Hippolochos sent him off to war with the instruction: 'always to be the best and to surpass the others' (*Iliad* 6.208), and Peleus, we are told, gave the same advice to his son Achilles (*Iliad* 11.782).[5] The context of this advice of course is military, but the drive for supremacy in the more peaceful arts of athletic and equestrian competition is also well attested in the Homeric poems. When the funeral pyre for Patroklos has finally died down, Achilles invites all the Greek heroes to take part in splendid Funeral Games in honour of his dear friend and companion, for whose death he feels responsible. Achilles himself does not take part, but presides over the Games as organizer, arbiter and dispenser of prizes (*Iliad* 23.257f.) The first and most important event – it occupies more than half of the total narrative of the Games – is the chariot-race, won, after some divine intervention, by Diomedes. This is followed by boxing, wrestling, a foot-race out and back around a turning-post, a fight in armour between Aias and Diomedes, which is stopped by Achilles before anyone gets hurt, weight-throwing and archery. The prize for a final event, spear-throwing, is awarded to Agamemnon without contest. Again, in the Odyssey, the Phaiakians amuse themselves and entertain their guest Odysseus with after-dinner Games (*Odyssey* 8.100f.), and there are other references to athletic competition besides. For example, in the course of the Funeral Games for Patroklos, even the aged Nestor, who did not compete, is given a prize after the chariot-race, in recognition of his youthful prowess in the past. This gives him a wonderful opportunity to reminisce, and he relates how once, at the Funeral Games for Amarynkeus, he won every event except, interestingly, the chariot-race, in which he was defeated, unfairly, he claims, by the twin sons of Aktor (*Iliad* 23.629-42).

Thus the idea of competition is deeply embedded in the mythology, which must surely reflect in some way the values and practices of the mainland Greeks of the Bronze Age. Other examples include the story of Pelops, the son of Tantalos, who established himself at Pisa (and in some quarters was credited with the founding of the Olympic Games) after winning as his bride the lovely Hippodameia, by defeating her father Oinomaos in a chariot-race.[6] Similarly, Atalanta swore that she would only marry the man who could defeat her in a foot-race; the story of how this was achieved by Hippomenes (with the help of Venus) is told at length by Ovid (*Metamorphoses* 10.560f.). There are also references to Funeral Games, held, like those described by Homer (see above), to honour a dead hero. Bacchylides himself alludes to what was in fact the standard foundation-myth of the Nemean Games – the Funeral Games held by the Argive heroes at Nemea in honour of the king's infant son Opheltes (see Bacchylides 9.10-12, and intro. to Ode 9).

The descriptions of these Games and contests, and in particular the Games in Homer, may indeed have things to tell us about the history of competitive sport, but there are difficulties. How much can we extrapolate from literary description to historical practice? The Funeral Games for Patroklos, for example, have a clear literary function within the epic. The quarrel between Achilles and Agamemnon which began the poem is echoed and reflected in the resolution of conflict by Achilles during the Games. Achilles has acquired a new level of compassion and understanding, and the Games present the transition from violence to reconciliation, culminating in the ransoming of the body of Hektor. Again, how can we be sure what period the Homeric descriptions reflect? It is widely accepted that the Homeric poems acquired something close to their present form towards the end of the eighth century BC, after a long period of oral composition and transmission, so that the epics probably present a patchwork of reminiscences, covering the many hundreds of years between the end of the Bronze Age and the eighth century. But hard (i.e. non-literary) evidence for athletic activity during this period is scant in the extreme, and in any case, many of the activities and practices described in Homer do not appear in the Games of the post-Homeric era, while others were reintroduced only much later. Thus, when the single event of the stadion-race was made part of the Olympic festival (traditionally in 776 BC) it seems as if the history of athletic competition was beginning all over again.

The festivals and the Games

Four festivals were especially important, and of these the oldest and most prestigious was the festival in honour of Zeus, held every four years at Olympia, in the north-west of the Peloponnese. There is archaeological evidence for a religious cult at Olympia from as early as the eleventh century, and over the following centuries Olympia seems to have developed into a significant focal point for the whole of the surrounding area, centred on the growing importance and prestige of its sanctuary and the cult of Zeus. It was not until 776 BC, however, that an athletic competition was introduced as part of the Olympic festival.[7] The first, and for a long time only, event was the stadion, a foot-race over a single length of the stadium.[8] Thereafter, over the following decades, other athletic and equestrian events were added, including, from 632 BC onwards, various events for boys, and the Olympiad gradually expanded into a spectacular five-day festival, combining religious worship, athletic competition and celebration, which attracted visitors and competitors from all over the Greek world.

The full programme at Olympia, with the date when each event was introduced, was as follows (distances in modern equivalent are of course only approximate):

Stadion	(200 metres)	776 BC
Diaulos	(400 metres)	724 BC

The diaulos was a foot-race over two lengths of the stadium, out and back around a turning-post at the far end. The name, which means 'double pipe', is reminiscent of, and was probably suggested by the standard musical practice of playing two aulos-pipes together. (See note on Ode 2.12.)

Dolichos	(4800 metres ?)	720 BC

A long-distance race (*dolichos* is the Greek for 'long'). There is no certain evidence for its length, but Miller suggests that it covered 24 lengths of the stadium.[9]

Pentathlon	708 BC

As the name suggests, the pentathlon was for all-rounders, involving a combination of five events. These were the discus, long-jump, stadion, javelin and wrestling. It is noteworthy that the discus, the javelin and the long-jump were not part of the Olympic programme as separate events. The order in which these events were contested remains uncertain, although there is general agreement that the wrestling was last of the five. Likewise the manner of determining the winner is unknown, except that success in three of the five events was sufficient for overall victory. But what happened if there was no clear winner after the first four events? If, for example, there were four contestants with one victory each, or one with two and two others with one each? If two athletes had two victories each, were the others eliminated, while these two contested the wrestling? The whole issue is beset with problems; many opinions have been offered, but in the absence of further evidence, we simply do not know the answers.

Pale	(wrestling)	708 BC

Pux	(boxing)	688 BC

There was no time-limit in the boxing. The contest continued without intermission until one contestant submitted, as in the pankration.

Tethrippon	(four-horse chariot)	680 BC

The four-horse chariot-race was probably the most spectacular event in the Games; it was certainly the most dangerous as well as the most prestigious. The expense involved in maintaining and training teams of horses meant that only the richest citizens could enter. We are told that the wealthy Athenian Alcibiades once entered seven teams at Olympia, which took first, second and fourth places (Thucydides 6.16.2). A word of caution: the length of the four-horse chariot-race, as of all the other equestrian events, is unknown, despite the confident assertions made by some scholars. The only real evidence is in Pindar, and that has, I believe, been generally misunderstood. At *Olympian* 3.33 Pindar describes how Herakles was filled with desire to plant olive trees 'around the twelve-times-turned limit of the course (*dromos*) of horses'. Most writers seem to understand this 'limit' to refer only to the turning-post at the far end, which, if turned twelve times, would mean that the full race covered 24 lengths of the hippodrome, and this is indeed what most claim, speaking of 12 'laps' and/or 24 lengths. But why would Herakles want to plant his olive trees only at the far end? Surely Pindar's expression is not so precise; surely he means rather that Herakles wanted to plant the trees all around the hippodrome, including both ends; that is, 'around the course for horses[10] which involves twelve turns'. The meaning must therefore be that the chariot-race covered twelve *lengths* of the hippodrome, not twelve 'laps'.[11] This is borne out especially by Bacchylides 10.25, written for a victory in the *hippios*. The *hippios*-race was unquestionably run over four lengths of the stadium; Bacchylides describes it as 'the course (*dromos*) with four turns' in reference to these four lengths, and Pindar's expression is surely of the same kind. We might compare also Pindar *Olympian* 2.50, referring to victories at the Isthmia and the Pythia 'for the chariots that run twelve courses (*dromoi*)'. A similar expression is used at *Olympian* 6.75: 'for those who drive foremost around the twelfth *dromos*', but this ode is for a victory in the mule chariot-race (*apene*), and may not be relevant. See also note on Ode 10.25.

In the end, however, none of this is very helpful, for we do not know how long the track actually was. No hippodromes have been excavated; that at Olympia was inundated and destroyed by flooding of the river Alpheos in the Middle Ages; at the Pythia the horse-races took place down below, on the plain of Krisa, but exactly where is anyone's guess, while the hippodromes at Nemea and the Isthmus have not yet been discovered.

Pankration	648 BC

The pankration was a particularly brutal form of physical combat, in which nothing was barred except eye-gouging and biting. Victory was achieved when one's opponent either died or submitted.

Keles	(ridden horse-race)	648 BC
Stadion	(for boys)	632 BC
Pale	(for boys)	632 BC
Pentathlon	(for boys)	628 BC

The boys' pentathlon was discontinued immediately after this Olympiad, for unknown reasons.

Pux	(for boys)	616 BC
Hoplitodromos	(race in armour)	520 BC
Apene	(mule chariot-race)	500 BC

Discontinued in 444 BC.

| *Kalpe* | (race for mares) | 496 BC |

According to Pausanias (5.9.2) riders in the *kalpe* jumped off their horses in the last lap and ran alongside, holding the reins. The *kalpe*, like the *apene*, was discontinued in 444 BC.

Sunoris	(two-horse chariot)	408 BC
Salpinktes	(trumpeters)	396 BC
Kerukes	(heralds)	396 BC
Tethrippon	(for foals)	384 BC

The four-horse chariot-race for foals was open to both colts and fillies; the Greek *polos* ('foal') is used for both sexes. The age at which a foal was regarded as becoming an adult horse is unknown.

Sunoris	(for foals)	264 BC
Keles	(for foals)	256 BC
Pankration	(for boys)	200 BC

As at Olympia, so too at Delphi, there is evidence of a religious cult from very early times, but the site seems to have been largely abandoned around 1100 BC. Substantial cult activity does not reappear until the ninth century, when large numbers of bronze male figurines and tripods begin to appear, characteristic of the worship of Apollo and testifying to the arrival and establishment of that god at Delphi.[12] The Homeric Hymn to Apollo relates how the god travelled about the earth looking for a place to found his oracle, until he finally settled on Delphi (Homeric Hymn 3.214f.) and the myth, as usual, reflects a reality. The oracle was at the core of the cult from the beginning. The sanctuary of the god, and his oracle, developed hand in hand, each contributing to the renown of the other, so that Delphi rapidly became one of the most important religious centres in Greece, as individuals, as well as state delegations, came from far and wide to worship the god and seek advice from his oracle.[13]

In the seventh century Delphi came under the control of the Amphictyonic League – a federation of city-states in central Greece – which enhanced its role in the political affairs of Greece still further. After the First Sacred War (600-590 BC) the League decided to reorganize and upgrade Apollo's festival. Hitherto, the only competitive event had been the *kitharodia* (singing to the accompaniment of the kithara); this was retained, but in 586 BC a wide range of musical, athletic and equestrian

Fig. 3. A competitor in the *kitharodia* (singing to the lyre), originally the only event at Delphi. Red-figure amphora by the Berlin painter, 490 BC. New York, Metropolitan Museum of Art.

competition was added to it. The Pythia was thus transformed at a stroke into a five-day festival which took place every four years, and which was now truly worthy of the god whom it honoured and of his great panhellenic sanctuary.[14]

The Isthmian Games took place in a sanctuary located in what is now the modern village of Kyra Vrysi, at the east end of the Corinth Canal, and close to the Isthmus itself. The foundation-myth of the Games involved the infant Melikertes, whose father, king Athamas of Thessaly, drove him and his mother Ino into the sea, where they drowned. The child's body was carried by a dolphin to the Isthmus, where it was found by Sisyphos, the king of Corinth. Sisyphos renamed the child Palaimon, buried him and established Funeral Games in his honour.[15] There are remains in the sanctuary of what may have been a cult-precinct of Melikertes/ Palaimon dating to the late fifth century BC, while in the Roman period (second century AD) a circular open temple was built housing a statue of a dolphin with a child on its back. It is possible that this was the original cult, but if so it continued only in a very subordinate role, supplanted at an early date by worship of the god to whom the sanctuary truly belonged, Poseidon, god of horses and the sea.

The ancient city of Corinth lay only a few kilometres to the west, at the head of the Corinthian Gulf. This strategic geographical position not only allowed Corinth to take charge of the sanctuary, which it controlled from an early date; it enabled the city also to control traffic and trade through the Isthmus, the only land access from northern Greece to the Peloponnese.[16] In addition, Corinth enjoyed direct sea-access to the west through the Gulf. Consequently, from the eighth century onwards, the city developed into the most important sea-going and mercantile power in Greece, as well as a centre of culture renowned throughout the Greek world for its artistic innovation and achievement. The first temple of Poseidon at the Isthmus was built in the seventh century BC – one of the earliest examples of monumental temple architecture in Greece – while the number of dedications increases rapidly from the same period, testifying to the god's growing reputation. The wealth, power and prestige of Corinth at this time was certainly a major factor in spreading abroad among the Greeks the fame of Poseidon's sanctuary.

In the early sixth century the ruling elite in Corinth decided to enhance their Isthmian festival by introducing Games, probably in direct imitation of Olympia, and perhaps in rivalry with the Amphictyons, who had done the same thing at Delphi only a few years before. In 582 BC the festival was reorganized as a biennial event, and a wide-ranging programme of competition was introduced, including, as at Delphi, a number of musical events. The programme was further enhanced by the unique *hamilla neon* ('contest of ships'), perhaps a rowing race, and by the *hippios*, a middle-distance foot-race over four lengths of the stadium, which appeared on the Nemean programme also, but not at Delphi or Olympia. The events at the Isthmia were organized in three age-classes: 'boys', 'youths' and 'men', another point of difference from the Pythian and Olympic Games, where only two classes, 'boys' and 'men', were used.

The Nemean Games probably owed their origin to the political ambitions of Argos, and the desire of the Argives to establish themselves as a major power in the region. One sure way to achieve this was to have control of an important religious site and festival, and in 573 BC the Argives decided either to found their own Games at Nemea or to take over and expand a local festival already there. According to the myth, the Nemean Games were established by the Argive heroes on their way to Thebes, as Funeral Games in honour of the infant Opheltes;[17] no doubt Argos encouraged the dissemination of this story to support and validate its claim to organize and control the Games. Like the Isthmia, the Nemean festival was celebrated every two years; if a hero-cult of Opheltes did exist at the site previously, it was replaced by the worship of Zeus when the Games were established. The programme was substantially similar to that at Olympia, although there were apparently fewer equestrian events, and there were three age-classes, as at the Isthmia. Musical competitions appeared only much later, in the Hellenistic and Roman periods.

These four festivals, the Olympia, Pythia, Isthmia and Nemea, with their attendant Games, were the most important of them all – the great panhellenic festivals. Together they constituted what the Greeks called 'the circuit' (*periodos*) and the athlete who was successful at all four was called a 'circuit-winner' (*periodonikes*). They were also known as the 'crown' or 'stephanitic' Games (from the Greek *stephanos* meaning 'crown' or 'wreath'); the name derives from the practice of awarding to the successful athletes as their prize a simple garland or wreath to adorn the head. At Olympia the crown was a wreath of olive, at Delphi of laurel and at Nemea of wild celery.[18] For the Isthmian Games it was made originally of pine, and again later, but during the Classical and Hellenistic periods dried wild celery was used, perhaps in imitation of Nemea.[19] No other prize was awarded, and there were no prizes for second or third. In this respect the panhellenic Games were clearly distinguished from the less prestigious, more local Games, at many of which cash and other valuable prizes were awarded. For example, large parts of an inscription from Athens survive, detailing the prizes on offer at the Panathenaia; huge quantities of olive oil were given as prizes, in many events for second and lower places as well, while in the *kitharodia* (singing to the kithara) even fifth place received 300 drachmas![20]

The poets and the poems

More important than the prizes, however, whether symbolic or material, were the honour and glory which attended success in the Games. The victory brought great honour not only to the athlete himself, but also to his home-town or city, and this was regularly acknowledged and rewarded by the granting of cash rewards and other valuable privileges, as was re-marked above. For example at Athens, successful athletes in the stephani-tic Games were entitled to free meals for life in the Prytaneion; other privileges might include such things as exemption from taxes and seats of honour at the theatre and the Games. Sometimes too, the city would approve the erection of a statue in a conspicuous position, to commemorate the victor's glorious achievement, while the victor himself, if he could afford it, might erect a statue or make other elaborate dedication to the god in whose sanctuary the victory was won. These statues were not, at least in the early period, what we would call portrait-statues; they did not represent the physical likeness of the victor, for it was not until the Early Classical period (from about 480 BC onwards) that the sculptors, having mastered the art of representing the body as a co-ordinated whole, began to experiment with the expression of feeling, emotion and character in the face, so that individual portraiture became possible.[21] Before that, monu-mental sculpture was an idealization, in which no distinction of form or style was made between god, hero and human. Having said that, it must be remembered that these statues and dedications would always have carried the name of the victor, either as dedicator or honorand, so that, even as notional dedications to the god, they served to blur the distinction between god and man, and thus played a major role in marking the elevation of the athlete to the world of gods and heroes, as well as keeping alive the renown of his achievement and spreading his fame among his fellows.

The victory, naturally, was the occasion for a great party. Held either at the god's sanctuary immediately after the Games, or in the victor's home-town after his return, or, no doubt frequently, both, the party was an opportunity for the athlete's family and friends to gather to celebrate his success with a night of feasting, drinking, singing and dancing, and it became common practice from a very early date to engage a well-known poet to compose a song in the athlete's honour and in praise of his achievement. It might be thought that these epinician songs (from the Greek *epinikios* = 'for victory') were an ephemeral honour, sung once at the victory party and soon forgotten, while a statue of bronze or stone, erected in a public place and carrying the victor's name, would provide a surer guarantee of immortality, but in fact the reverse has proved to be the case. Pausanias (second century AD) devotes the greater part of Book 6 of his *Traveller's Guide to Greece* to listing and describing well over 200 statues which he saw in the Altis (the sacred enclosure) at Olympia,[22] but how many of these are still there today? None. On the other hand, around sixty victory poems have survived to the present day, in whole or in part, and these constitute one of our major sources for information on the Games and the athletes who took part in them.

Three names especially have long been associated with the creation of epinician songs – Simonides, Pindar and Bacchylides. More recently, however, some papyrus fragments have been found containing parts of poems written by Ibycos, a lyric poet from the Greek colony of Rhegium in the south of Italy, although his mature work was written in Samos under the patronage of the tyrant Polycrates (second half of the sixth century BC).[23] Ibycos is known to have written both narrative and erotic poems,[24] but these new fragments are clearly epinician, for they illustrate already many of the characteristics of the later victory songs. One of them refers to an Athenian, Callias, who may be the Callias known to have won the Olympic chariot-race in 564 BC. If this is right, it would push the history of epinician poetry back into the first half of the sixth century, not many years, in fact, after the establishment of the great panhellenic Games at Delphi, the Isthmus and Nemea. Thus it would appear that the emergence of victory poetry as a distinct genre coincides with, and was presumably driven by, the sudden increase in opportunities for competition, as the successful athletes sought to spread their renown and immortalize their achievement.

The victory poems of Bacchylides (and of Pindar) reveal a depth and seriousness of purpose, a concern with values and metaphysical issues, which belies their origin as casual songs for a party, and this is true even of the shorter works. It was probably Simonides of Ceos[25] who was initially responsible for this shift of focus, although not enough of his extensive output now survives to allow a definitive judgment. When we turn to Bacchylides and Pindar, however, we find these characteristics well established. Thus the poems are replete with invocations and prayers to the gods, as well as, in the longer poems at least, a mythological narrative, which elevates the audience at once into the world of gods and heroes. In addition there are regularly 'gnomic' passages,[26] consisting of a series of maxims which the poet uses both to express the moral framework which underpins the poems, as well as to give advice to his client (see e.g. Ode 1.160f.). In short, the religious and moral background to the poems is evident on every page.

It must be remembered, however, that the poems are in the first instance songs of praise; they were commissioned and designed to eulogize the successful athlete, and this remained always their primary, indeed their only, function. Thus we find interspersed at intervals throughout the poem overt praise of the athlete and the prowess of his victory. This is often enhanced by the enumeration of previous victories, and by praise of the victor's father or other members of his family, especially if they too had been successful in the Games. The contest itself is never described in any detail, although Bacchylides liked occasionally to enliven his narrative with a vividness which transports us instantly into the arena (see e.g. 9.31 and 10.21, with the notes there). Sometimes too, the victor's hometown is singled out for special praise. Just as the victory brought great honour to his city, so too the athlete's renown was enhanced by the splendour of the city from which he came. In addition to these more obviously 'programmatic' parts of the poem, the Games themselves, especially the great panhellenic festivals and the gods who presided over them, are also given their due share of praise, regularly with the reminder that the athlete owes his success to the grace of god. The victor may have, indeed does have, a natural inborn talent, but nature (*phua*), even when supplemented by rigorous training,[27] is not enough, and the victory is always seen as a gift of the god. From here it is a short step to praise of the athlete's character in general; the surest pathway to success is to display those qualities of excellence (*areta*), such as generosity and hospitality, respect for one's fellow men and reverence towards the gods, which especially characterized the leisured and aristocratic classes for whom the poets wrote.[28]

A final important feature of the poems has already been alluded to; that is, the parallel which both Bacchylides and Pindar are frequently at pains to draw between the victor's achievement as athlete, and their own as poet. Both are on the same level and of equal merit. As the victory elevated the athlete to the realm of gods and heroes, so the poem elevates the victory to the realm of the noble and valuable. The victory may be the gift of god, but it is the poet's job to reveal it and give it permanence. As Bacchylides puts it: 'the light of a man's worth does not fade with his body, but the Muse sustains it' (3.90-2).

There were no rules or conventions regarding the arrangement of these many disparate elements within the poem, and in fact Bacchylides shows great skill in varying the structure of his odes. But this very disparity has often been regarded as a negative element, and the epinicians have been criticized for lack of unity and coherent structure, involving abrupt and arbitrary transitions from one theme to another, inconsequential digression and rambling irrelevance. Especially the mythic narrative in the longer odes has been seen in this light. What, after all, can the story of the persecution of the daughters of Proitos by Hera (Ode 11) have to do with a young boy from Metapontion in the south of Italy, or the descent of Herakles to the Underworld (Ode 5) with Hieron, king of Syracuse in Sicily? But this is to misunderstand fundamentally the meaning and function of the mythology within ancient Greek society. The mythological stories did not constitute simply a fixed body of decorative material from which the poets could select at random in order to adorn their work; rather the mythology was a vital and living organism, constantly present to the consciousness of the Greeks. It represented, as we might say, their 'Dreamtime'; it told them who they were and how they related to the world in which they found themselves.[29] As such, it was a fluid and always changing entity, as the poets drew upon it and modified the received stories as they saw fit, in order to express their understanding of the world and interpret their experience. Thus the mythic narratives in the odes of Bacchylides are *always* relevant to the occasion. Sometimes the relevance is obvious, when the myth and its hero have some direct association with the victor's family or city (e.g. Odes 1 and 9); at other times it is possible to see how Bacchylides has changed the traditional version of the myth to suggest its relevance to the victor and his situation (e.g. Odes 3, 5 and 11).[30]

So too, other parts of the odes which have been similarly criticized on structural or thematic grounds – the apparent digressions, the abrupt transitions, the gnomic passages, the self-reference, bordering on self-advertisement at times – all have their own contribution to make to the 'programme' of the ode, that is, to the praise of the successful athlete. This insight is largely due to the work of E.L. Bundy,[31] who, in a detailed study of two odes of Pindar (*Olympian* 11 and *Isthmian* 1) analysed the rhetorical and stylistic conventions of epinician poetry and finally laid to rest the notion of irrelevance. For example, when Pindar seems to be embarrassed by poverty of expression, this is not irrelevant self-deprecation; rather 'these inadequacies have been rigged as foil for the greatness of the *laudandus*' (i.e. the victor). Again, when he claims to be truthful, this is not self-assertion; he means rather that his praise is no less than the victor deserves.[32]

The unity of the victory odes, then, arises primarily from the fact that *all* parts of the ode contribute to the praise of the victor. But there is a still deeper level at which poetic unity may be sought and found, a unity which derives from the fact that the odes are suffused in every part by a world-view clearly shared by poet and client, a world-view based on the aristocratic values of natural and inherited excellence, together with the concomitant obligation to realize the full potential of that excellence, so as to enjoy the favour of the gods. 'I say this now and always: excellence brings the greatest glory' (Bacchylides 1.159-60), or, in the words of Pindar: 'when the god-given brightness comes, there is a shining light upon men, and their life is sweet' (*Pythian* 8.96-7).

Bacchylides was born on the island of Ceos (now Kea or Tzia), just off the east coast of Attica, probably close to the end of the sixth century. The most widely accepted date is *c.* 507-505 BC. His great rival Pindar was born in Thebes in Boeotia only a little earlier in 518 BC. Both poets belonged to distinguished families, although neither seems to have been personally wealthy, and they travelled widely around Greece and Sicily cultivating the friendship and patronage of the rich and powerful as they sought commissions for their work. Simonides had done the same before them; indeed Bacchylides was probably introduced to Hieron, king of Syracuse, by his older relative. It is uncertain when either poet died; there is some (dubious) evidence to suggest that Bacchylides survived to the beginning of the Peloponnesian War (431 BC) but his latest datable poems are Odes 6 and 7 from 452 BC, while the latest work of Pindar for which there is a reliable date is *Pythian* 8, written in 446 BC. Thus the creative life of both of these great poets came to an end around the middle of the fifth century BC, and they had no successors. When Bacchylides and Pindar ceased to produce victory poems, the genre simply disappeared from the landscape. Victories were still won, but they were celebrated differently, and the commemorative statue, with a dedicatory epigram on the base honouring the victor and his achievement, became the norm.[33]

The text of the poems of Bacchylides

For a very long time the poems of Bacchylides were hardly known to the modern world. Only a few scraps of papyrus survived, together with some quotations in the works of other ancient authors. But in 1896 a papyrus roll came to light in Egypt which was found to contain fourteen epinician odes and six dithyrambs.[34] These were at once recognized as the work of Bacchylides, for the text of some of the previously known fragments reappeared in the new papyrus. The circumstances of its discovery are mysterious; it was apparently offered for sale to an Englishman and eventually smuggled out of Egypt to London, where it now resides in the British Library (Pap. BM 733). This papyrus (referred to conventionally as Pap. A) is now our major source for the text of Bacchylides. Unfortunately it is sadly mutilated; no doubt the clandestine nature of its transport from Cairo to London has much to do with its present condition. The papyrus was cut or broken into several sections, probably for ease of concealment, and it is clear that several columns of text have been lost at these breaks. In addition, the first four columns, which were at the outside of the roll, and thus particularly exposed to casual damage, survive only in a handful of isolated fragments. These have been painstakingly identified and inserted in their probable positions by the early editors,[35] and it is a tribute to their skill and scholarship that any sense can be made of this opening section at all.[36]

But there have been gains as well as losses. In 1938 two further fragments of Pap. A were found, which gave us the text of Ode 4.6-12 and Ode 12.33-42. In addition, the second of these two fragments has allowed us to calculate the number of columns actually missing between Odes 12 and 13.[37] Every little helps. Finally, a piece of papyrus from another copy of Bacchylides was found at Oxyrynchus in Egypt, which provided parts of two hitherto unknown odes.[38] These must have stood after Ode 14, since there appears to be no room for them anywhere else; numbered 14A and 14B, they were probably the last on the roll of epinicians. This in turn indicates that at least two columns, and probably more, have been lost after column 35 of Pap. A, containing the remainder of Ode 14, as well as Odes 14A and 14B.

The poems are written in verse, which means, as it does for all ancient Greek poetry, that the lines are organized in metrical patterns involving complex arrangements of long and short syllables. The majority of the odes are 'triadic', that is, they comprise groups of three stanzas, of which the first two (called 'strophe' and 'antistrophe'), are identical in their metrical structure, while the third (the 'epode'), is different. Within any ode, all the strophes and antistrophes are the same, metrically, and all the epodes are likewise identical to one another. A few of the shorter odes, however, consist only of a single pair of corresponding strophe and antistrophe. The beginning of each strophe, antistrophe and epode is indicated in the translation, in the right-hand margin.

Notes

1. The wonderful statue of Apollo at the centre of the west pediment of the temple of Zeus at Olympia (see p. 3 above), especially embodies this ideal in its serene and tranquil majesty.

2. For details, with references and bibliography, see Mark Golden, *Sport and Society in Ancient Greece*, Cambridge 1998, pp. 28-9.

3. Golden, op. cit., pp. 30-2.

4. Golden, op. cit., p. 32.

5. Cf. Aischylos *Seven Against Thebes* 592. In this play Aischylos singles out the wise and pious seer Amphiaraos from the other Argive leaders, who are motivated by greed and the lust for power. The difference is symbolized by their shields, and in contrast to the vainglorious pretence of valour displayed by the others, the shield of Amphiaraos bears no device: 'for he wants to be, not merely seem, the best'.

6. See Pindar *Olympian* 1.67f., and the notes on Bacchylides 5.182, 7.5 and 8.32. The magnificent sculptures of the east pediment of the temple of Zeus at Olympia (i.e. looking towards the hippodrome) depict the preparations for this race, under the supervision of Zeus himself.

7. This date has become enshrined in our tradition as one of the very few precise and reliable dates in ancient history, but in fact it was already disputed in antiquity. It goes back to Hippias of Elis, who, around 400 BC, compiled the first list of Olympic victors, but Plutarch, writing in the first or second century AD, claimed that Hippias had no evidence for this starting point (Plutarch *Numa* 1.4; see also Golden, op. cit., p. 63). Modern scholarship tends to agree with Plutarch, and the archaeological evidence suggests a date closer to 700 BC).

8. The stadion was a measurement of length equivalent to 600 Greek feet, but since the foot was not standardized, the actual length of the stadion-race varied from one locality to another. At Olympia it measured 192 metres, while the full length of the fifth-century BC stadium, as it exists today, is a mere 212 metres. This cannot have left much room for deceleration. A similar situation must have existed at the Isthmian stadium, where, as Bacchylides describes it, the victorious runner falls into the crowd at the end of his race (10.23f.) See also note on Ode 10.21.

9. S.G. Miller, *Greek Sports from Ancient Sources*, Berkeley, CA 1991, p. 212.

10. Pindar clearly means 'chariots' here, since he is writing for a chariot-race victory.

11. But see H.M. Lee, 'Pindar, *Ol.* 3.33-34: The Twelve-Turned Terma', *AJPh* 107 (1986), pp. 162-74. Lee argues vigorously for twelve 'laps'.

12. Delphi was originally known as Pytho, whence the god himself was the Pythian god, and his festival was called the Pythia. For the derivation and meaning of this name, see note on Ode 8.17.

13. In the *Iliad*, Achilles alludes to the huge wealth of Pytho (9.404-5), while at *Odyssey* 8.79-81, Agamemnon is said to have consulted the oracle. These are certainly anachronistic references, but they show the fame of Delphi already at the time these parts of the epic were created (presumably late eighth century).

14. No doubt the League organizers had the Olympic Games in mind in designing their new programme, for the list of events at the two festivals is remarkably similar, especially after the *tethrippon* (four-horse chariot-race) was added at the second Pythia in 582 BC. However the Pythia had a much earlier and stronger emphasis on music, reflecting the close connection of Apollo with the lyre. For a convenient list of the events at both festivals and the date of their introduction, see S.G. Miller, op. cit., p. 203.

15. See Pindar, fragment 5 (from an Isthmian Ode).

16. 'the gates of Pelops' island', as Bacchylides calls it (1.13-14).

17. See the intro. to Ode 9.

18. See Pausanias 8.48.2-3; also Lucian *Anacharsis* 9f.

19. Plutarch *Moralia* 675Dff.

20. *IG* II 2, 2311 (first half of the fourth century BC)

21. See e.g. G.M.A. Richter, *A Handbook of Greek Art*, Phaidon 1959, pp. 85 and 91.

22. Pausanias 6, chs 1-18. Even this list is far from complete, as Pausanias himself acknowledges. He excludes those victors who in his opinion were less worthy, their victories being due as much to good luck in the draw as to skill and strength, while he includes: 'only those who themselves achieved some distinction or whose statues were better made than others' (6.1.2). Interestingly, he includes what he claims were the first two statues ever erected at Olympia – those of Praxidamas of Aigina (boxing, 59th Olympiad, 544 BC) and Rexibios of Opous (pankration, 61st Olympiad, 536 BC); these two were made of wood, and were already, when Pausanias saw them, 'much decayed' (6.18).

23. See D.A. Campbell, *Greek Lyric* (Loeb Classical Library), vol. III, pp. 236-9 (fragments 282 B i and B ii).

24. For the latter see note on Ode 10.42.

25. Simonides (556-468 BC) was a relative of Bacchylides, probably his uncle (see Strabo 10.5.6), and the younger poet no doubt learned much of his technique from his kinsman.

26. The word comes from the Greek *gnome*, 'opinion', or 'judgment'; the words *gnome* and 'gnomic' are used frequently in the commentary in this sense.

27. This aspect of athletic endeavour is largely ignored by the poets, no doubt to avoid diminishing the glory of the athlete himself. Bacchylides only once mentions a trainer by name, Menandros of Athens (13.192; see note there).

28. See especially the intro. to Ode 1.

29. The term is borrowed from Australian Aboriginal culture. The songs and stories of the 'Dreamtime' not only provide the Aboriginal people with a connection to their spirit-ancestors; they also create and define their relation to the land to which they belong and which gives them their identity. These meanings are continually revalidated through ceremonial performance.

30. The introductions to individual odes will discuss these matters in some detail.

31. Elroy L. Bundy, *Studia Pindarica*, Berkeley, CA 1986.

32. Bundy, op. cit., p. 4. Bundy's book requires a substantial command of ancient Greek, but his conclusions can, and should, be understood by all. The commentary on individual odes will highlight the importance of Bundy's insights from time to time. See e.g. note on Ode 3.86-92, on the 'priamel'.

33. Golden (op. cit., p. 85) seeks to explain this change of fashion. He argues that the competitive elite had grown tired of having their successes represented as a public good, a 'benefaction from the victor upon the city', so that they began to seek a more personal recognition. But this can be at best only a small part of the reason,

for the glory that the victory reflected upon the athlete's city was always secondary in the epinician to the praise of the athlete himself.

34. The dithyramb was a choral song involving a mythic narrative, sometimes specifically in honour of Dionysos, but often not, and sometimes including dialogue of a quasi-dramatic nature. There were competitions for dithyrambic composition at the Dionysia in Athens, at which Simonides claimed to have excelled.

35. Especially Prof. F. Blass: *Bacchylidis Carmina*, Leipzig 1898, 1899 and 1904.

36. The papyrus was edited in the first instance by F.G. Kenyon, *The Poems of Bacchylides*, London 1897, and subsequently by (among others) R.C. Jebb, *Bacchylides, The Poems and Fragments*, Cambridge 1905, and H. Maehler, *Die Lieder des Bakchylides*, Leiden 1982 (2 vols). These two (Jebb and Maehler) are the works chiefly referred to in my commentary. It might be worth noticing that Jebb's numbering of the columns is no longer valid. Not only did he disregard the first four columns reconstituted from the fragments, but he did not have the benefit of the more recent papyrus discoveries. Column numbers are indicated in the left-hand margin of my translation.

37. See intro. to Ode 12.

38. Pap. Oxy. 23. 2363, conventionally known as Pap. L. See intro. to Ode 14B.

Works Cited with Abbreviations

Ancient authors

Aelian (2/3 cent. AD)
  Var. Hist. = Varia Historia
Aisch. = Aischylos, tragic poet (5th cent. BC)
  Agam. = Agamemnon
  Eum. = Eumenides
  Libation Bearers
  Pers. = Persai
  Prom. = Prometheus
  Seven = Seven against Thebes
  Supp. = Suppliant Maidens
Akusilaos, historian (5th cent. BC)
Alcman, lyric poet (7th cent. BC)
Alkaios, lyric poet (7/6 cent. BC)
Anacreon, lyric poet (6th cent. BC)
Apollod. = Apollodoros, mythographer (1st cent. AD)
Ap. Rhod. = Apollonios Rhodios, epic poet (3rd cent. BC)
  Argonaut. = Argonautica
Archil. = Archilochos, lyric poet (7th cent. BC)
Arctinos, epic poet (7th cent. BC)
  Aithiopis
Arist. = Aristophanes, comic poet (5th cent. BC)
  Birds
  Clouds
  Frogs
Athenaeus, grammarian (2nd/3rd cent. AD)
Bacch. = Bacchylides
Call. = Callimachos, poet (3rd cent. BC)
  Aitia
  Hymns
Cic. = Cicero, Roman politician and orator (1st cent. BC)
  Verr. = Verrine Orations
Corinna. lyric poet (6th cent. BC)
Diod. = Diodoros, historian (1st cent. BC)
Dion. Hal. = Dionysios of Halicarnassos, rhetorician (1st cent. BC)
Epicharmos, comic poet (5th cent. BC)

Eur. = Euripides, tragic poet (5th cent. BC)
  Alc. = Alcestis
  Bacch. = Bacchae
  El. = Electra
  Helen
  Herakles
  Hipp. = Hippolytos
  Hypsipyle
  Iph. Aul. = Iphigeneia at Aulis
  Iph. Taur. = Iphigeneia in Tauris
  Med. = Medea
  Meleager
  Or. = Orestes
  Phoin. = Phoenician Women
  Supp. = Suppliant Women
  Troad. = Trojan Women
Favorinus, sophist and historian (2nd cent. AD)
  On Exile
Hdt. = Herodotos, historian (5th cent. BC)
Hes. = Hesiod, epic poet (8th/7th cent. BC)
  Shield
  Theog. = Theogony
  Works and Days
Hom. = Homer, epic poet (8th cent. BC)
  Il. = Iliad
  Od. = Odyssey
[Homer]
  Cypria
Hom. Hymn = Homeric Hymns (various dates)
Horace, Roman Lyric Poet (1st cent. AD)
  Odes
Ibycos, lyric poet (6th cent. BC)
Lucian, sophist (2nd cent. AD)
  Anacharsis
Nicander, epic poet (2nd cent. BC)
Nonnos, epic poet (4th/5th cent. AD)
Old Testament (various dates)
  Exodus
  Genesis
  Jeremiah
  Job
  Psalms
  I Samuel
Orphic Argonautica (?1st cent. BC)
Ovid, Roman poet (1st cent. AD)

Ibis
Metamorph. = Metamorphoses
Paus. = Pausanias, travel writer (2nd cent. AD)
Pherek. = Pherekydes, historian (5th cent. BC)
Phrynichos, tragic poet (5th cent BC)
Pind. = Pindar, lyric poet (5th cent. BC)
  Ol. = Olympian Odes
  Pyth. = Pythian
  Nem. = Nemean
  Isth. = Isthmian
  Paians
Plato, philosopher (5th/4th cent. BC)
  Tim. = Timaios
Pliny (the Elder), natural scientist (1st cent. AD)
  Nat. Hist. = Historia Naturalis
Plut. = Plutarch, biographer and philosopher (1st/2nd cent. AD)
  Moral. = Moralia
  Num. = Numa
  Thes. = Theseus
Rufinus, epigrammatist (late)
Sappho, lyric poet (7th cent. BC)
Semon. = Semonides, iambic poet (7th/6th cent. BC)
Simon. = Simonides, lyric poet (6th/5th cent. BC)
Solon, elegaic poet (7th/6th cent. BC)
Soph. = Sophocles, tragic poet (5th cent. BC)
  Aias (= Ajax)
  Ant. = Antigone
  El. = Electra
  OC = Oedipus at Colonos
  OT = Oedipus Tyrannos (= Oedipus the King)
  Phil. = Philoktetes
  Trach. = Women of Trachis
Stesichoros, lyric poet (7th/6th cent. BC)
Strabo, geographer (1st cent. BC/1st cent. AD)
Theocrit. = Theocritos, pastoral poet (3rd cent. BC)
Theog. = Theognis, elegaic poet (6th cent. BC)
Theophrastos, philosopher (4th/3rd cent. BC)
  Hist. Plant. = Historia Plantarum
Theopompos, historian (4th cent. BC)
Thuc. = Thucydides, historian (5th cent. BC)
Timaios, historian (4th/3rd cent. BC)
Verg. = Vergil, Roman epic poet (1st cent. AD)
  Aen. = Aeneid
  Ecl. = Eclogues
  Georg. = Georgics

Xen. = Xenophon, historian (4th cent. BC)
  Anabasis
  Hell. = *Hellenica*

Other abbreviations

ABV = J.D. Beazley, *Attic Black-Figure Vase-Painters*, Oxford 1956.
AJPh = *American Journal of Philology*, Baltimore.
Anth. Pal. = *Anthologia Palatina* (a collection of Hellenistic and later epigrams, put together in the 10th cent. AD).
ARV = J.D. Beazley, *Attic Red-Figure Vase-Painters*, 2nd edn, Oxford 1963.
ASNP = *Annali della Scuola Normale Superiore di Pisa*, Classe di Lettere e Filosofia, Pisa.
BCH = *Bulletin de Correspondence Hellenique*, Paris.
Blass = F. Blass, *Bacchylidis Carmina*, Leipzig 1898; 3rd edn 1904.
Bundy, *Stud. Pind.* = E.L. Bundy, *Studia Pindarica*, Berkeley, CA 1986.
CAH = *Cambridge Ancient History*, Cambridge.
Drach. = A.B. Drachmann, *Scholia Vetera in Pindari Carmina*, 3 vols, Leipzig 1903-27.
Et. Mag. = *Etymologicum Magnum*, ed. T. Gaisford, 1841 (a 12th-cent. AD lexicon, based in part on the earlier (9th/10th-cent.) *Etymologicum Genuinum*, not yet fully edited).
FGH = *Die Fragmente der Griechischen Historiker*, ed. F. Jakoby, Berlin and Leiden, 1923-.
fr. = fragment.
HSCP = *Harvard Studies in Classical Philology*, Cambridge, MA.
IG = *Inscriptiones Graecae*, Berlin.
Jebb = R.C. Jebb, *Bacchylides, The Poems and Fragments*, Cambridge 1905.
JHS = *Journal of Hellenic Studies*, London, Society for the Promotion of Hellenic Studies.
LCM = *Liverpool Classical Monthly*, University of Liverpool.
Maehler = Herwig Maehler, *Die Lieder des Bakchylides*, 2 vols, Leiden 1982.
Pap. Oxy. = *The Oxyrhynchus Papyri*, ed. B.P. Grenfell, A.S. Hunt et al., London 1898-.
PMG = *Poetae Melici Graeci*, ed. D.L. Page, Oxford 1962.
PP = *La Parola del Passato*, Rivista di Studi Antichi, Naples.
PSI = *Publicazioni della Societa Italiana*, ed. G. Vitelli, M. Norsa et al., Florence 1912-.
schol. = *scholia*: comments and interpretations written by ancient scholars in the margins of the manuscripts.
ZPE = *Zeitschrift für Papyrologie und Epigrafik*, Bonn.

Further Reading

Alexandre, O. (ed.), *Mind and Body: Athletic Contests in Ancient Greece*, Athens 1989.

Bowra, C.M., *Greek Lyric Poetry, from Alcman to Simonides*, Oxford 1961.

Burnett, A.P., *The Art of Bacchylides*, Cambridge, MA 1985.

Cartledge, P., 'The Greek Religious Festivals', in P.E. Easterling and J.V. Muir (eds) *Greek Religion and Society*, Cambridge 1985.

Easterling, P.E. and B.M.W. Knox (eds), *The Cambridge History of Classical Literature: I. Greek Literature*, Cambridge 1985.

Fagles, R. (tr.) and A. Parry (comm.), *Bacchylides: Complete Poems*, New Haven 1961.

Fearn, D., *Bacchylides: Politics, Performance, Poetic Tradition*, Oxford 2007.

Finley, M.I. and H.W. Pleket, *The Olympic Games: The First Thousand Years*, London 1976.

Golden, M., *Sport and Society in Ancient Greece*, Cambridge 1998.

Harris, H.A. *Greek Athletes and Athletics*, London 1964.

———, *Sport in Greece and Rome*, London and Ithaca, NY 1972.

Hornblower, S. and C. Morgan (ed.) *Pindar's Poetry, Patrons and Festivals*, Oxford 2007.

Koursi, M. (ed.), *The Olympic Games in Ancient Greece*, Athens 2003.

Kyle, D.G., *Athletics in Ancient Athens*, Leiden 1987.

Lefkowitz, M. (tr. and ed.), *The Victory Ode: an Introduction*, Park Ridge 1976.

Maehler, H., *Bacchylides: A Selection*, New York 2003.

Miller, S.G., *Arete: Greek Sports from Ancient Sources*, Berkeley, CA 1991.

———, *Nemea: A Guide to the Site and Museum*, Berkeley, CA 1990.

———, *The Ancient Stadium of Nemea*, Greek Ministry of Culture (no date).

Poliakoff, M.B., *Combat Sports in the Ancient World*, Yale Univ. Press, 1987.

Segal, C., *Aglaia: The Poetry of Alcman, Sappho, Pindar, Bacchylides, and Corinna*, Lanham, MD 1998.

Steiner, D., *The Crown of Song: Metaphor in Pindar*, London and New York 1986.

Swaddling, J., *The Ancient Olympic Games*, London 1980.

Valavanis, P., *Games and Sanctuaries in Ancient Greece*, Los Angeles 2004.

Young, D.C., *The Olympic Myth of Greek Amateur Athletics*, Chicago 1984.

The Victory Poems

Translation

ODE 1

FOR ARGEIOS OF CEOS

Boys' Boxing, Isthmian Games, before 452 BC

1 Col. 1   Daughters of Zeus who rules on high,   Str. 1
Pierian maidens
..... famed for the lyre,
.... weave .....
songs] to [honour
the lord] of the Isthmus,
husband of wise ....
...... Nereus' daughter,

    .... and the ... of the island   Ant. 1
10   .... where ....
    ....
    ....
O god-built gates
of Pelops' shining island,

    (15-18 missing)

17   Epode 1

19   yoked] the horses to his chariot
20   .... they] flew ......
    ....
    ....
.... others ....

Ode 1

(24-46 missing or too fragmentary to translate)

24   Str. 2
32   Ant. 2
35 Col. 2
40   Epode 2

47   .... shrewd   Str. 3
            .... the maidens
              ......]agora
50   ...... from sleep that soothes the mind
              ? leave] our
            ...... ancient city

                    ....
            and ...... a home at the sea's edge

55   that stands] in the light of the sun   Ant. 3
                    ....

                    (57-70 missing)

63   Epode 3
69 Col. 3
70   Str. 4
71   ....
            ......]sagora
            ...... but Makelo ....
              ...... she who loves to spin,
            ...... and by the fair-flowing stream
            ...... and she addressed them
            with [soft] voice comforting

            .... I have lost   Ant. 4
            ....`with a two-fold, cutting pain
80   .... in poverty
            .... altogether
                    ....
                    ....
                    (84-110 missing)

86   Epode 4
93   Str. 5

101   Ant. 5
104 Col. 4
109   Epode 5

111   ....
                 ...... on the third ......
                 day Minos, the warrior,
                 came – fifty ships with shimmering sterns
                 and a host of Cretans with him.

                 There he took the lovely girl   Str. 6
                 Dexithea –
                 Zeus, god of glory, willed it.
                 He left her half his people,
120   heroes, lovers of war,
                 and sharing out the craggy land among them
                 the king, Europa's son,
                 sailed off

                 to Knossos' lovely city.   Ant. 6
                 When the tenth [month] came
                 his lovely-haired [bride
                 brought forth Euxantios,
                     ...... ruler of that glorious [island
                         ....

                         (130-7 missing)

132   Epode 6
138   .... daughters [fled ?

Col. 5   .... a city   Str. 7
140   deep in the light of the setting sun.
                 And of his race was born
                 Argeios, [strong] of hand
                 ...... and lion-hearted when
                 the call to battle came;
                 light-footed too, and
                 ...... mindful] of those blessings

                 which bow- [famed] Apollo   Ant. 7
                 granted] to Pantheides, his father,

for his healing art,
150   for his respect and love for guests.
He won his share of the Graces' gifts
and was admired by many men;
at the end of his life he left behind
five children who have won great praise.

To one of these the high-benched son of Kronos   Epode 7
gave victory at the Isthmus –
reward for his benefactions – and his share
of other shining crowns.
I say this now and always:
160   excellence brings the greatest glory;
wealth comes even to the unworthy,

and is wont to swell the mind of a man;   Str. 8
but he who is generous to the gods
can cheer his heart
with hope of a greater glory.
If a man has the gift of health
and can live from what he has,
he is second to none in fortune.
There is delight in every human life

170   – let it only be free of sickness   Ant. 8
and helpless poverty.
Just as the wealthy man's desires are great,
so the poorer man wants less;
Col. 6   but men take no pleasure
in having all their needs at hand;
always the goal is
that which eludes the grasp.

He whose spirit   Epode 8
worthless ambitions drive
180   + may win honour in his lifetime +
but excellence – not easily achieved –
when brought to its proper end,
leaves for a man, even when he is dead,
an enviable monument of renown.

ODE 2

FOR ARGEIOS OF CEOS

Boys' Boxing, Isthmian Games, before 452 BC

<table>
<tr><td>1</td><td>Fame, giver of proud gifts,
go quickly] to sacred Ceos,
bearing the glad news
that Argeios has won the victory
in the boxing, bold of hand.</td><td>Strophe</td></tr>
<tr><td></td><td>And he brought to mind the splendid deeds –
seventy winners' crowns in all –
which, leaving Euxantios' holy island,
we have celebrated</td><td>Antistrophe</td></tr>
<tr><td>10</td><td>at the far-famed neck of Isthmus.</td><td></td></tr>
<tr><td></td><td>The Muse of this place
calls forth the sweet sound of the pipes,
honouring Pantheides' own dear son
with songs of victory.</td><td>Epode</td></tr>
</table>

ODE 3

FOR HIERON OF SYRACUSE

Chariot-Race, Olympic Games, 468 BC

Sing, Klio, you whose gifts are sweet,   Str. 1
of Demeter, queen of Sicily where the best grain grows,
of Kore violet-crowned,
and of Hieron's swift Olympic-racing mares.

For beside the wide-swirling stream of Alpheos they   Ant. 1
       sped –
Victory pre-eminent and Splendour attended them –
and there they brought good fortune to Deinomenes' son,
giving him the crown.

The people shouted [...   Epode 1
10   Ah, thrice-blessed [is the man
Col. 7   who has won from Zeus the privilege,
more than all others, of ruling over Greeks,
yet knows not to conceal his towered wealth
in the black shroud of darkness.

The holy places teem with festal sacrifice of oxen,   Str. 2
the streets are filled with guests made welcome;
gold gleams amid the sparkle
of tripods, finely crafted, standing high

before the temple, where the people of Delphi   Ant. 2
20   tend Apollo's greatest precinct
by the flowing waters of Kastalia.
Glorify the god, yes, the god, for that
is the best kind of happiness.

For once, as Sardis fell to the Persian host,   Epode 2
when Zeus fulfilled
his fated judgment,
Apollo, lord of the golden sword,
saved Croesus too, high king
of the Lydians, horse-breakers.

He, come to that day for which none hope,   Str. 3
30 purposed to wait no longer
for tearful slavery,
and out in front of the bronze-walled court

heaped up a pyre. There with his cherished [wife Ant. 3
and lovely-haired daughters, inconsolable in grief,
he climbed up on to it;
and raising his hands to the towering sky

cried aloud: 'All-mastering divinity,   Epode 3
where now the gratitude of gods?
Where is the lord Apollo, Leto's son?
40 The house of Alyattes falls to [ruin
.... of countless
....

............] the city;   Str. 4
the swirling waters of Paktolos, [rich in gold
Col.8 run red with blood.] In shame the women
are taken from their well-built homes.

What was hateful before is welcome now;   Ant. 4
to die is sweetest.' This much he said, and commanded
the soft-stepping servant to fire his house of wood.
50 The young girls screamed, stretched out their hands

to their mother; for death foreseen   Epode 4
is the most hateful of all for mortals.
But when the flashing force of
the terrible fire was taking hold,
Zeus set above it a black, concealing cloud,
and quenched the yellow flame.

Nothing is beyond belief, if the will of god   Str. 5
contrives it. Then Apollo, Delos-born,
carried off the old man to the Hyperboreans,
60   and set him down to dwell there
with his slender-ankled daughters,

for his piety, because his offerings   Ant. 5
to holy Pytho were greatest among mortals.
Hieron, whose praise is great,
no mortal man, who dwells in Greece,

will wish to say that he has sent to Loxias   Epode 5
more gold than you.
He who does not feed on envy
can give praise
to ......] the horse-loving man of war,
70   who holds] the sceptre of [...] Zeus,

and shares in the gifts of the Muses, violet-haired,   Str. 6
....
......] of a day
.........] you see; [Life is] short.

Fluttering hope undoes the reason   Ant. 6
of creatures of a day. The lord [Apollo
......] spoke to the [son of] Pheres:
Col. 9   'You are but mortal; so you must hold to a faith

twofold: believe that the light of tomorrow's sun   Epode 6
80   will be the last you see,
and that you will live out your life
for fifty years in deep prosperity.
Delight your heart with holy deeds, for this
is the highest gain.'

He who has sense understands what I say.   Str. 7
The deep sky is not corrupted; the sea's water
is not fouled; gold brings delight;
but for a man it cannot be, that he thrust aside

grey age, and bring again the bloom   Ant. 7
90   of youth. The light of a man's worth
does not fade with his body,
but the Muse sustains it. You, Hieron,

have displayed before men   Epode 7
the finest flowering of wealth; silence
brings no ornament to the man who has won success;
but in true report of glorious achievement
people will sing my song also,
gift of the honey-tongued nightingale of Ceos.

ODE 4

FOR HIERON OF SYRACUSE

Chariot-Race, Pythian Games, 470 BC

1	Still Apollo golden-haired	Strophe
	loves the city of Syracuse,	
	and honours Hieron, its upright ruler.	
	For by the navel-stone in the land of the high glens	
	he is celebrated – winner at Delphi for the third time –	
	he and his splendid swift-running mares.	
	...... the sweet-voiced	
	rooster of Urania, [queen] of the lyre	
	...... but with willing mind	
10	...... showered with songs.	

	And] now for a fourth time [too], if a ...	Antistrophe
	... had [rightly] poised the scales of Justice,	
Col. 10	we would be honouring Deinomenes' son;	
	But as it is] we may crown him now with garlands –	
	him who, alone of men that walk the earth,	
	by the deep folds of Kirrha's bay	
	achieved this feat –	
	and sing besides of two Olympic prizes.	
	What better than to be loved by gods	
20	and win one's share of blessings of every kind?	

ODE 5

FOR HIERON OF SYRACUSE

Horse-Race, Olympic Games, 476 BC

<table>
<tr><td>1</td><td>Fate-favoured leader of Syracusans,</td><td>Str.1</td></tr>
<tr><td></td><td>riders of wide-wheeling chargers,</td><td></td></tr>
<tr><td></td><td>you, beyond all who now walk this earth,</td><td></td></tr>
<tr><td></td><td>will surely recognize this ornament,</td><td></td></tr>
<tr><td></td><td>sweet gift from the Muses violet-crowned.</td><td></td></tr>
<tr><td></td><td>Set aside your cares from your straight-judging heart</td><td></td></tr>
<tr><td></td><td>and in peace</td><td></td></tr>
<tr><td></td><td>direct your mind this way,</td><td></td></tr>
<tr><td></td><td>where a guest-friend,</td><td></td></tr>
<tr><td>10</td><td>famed servant of gold-garlanded Urania,</td><td></td></tr>
<tr><td></td><td>with the lovely Graces</td><td></td></tr>
<tr><td></td><td>weaves a song and from his holy island</td><td></td></tr>
<tr><td></td><td>sends it to your glorious city.</td><td></td></tr>
<tr><td></td><td>He wishes to pour out from his breast</td><td></td></tr>
<tr><td></td><td>his voice in praise of Hieron;</td><td></td></tr>
<tr><td></td><td></td><td></td></tr>
<tr><td></td><td>as the eagle, messenger of Zeus loud-thundering</td><td>Ant. 1</td></tr>
<tr><td></td><td>whose realm spreads wide,</td><td></td></tr>
<tr><td></td><td>cleaves the deep sky, high</td><td></td></tr>
<tr><td>20</td><td>on the pulsing beat of wings, swift,</td><td></td></tr>
<tr><td></td><td>confident, trusting in his mighty strength,</td><td></td></tr>
<tr><td></td><td>and the screeching birds cower in fear;</td><td></td></tr>
<tr><td></td><td>the mountain peaks of the great earth</td><td></td></tr>
<tr><td></td><td>do not confine him</td><td></td></tr>
<tr><td></td><td>nor the towering waves</td><td></td></tr>
<tr><td>Col. 11</td><td>of the tireless sea;</td><td></td></tr>
<tr><td></td><td>he, driving on restless wing, featherlight,</td><td></td></tr>
<tr><td></td><td>high in the endless, empty sky,</td><td></td></tr>
<tr><td></td><td>rides on the breath of the western wind,</td><td></td></tr>
<tr><td>30</td><td>a sight well known among men.</td><td></td></tr>
</table>

	So now, high-minded children of Deinomenes,	Epode 1
	I too have on all sides	
	numberless pathways of song	
	to praise your excellence,	
	by the grace of dark-haired Victory and the	
	bronze-armoured god of war.	
	I pray that the god will not grow weary doing good.	
	The morning sun whose arms are golden	
	watched him win, the chestnut colt Pherenikos,	
	the colt that runs on the wind,	
40	beside the wide-swirling stream of Alpheos,	
	and at holy Delphi too.	Str. 2
	Calling the earth to witness I declare:	
	never yet, as he rushed to the line in a race	
	was he stained by the dust	
	of horses in front.	
	For with onrush matching the wind from the North,	
	responsive to his rider's hand he flies,	
	aiming to bring again applause and victory	
	for Hieron, friend of guests.	
50	Blessed is he to whom god has given	
	his share of good,	
	and a life to live of wealth	
	and coveted good fortune.	
	For no man that walks this earth is born	
	god-favoured in all things.	
	Hear now, for they say that once	Ant. 2
	the never-conquered, the destroyer of cities,	
	son of Zeus bright-thundering,	
Col. 12	went down to the halls of slender-ankled Persephone,	
60	to bring to the light from Hades	
	the saw-toothed hound,	
	child of the terrible Echidna.	
	There by the flowing waters of Kokytos	
	he discovered the souls of the unhappy dead,	
	flittering like the leaves that the wind swirls	
	along the snow-bright glittering	
	goat-grazing ridges of Ida;	
	and among these souls shone forth the ghost	
	of Porthaon's bold-spirited son,	
70	spear-fighter.	

And when the awesome hero, son of Alcmena,   Epode 2
saw him, shining in his armour,
he set the sweet-sounding bowstring
over the bow's curved tip;
then, folding back the quiver's cover
drew out a bronze-head arrow.
The soul of Meleager stood out to face him,
and, knowing well the truth, addressed him:
'Son of great Zeus,
80   stand as you are; make light your heart,

and do not let fly from your hands   Str. 3
the tearing arrow,
to no purpose, against the souls of the dead.
You need have no fear.'
So he spoke, and the lord
Amphitryon's son was amazed, and answered:
'Who of immortals or of those who die
nurtured such a son? On what soil?
And who killed you? For it may be
90   that the lovely Hera will send that man to take my life.
Still, the fair-haired Athena will
Col. 13   no doubt take care of that.'
And Meleager addressed him,
weeping: 'It is hard
for men that walk the earth

to turn aside the will of gods.   Ant. 3
Were it not so, my father Oineus, rider of horses,
with prayer and sacrifice
of many goats and blood-red cattle
100   had surely stilled the anger
of holy Artemis,
white-armed goddess, flower-crowned.
But the Maiden held her anger unsubdued;
and against the lovely dancing-grounds of Calydon
she loosed a wild wide-ranging boar
implacable in fight.
There with tearing tusk and force of flood
it rooted out the ordered rows of vines,
slaughtered the flocks and any man
110   who came to face it.

Six days unceasing we, greatest of Greek heroes,   Epode 3
stood in hateful battle against it,
not giving ground;
and when the god gave victory to the Aitolians,
we buried those whom the boar loud-roaring
had slain in violent onset,
Ankaios, and Agelaos
best of my dear brothers
born to Althaia in the far-famed
120   palace of my father Oineus.

But deadly Fate destroyed [more still.   Str. 4
For not yet did the daughter of Leto,
fierce-hearted huntress,
Col. 14   stay her anger, but still we fought
not giving ground against the steadfast Kouretes
over the lurid skin.
Then among many others I slew Iphiklos,
and noble Aphares,
swift-running brothers of my mother.
130   For the staunch-hearted god of war does not mark out
a friend in the fighting.
But blind from the hand the spear-shafts go
to take the lives of enemy men
and bring death to those
for whom god wills it.

Heedless of this my ill-starred mother,   Ant. 4
fierce-hearted daughter of Thestios,
planned my death – ah, reckless woman.
140   From its ornate chest she took
the log, my sudden doom –
the log which Klotho once,
as she spun the thread of my life,
had set to mark its end –
and burned it.
Just then I was stripping the armour from the
          flawless hero Klymenos,
Daipylos' valiant son,
encountered in front of the towered walls,
and they in flight to their well-built
150   ancient city Pleuron.

So the sweet life in me ebbed away   Epode 4
and I knew my strength was gone.
Alas! – I drew my last breath and wept in my sorrow,
as I left behind my splendid youth'.
This, they say, was the only time
Col. 15   that Amphitryon's son,
the fearless warrior, wept,
in pity for the grieving hero's fate.
And answering him he spoke these words:
160   'Not to be born is best for mortals,

not to see the sun's light.   Str. 5
But there is no profit in such lament –
so one must speak of that which
one intends to bring to pass.
Is there then in the palace
of Oineus, lover of war,
a daughter, still unwed,
whose noble stature matches yours?
Such a one I would gladly make my shining wife.'
170   The soul of Meleager,
steadfast in war, replied:
'I left in my house Deianeira,
the pale skin glowing at her throat,
innocent still of golden Aphrodite,
enchantress of mortals.'

White-armed Kalliope,   Ant. 5
stop here the well-built chariot;
sing of Zeus, son of Kronos,
Olympian leader of the gods,
180   and of Alpheos' tireless flow,
and mighty Pelops,
and Pisa, where Pherenikos
famed for speed, won in the race
and came to towered Syracuse,
bringing to Hieron
the garland of god's favour.
Col. 16   Praise must be given as truth requires,
and malice thrust away with both hands,
190   when any man enjoys success.

A Boeotian it was,   Epode 5
the sweet Muses' servant Hesiod, who declared:
'whom the immortals honour,
fame among men attends him also.'
I am easily persuaded
to send to Hieron a glorious song of praise,
which does not stray from the path of what is proper.
For thus the stock of blessings flourishes.
May Zeus, the greatest father,
200   protect them in peace, unshaken.

ODE 6

FOR LACHON OF CEOS

Stadion, Olympic Games, 452 BC

<table>
<tr><td>1</td><td>Lachon has won from greatest Zeus
renown unparalleled for speed of foot,
where the Alpheos runs to the sea [...
for which at Olympia in the past,
with victory-garlands abundant in their hair,
young men have sung
in praise of Ceos rich in vines,
for her success in boxing and the foot-race.</td><td>Strophe</td></tr>
<tr><td>10</td><td>And now, by the grace of Victory's goddess,
praise from Urania, queen of song,
honours you,
child of Aristomenes,
swift-footed as the wind,
with songs before your house,
because, successful in the foot-race,
you have brought fame to Ceos.</td><td>Antistrophe</td></tr>
</table>

ODE 7

FOR LACHON OF CEOS

Stadion, Olympic Games, 452 BC

<table>
<tr><td>1</td><td>O shining daughter of Time and Night,
sixteenth day of the fiftieth month,
by the grace of loud- [thundering Zeus …</td><td>Strophe</td></tr>
<tr><td>Col. 17</td><td>……] at Olympia ….
… [Alcmena's son appointed] you
to judge for the Greeks the speed
of swift feet and the heroic strength of mighty limbs.
He to whom you grant the victory – most honoured prize –
is called renowned among men, and envied.</td><td></td></tr>
<tr><td>10</td><td>Lachon, Aristomenes' son,
you adorned with the victor's crown.</td><td></td></tr>
</table>

Antistrophe

………
……] Chairolas […
………] pious [……
……] death [……
……] native land [……
……] newly judged [……
………] childless [……

(19-22 missing)

ODE 8

(FOR LIPARION OF CEOS?)

(1-7 missing)

<table>
<tr><td>1</td><td></td><td>Strophe</td></tr>
</table>

8   ...... contest ......
       ...... Lipa[ros ? ......
10   ....
       ...... sons of the Greeks ...
       ...... rich in vines ......
       .... song (?) ......
       .... in Ceos (?)
       ...... although (?)] without horses ...
       ....

Col. 18   singing in praise of Pytho, where sheep are
          sacrificed,   Antistrophe
    and Nemea, and the Isthmus.
    Laying my hand upon the earth
20   I shall make this boast – and the whole debt
    of praise shines clear and truth attends it –
    no man among the Greeks,
    competing in his age group
    as boy and man,
    has won more victories.
    O Zeus whose spear is the thunderbolt,
    may you bring also to fulfilment
    by the banks of Alpheos, silver-swirling,
    his prayer for great renown, god-given,
30   and give to go with him, about his head,
    the Aitolian olive's silvery coronal,
    at the far-famed Games of Phrygian Pelops.

ODE 9

FOR AUTOMEDES OF PHLEIUS

Pentathlon, Nemean Games

1	Graces of the golden distaff, grant renown that sways mankind, for the voice of the Muses violet-eyed is ready to sing, inspired, in praise of Phleius and the verdant plain of Zeus of Nemea, where Hera, white-armed goddess, reared the lion, deep-throated, slayer of sheep, for Herakles, first of his far-famed Labours.	Str. 1
10	There the men of the blood-red shields, pick of the Argive heroes, first competed in games to honour Archemoros, slain as he slept by the monstrous serpent, yellow-eyed, token of death to come. O Destiny whose power is great, the son of Oikles could not persuade them to go back to the streets of heroes. Hope steals away men's reason,	Ant. 1
20 Col. 19	hope, which even then sent Adrastos, Talaos' son, to Thebes for Polyneices [... From those renowned Games in Nemea they win fame among mortals who each second year bedeck their fair hair with the crown. Now god has given it to Automedes for his victory.	Epode 1

For among his pentathlon rivals he stood out   Str. 2
as bright Selene on a full-moon night
outshines the light of stars.
30   So before the endless sea of Greeks around him
he displayed his awesome form,
in the throw of the wheel-shaped discus,
and hurling from his hand into the towering sky
the shaft of dark-leaved elder
he raised the roar of the crowd.

He brought to its end the wrestling's glittering dance,   Ant. 2
with such high strength of courage throwing
strong-limbed bodies to the ground;
then came to the dark swirling waters of Asopos,
40   whose fame has spread to every land,
even to distant Nile;
and they who dwell by Thermodon's fair-flowing stream,
spear-skilled daughters of Ares,
driver of horses,

they too, much-envied lord of rivers,   Epode 2
have encountered your descendants,
as has the seat of lofty-gated Troy.
On all sides, along a broad pathway,
spread countless stories of your family,
50   your shining-girdled daughters,
whom with good fortune the gods set down
as founders of cities never sacked.

For who does not know of dark-haired   Str.3
Thebe's well-built city,
Col. 20   or of Aigina, whose [name is great,
she who, [brought to] the bed of greatest Zeus
gave birth to the hero ......
        ......
who] in trials (?) ... of the land of the Achaeans
        ....
60   ......
        ...... of the lovely robe,

and [Peirene, maiden] with the braided crown,   Ant. 3
and all the other honoured daughters
of the ancient singing river,
taken in the exalting beds of gods.
    ......] city
    ....] victory [......
    ....] the sound of pipes
    ....
70   ....

    ....   Epode 3
......] to praise golden [Aphrodite] violet-haired,
mother of the unyielding Loves,
......] famed among mortals
    ....
......] guest-friend [......
    ....
    ....] the song

which ....] both for you when you are dead   Str. 4
80   and for] those who come after
will forever proclaim [.. through] endless time
your] victory at Nemea. Splendid success,
when it wins real praise,
is treasured on high among the gods.
When men speak truly there remains,
even if [a man should die,
the loveliest plaything of the [deep-girdled] Muses.

Many are the ...... of men,   Ant. 4
Col.21 but God's will brings to light
90   what is [hidden] in the [dark] of night;
    ....] and the better
    ....
    ....
    ....
    ....] to few
men [is it given to know] the future.

Epode 4

...... ? Zeus] granted his favour
and the god-honoured city ...... [? of] Dionysos
to dwell in ....
100   golden-sceptred ......
praise him ...... who wins success;
with revels [of young men
sing] for Timoxenos' son
the praise of his pent[athlon victory.

ODE 10

FOR AN ATHENIAN

Stadion and Hippios, Isthmian Games

1   Fame … you visit   Str. 1
the races [of men?] and …

......

......

......

...... , that golden- [
… with the eyes …
rest and ease ......
… and now your sister's husband has stirred
10   the sweet-voiced honey-bee from the island where it dwells,

to have at hand a deathless   Ant. 1
monument of the Muses –
a delight for men to share –
declaring your prowess to those who walk the earth,
for the times when, by the grace of Victory's goddess,
garlanding your blond head with flowers,
you brought glory to broad Athens
and renown to the sons of Oineus
at Poseidon's far-famed games,
20 Col. 22 displaying to the Greeks the speed of your dashing feet.

For when he stood on the stadion's finishing line,   Epode 1
breath hot like a storm-wind, and again
when he spattered the watchers' cloaks with oil,
as he dashed into the close-packed throng,
after rounding the turns in the four-length course,
twice the heralds of the
fair-minded judges
proclaimed him Isthmian victor;

twice also at Nemea, by the holy altar of Zeus,   Str. 2
30 son of Kronos; and renowned Thebes
welcomed him, and the broad dancing-grounds
of Argos; Sicyon too, by god's will,
and those who hold Pellene,
who dwell in Euboia's rich [cornlands
and the sacred island of Aigina.
Each seeks a different path to tread,
hoping to win a clear renown.
Countless are the skills of men.

For indeed the clever man,   Ant. 2
honoured by the Graces' gift,
40 or with some skill in prophecy,
grows strong with golden hope;
another bends his artful bow at boys;
for others the heart swells over ploughed lands
and herds of cattle.
The future brings to birth ends unforeseeable
as chance weighs down the scale.
Best is – for a noble man to be
much-envied among men.

I know the great power that wealth has too;   Epode 2
50 it makes the useless useful.
Why in my zeal do I drive my song far off the track?
Good cheer appears for mortals
after the victory;
Col. 23 of pipes ......
mingle ...
must ......

ODE 11

FOR ALEXIDAMOS OF METAPONTION

Boys' Wrestling, Pythian Games

1	Goddess of Victory, whose gifts are sweet,	Str. 1
	to you [alone] the father	
	high-throned	
	and standing at the side of Zeus	
	on Olympos, rich in gold,	
	you determine the end of excellence	
	for immortals and for men.	
	Be gracious, daughter of long-haired	
	Styx, who judges straight; now again,	
10	by your favour, Metapontion, god-honoured city,	
	resounds with festal cheer	
	and the revels of strong-limbed young men.	
	They hail in song the Pythian victor,	
	Phaiskos' admirable son.	

	The lovely Leto's son,	Ant. 1
	god born on Delos, welcomed him	
	with gracious glance,	
	and many crowns of flowers fell	
	on the plain of Kirrha	
20	around the feet of Alexidamos	
	for the strength of his all-conquering wrestling.	
	That day at least the sun did not see him	
	thrown to the ground.	
	And I will say this –	
	on the hallowed soil of holy Pelops too,	
	by Alpheos' lovely stream,	
	he would, had not the pathway of straight justice been diverted,	
	have crowned his hair	

56

	with the silvery olive that welcomes all,	Epode 1
30	and come to calf-rearing [Italy] and his home.	
	For in that land of the lovely dance	
Col. 24	[many a] boy he brought [to the ground]	

with the silvery olive that welcomes all,

and come to calf-rearing [Italy] and his home.
For in that land of the lovely dance
[many a] boy he brought [to the ground]
with subtle skills.
Either a god was to blame,
or perhaps the wandering judgments of men
wrested the highest prize from his hands.
But now the goddess of the wild,
she of the golden distaff,
gentle Artemis, famed for archery,
has given him shining victory.
To her the son of Abas once
set up an altar, rich in prayer,
he and his daughters finely-robed,

daughters whom all-powerful Hera drove in flight
from the lovely halls of Proitos,
binding their minds
in the strong yoke of madness.
For they, in youthful spirit, maidens still,
went to the precinct of the goddess,
she who wears the purple girdle;
claimed that their father far outstripped in wealth
the fair-haired consort of august Zeus,
god of wide-ranging power.
Angered, the goddess
put in their hearts a wandering confusion.
And crying a shivering cry
they ran to the mountain, slender-leaved,

leaving the city of Tiryns
and its god-built streets.
For there the fearless warriors,
bronze-armoured demigods,
were living with their envied king –
ten years already since they left Argos,
dear to gods.
For there sprang up between the brothers,
Proitos and Akrisios,
a raging quarrel, from slight cause;

they, with conflict passing justice and
ruinous fighting, would have brought their people down.
But the people prayed to the sons of Abas,
70   heirs to the rich barley-land,

that the younger settle Tiryns   Epode 2
before they fell into some grim necessity.
Zeus son of Kronos assented,
honouring the race of Danaos
and Lynkeus the charioteer,
to give them rest from their hateful troubles.
The mighty Cyclopes came
and built a splendid wall
for the glorious city,
80   where the far-famed godlike heroes dwelt
when they left renowned horse-rearing Argos.
From there the virgin daughters of Proitos,
hair shining black,
rushed off in flight.

Grief seized their father's heart   Str. 3
and a strange thought struck him.
He had a mind to drive
the two-edged sword into his breast,
90   but his spearmen, with soothing words
and force of hands, restrained him.
A full twelve-month they wandered in flight distracted,
through thick-shaded forest,
through Arcadia's sheep pastures.
But when at last their father came
to Lousos' lovely stream,
he cleansed his body in its waters,
and raising his hands to the light

from the sun's swift chariot,   Ant. 3
100 Col. 26 called upon the soft-eyed daughter of Leto,
goddess who wears the crimson veil,
to free his wretched children
from their wandering frenzy.
'And I will sacrifice to you
twenty blood-red oxen, still unyoked.'
She whose father is supreme,

huntress of wild beasts, heard his prayer.
She persuaded Hera
and gave the flower-crowned maidens
rest from their godless madness.
110 At once they built a precinct and an altar,
stained it with blood of sheep
and founded dancing choruses of women.

From there you followed the Achaian heroes, Epode 3
lovers of war,
to their horse-rearing city,
and with good fortune
you dwell now in Metapontion,
golden mistress of your people.
By the fair waters of Kasas
[their ancestors founded] for you
120 a lovely hallowed sanctuary,
when at last, fulfilling the will of the blessed gods,
they sacked the well-built city of Priam
with the bronze-armoured sons of Atreus.
He whose mind is straight
will find in every age
countless deeds of valour among the Achaians.

ODE 12

FOR TEISIAS OF AIGINA

Wrestling, Nemean Games

1	Klio, queen of song,	Str. 1
	if ever before you have guided my mind,	
	so guide it now	
	like a skilled helmsman.	
5	For Victory, august goddess, bids me come	
	to Aigina's blessed island,	
	to honour the god-built city for guest-friends,	

and [to sing of] the strong-limbed wrestling at Nemea. Ant. 1

9 Col. 27   (9-32 missing)

15   Epode 1
24   Str. 2
31   Ant. 2

....
of a guest-friend ...... city- [?
35   at the Games of neighbouring peoples.
           For thirty splendid victories
           they were celebrated, some at [Pytho,

some at the throat, pine-fragrant,   Epode 2
of Pelops' holy island,
40   some in the precinct of Zeus of Nemea,
           god of the crimson lightning flash;
           ...... these, and by [Alpheos] silver-swirling

43 Col. 28   (43-69 missing)

ODE 13

FOR PYTHEAS OF AIGINA

Pankration, Nemean Games, before 481 BC

(1-7 missing)

Str. 1

1
8 Col. 29   ....
             ......] Klio
10   ....
              ....
              ....

(13-43 missing or too fragmentary to translate)

13	Ant. 1
25	Epode 1
34	Str. 2

44 Col. 30 'he will stay the sinner from his vaunting violence,
exacting from mortal men their punishment;

Ant. 2

such is the hand that Perseus' son
lays, hard on the neck
of the lion, raw flesh eater,
with wrestling skills of every kind.
50   For the flashing bronze that lays men low
will not pass through
that fearsome body,
but the blade bent back;
in truth I declare that here one day
the sweat will run
as the Greeks strain
for the pankration's crown.'

61

......] by the altar of Zeus whose rule is supreme   Epode 2
the flowers [of Victory] bringer of glory,
60   nourish for men – few among mortals always –
a golden renown
that shines afar in their own lifetime,
and when the dark cloud
of death conceals,
there remains – a destiny unshakeable –
the deathless fame of success.

You too, son of Lampon,   Str. 3
have won this glory, at Nemea,
and come, hair crowned with garlands
70   of flowers, all in bloom,
to the high-built streets of [Aiakos'] city;
so] the island of your fathers
swells] with the [sweet voice] of revelry
that brings delight to men,
for you displayed all-mastering
strength in the pankration.
Aigina gentle-minded, daughter
of the swirling river,

Col. 31   surely the [son of Kronos   Ant. 3
80   has given you great honour,
displaying before all the Greeks
the blaze of [new-won victory.
To praise your [power
a girl in high pride often sings
     ....
dancing, like a carefree fawn
on light feet leaping
to the flowered [hill-sides,
with her neighbours,
90   her famed [companions.

And the maidens, crowned   Epode 3
with crimson flowers and rushes –
their native ornament –
sing of your [child,
O queen of the land that welcomes all,

and of rose-armed Endais,
who, joined with Aiakos in his bed,
bore [godlike] Peleus
and the [warrior] Telamon.

100   Their battle-rousing sons   Str. 4
I shall celebrate –
swift Achilles
and the high-couraged son of lovely Eriboia,
Aias, hero of the mighty shield,
who stood upon the stern and held
bold-hearted Hektor,
bronze-[helmeted,
urgent to [burn the ships
with fire inhuman,
110   while the son of Peleus nursed
the tearing anger in his heart

and freed the Trojans   Ant. 4
from destruction.
For before they would not leave
Col. 32   the wondrous city
of Ilion, many-towered,
but cowered, fear-stricken for the painful fighting,
so long as Achilles raging
drove havoc over the plain,
120   shaking his murderous spear.
But when the fearless [son
of the Nereid violet-crowned
left off from war –

as the wind from the North   Epode 4
on the sea's dark swell,
encountered at the rising of the night,
sunders the [hearts of men] beneath the waves,
but with the dawn that brings light to mortals
it leaves off, and a fair wind soothes the sea;
130   on the breath of the South wind
they belly the sail
and gladly reach the land unhoped for –

so the Trojans when they heard   Str. 5
that Achilles, spear-fighter,
was staying in his tents
for the sake of a fair-haired woman,
Briseis – desire in her lovely limbs –
raised their hands to the gods,
seeing the sunlight bright
140   behind the storm.
Headlong they left
Laomedon's walls
and swept to the plain
to start the strong encounter.

They drove the Danaans to flight;   Ant. 5
Ares, spear-god, stirred them on,
and Apollo, Loxias, lord of Lycians;
they came to the sea's edge,
where they fought
150 Col. 33 by the splendid sterns of the ships.
The dark earth ran red
with the blood
of warriors slain
by the hand of Hektor.
    ......] for the heroes
    ....] through the on-rush of the godlike.

    ......] with proud hopes,   Epode 5
spirited, crying
a mighty cry
160   the Trojan horsemen
......] the dark-eyed ships
......] and banquets in
.........] would hold the god-built city.
But see, before that they would stain blood-red
Scamander's swirling waters,

dying at the hands of the sons of Aiakos,   Str. 6
destroyers of city walls.
If even their [.........
or on a [pyre] of wood deep-piled

Ode 13

(170-4 missing)

175   For far-shining excellence
is not obscured, hidden,
in the lightless [veil] of night,

      but, rich in renown   Ant. 6
      enduring, she spreads,
180   unfailing, over the earth
and the restless sea.
And she honours too,
Aiakos' glorious [island,
and guides the city
Col. 34   with Eukleia, lover of the crown,
and wise Eunomia,
she whose allotted realm is revelry,
and who keeps in peace
the cities of pious men.

190   Sing, boys, the great glory   Epode 6
of Pytheas' victory,
of Menandros' care and help as well,
which holy Athena, great-hearted
goddess of the golden chariot,
has honoured often already, by the waters of Alpheos,
and crowning the hair of countless men besides
with victors' garlands
at the panhellenic Games.

      If a man is not over-mastered   Str. 7
200   by envy, bold of tongue,
let him justly praise
the man of skill.
Mortal men find fault with all achievement,
but truth will prevail;
time that overcomes all things
always holds on high
success nobly won.
The idle [voice] of enemies
fades, unseen.

(210-19 missing)

65

211   Ant. 7

220 Col. 35 warms his heart with hope.
            I too place my trust in this,
            and in the Muses, crimson-veiled,

            as I display this [new-spun garland   Epode 7
            of praise; and I honour
            the splendid hospitality
            which you, Lampon, [have given me –
            may you in return regard my [gift] to your [son
            as no slight one.
            If indeed Klio rich in flowers
            has truly filled my mind with song,
230   words of delight shall herald him
            to all the people.

ODE 14

FOR KLEOPTOLEMOS OF THESSALY

Chariot Race, Petraian Games

1	To be fate-favoured of god	Str. 1

1   To be fate-favoured of god   Str. 1
    is best for men;
    fortune, falling, a heavy burden,
    crushes even the good,
    and when she prospers
    raises the bad to prominence.
    Each has a different kind of honour.

    Men win success in countless ways,   Ant. 1
    but one stands out before all –
10 he who] governs with just mind
    that which lies to his hand.
    The voice of the lyre,
    the sweet song of the chorus,
    do not belong in battles, heavy with grief,

    nor in festivities the ring   Epode 1
    of clashing bronze; but for every
    work of men the [right time
    is best; god also [...] him who succeeds.
    Now, as a gift for Kleoptolemos,
20 we must celebrate the sanctuary of Poseidon Petraios,
    and, for his chariot victory,
    the renowned son of Pyrrichos,

    who, of hospitable, right-judging ...   Str. 2

Col. 36   (the remainder is missing)

ODE 14 B

FOR ARISTOTELES OF LARISA

<table>
<tr><td>1</td><td>Hestia gold-enthroned,
you who, seated in mid-city, foster
the great prosperity of the renowned
Agathokleadai, wealthy men,
by sweet-smelling Peneios
in the valleys of sheep-rearing Thessaly;
from there to fertile Kirrha
came Aristoteles also,
and twice was crowned,</td><td>Str. 1</td></tr>
<tr><td>10</td><td>a grace upon horse-mastering Larisa
.........</td><td></td></tr>
</table>

(the remainder is missing)

Commentary

ODE 1
FOR ARGEIOS OF CEOS
Boys' Boxing, Isthmian Games, before 452 BC

The event

Odes 1 and 2 were composed to celebrate the same victory. The successful athlete would naturally be honoured twice, first at the festival itself, and then again on his return home, where the victory was a source of great pride to his fellow citizens. Sometimes, as on this occasion, a formal ode was commissioned for both celebrations. The short Ode 2, it seems, was written to be sung at the Isthmus, at the celebration immediately after the Games, whereas Ode 1 was the major epinician, presented on the return of Argeios to his home in Ceos. (Cf. Odes 6 and 7, for Lachon, also of Ceos.)

The title of Ode 1 has disappeared in the damage to the opening of the papyrus. Ode 2 has merely the abbreviated title 'for the same', but the occasion of the odes can be discovered from internal evidence. It is clear from 1.156 and 2.7 that the victory was won at the Isthmian Games, and from 2.4 that the victor's name was Argeios. At 2.2 we learn that he came from Ceos, while at 1.148 and 2.13 his father is named as Pantheides. Further, part of an inscription from Ceos survives which recorded the names of athletes from Ceos who won at the Isthmian and Nemean Games (*IG* XII 5 608; the inscription itself was engraved much later than the fifth century, but it certainly depended on contemporary records). In line 15 of this inscription, in the list of winners at the Isthmus, the name of Argeios son of Pantheides is found, as victor in an unidentified event in the 'boys' age class. This is surely the victory celebrated in Odes 1 and 2. The event was probably boxing; the descriptions at 1.142-5 and 2.4 ('strong of hand', 'lion-hearted', 'light-footed', 'bold of hand') are perhaps best suited to a boxer, and we learn from Ode 6.8 that there had been at least one victory in boxing by an athlete from Ceos prior to that ode. The pankration and wrestling are also possible, but less likely (for nimbleness of foot in a wrestler, however, see note on 9.36).

The date of the ode cannot be exactly determined. However, in the Cean inscription mentioned above (*IG* XII 5 608) the name of Argeios appears again (line 26) in the list of Nemean victors, this time in the 'youths' age class, and this Nemean victory stands immediately before the record of two successes in boys' events at Nemea by Lachon, son of Aristomenes. Now this Lachon also won the boys' stadion at Olympia, celebrated in Odes 6 and 7, and securely dated to 452 BC. Lachon's Nemean victories are probably not earlier, for they are not mentioned in Odes 6 or 7, although it was common practice to enhance the praise of the victor by referring to earlier successes (cf. e.g. 1.157-8). But they cannot be much later either. The upper age limit for 'boys' at Nemea was probably 16, while at Olympia, where there were only two classes ('boys' and 'men') it was probably 18. If Lachon won both of his Nemean victories at the same Nemea in 451 BC, that is, if he was still a 'boy' (maximum 16) in 451, he could have been 15 at the Olympiad of 452, competing against others up to 18 years old. But if he won one (or both) of his listed successes at the following Nemea of 449 BC, he must have been only 13, perhaps even 12, at the 452 Olympiad. Victory at such an age against 18-year-olds is hardly plausible. We should therefore place both of Lachon's Nemean victories in 451 BC.

Now Argeios was victorious at Nemea as a 'youth' (17-19 years, probably), and this is recorded on the inscription above – i.e. not later than – the victories of Lachon (see above). If he won this victory in the same year as Lachon (451), and if he was only 17 at the time, he could have been 16 (i.e. a 'boy') at the Isthmian Games of 452 BC. 452 is therefore absolutely the latest date at which we can place Argeios' Isthmian victory. It is more probable, however, that Argeios' Nemean victory was earlier than those of Lachon, and there is no need to suppose that he was at the bottom end of the age range, so that an earlier date is likely. For example, if he won at Nemea in, say, 455, and was 18 at the time, the latest date at which he could win as a 'boy' at the Isthmus would be 458 BC.

The myth

At 112f. Bacchylides tells the story of Dexithea, her union with the legendary king Minos of Knossos in Crete, and the birth of their son Euxantios. But this myth is not told in isolation; Minos arrives in Ceos 'on the third day' (112-13), that is, presumably, on the third day after the events just described in the preceding fragmentary part of the ode. So the story of Dexithea is connected to what has gone before. Further, at line 73 most of a word is preserved which is almost certainly the woman's name 'Makelo', who is known from other sources for this legend (see further below) either as the mother or the sister of Dexithea. It seems probable, therefore, that the whole central section of Ode 1 (perhaps from as early as Epode 1, line 17) was devoted to a single continuous mythic narrative, describing the fortunes of the family of Makelo and Dexithea.

The first four columns of the papyrus are very badly damaged; much of the first 140 lines of the ode is missing, and what survives must be reconstituted from a number of small fragments, so that few details can be recovered with certainty. Fortunately, the story is known to us from other sources (with insignificant variations in the forms of some of the names).

Ovid (*Ibis* 475) alludes briefly to the destruction of Makelo, together with her husband, by the thunderbolt of Zeus, and in their attempts to explain this passage the ancient commentators (*scholia*) give us the full story. There lived in Ceos a race of semi-divine creatures called Telchines, volcanic demons, who were at once metal-smiths and malicious wizards. Originally from Rhodes, they had been driven out from there and had settled (some of them at least) in Ceos. Their chief in Ceos was Damon, and among the daughters of Damon were Makelo and Dexithea. Now when Zeus (according to Nonnos 18.35, Zeus and Apollo) had occasion to visit Ceos, he was hospitably entertained by Makelo and her sisters, who thus earned the gratitude of the gods. The Telchines themselves, however, had by their evil arts blighted the crops and the fruits of the earth (according to Nonnos, 14.42f., this happened in Rhodes and was the cause of their expulsion from that island, but the *scholia* on Ovid at least imply that it happened in Ceos). Zeus therefore determined to wipe out the entire race of the Telchines, but because of their hospitality to the gods the daughters of Damon were spared. (The death of Makelo, to which Ovid alludes (*Ibis* 475, see above) remains unexplained; notice however that Pindar also (*Paian* 4.42f.) mentions only the mother of Euxantios (i.e. Dexithea) as being spared when Ceos and her people were wiped out. Callimachos on the other hand (*Aitia* 3 fr. 75.64f.) makes Makelo the mother of Dexithea, and says that these two alone were spared when the Telchines were destroyed. Evidently two versions of the legend were current. See further note on 73, below.) Dexithea (her name means 'she who receives the god') was then further rewarded and honoured by the arrival of Minos and her marriage to that great king, resulting in the birth of a son Euxantios, who became the eponymous founder of the distinguished clan of the Euxantidai in Ceos.

Thus we have a straightforward mythological narrative of a familiar type, a story of sin and punishment on a grand scale. The gods destroy the wicked and begin again. The whole race of sinners is wiped out from the face of the earth, and only the good survive to renew the line. Exactly how Bacch. handled this story, how much of it he included, and where he placed the emphases, must remain unclear, but it is probable that, in such a long poem, his treatment was full and extensive. The surviving fragments may provide some clues. Lines 19-20 (if in fact this fragment is correctly placed) seem to indicate that someone starts out on a journey – perhaps Zeus on his way to Ceos for the visit during which he was hospitably entertained by Makelo and Dexithea. Then (perhaps in consequence of a dream warning of the impending destruction of the Telchines) one of the women, on rising from sleep, advises the others to leave their ancient city and seek a new home by the shore (50-5). In the next major fragment Makelo addresses some persons, probably Dexithea and her sisters, and laments the loss of home and family (73-81), although others (e.g. Jebb, p. 445) suppose that she is speaking to the disguised Zeus and Apollo, and that it is at this point that the hospitality for which they were saved is offered. On this view, Makelo would be here apologizing for the inadequacy of that hospitality. After another long gap in the papyrus, the narrative resumes with the arrival of Minos (112f.) and the birth of Euxantios, who subsequently founds a new city at that place on the shore to which his mother and her sisters had fled (139-40; cf. 54-5). It is from this city and from the line founded by Euxantios that Argeios stems, and so the poet returns from the myth to the present and to the praise of the victor. (For an even more imaginatively romantic reconstruction, see Jebb, pp. 447-8.)

In all of this there has been no mention of the Telchines themselves, of their sinful *hubris*, as Callimachos calls their behaviour (*Aitia* 3, fr. 75.68-9), or of their destruction. But in the large gaps between the surviving fragments of the ode there is plenty of room for this story, and we may be fairly sure that Bacch. included it. Fr. 52 of Bacch. is a quotation from Tzetzes, which tells us that Bacch. somewhere mentioned the names of four Telchines, and this ode is a likely place for that mention. But more importantly, the meaning and implications of the myth of the Telchines seem very relevant to Bacchylides' purposes in this ode, and he would surely have included the story for this reason.

There is a very clear parallel between the myth and the situation of Argeios and his family, which Bacch. is at pains to draw to our attention. Dexithea was rewarded and honoured for her respect for, and hospitality to, strangers, who turned out to be gods in disguise. So Pantheides, the victor's father, and descendant of Dexithea, continued that tradition of hospitality and respect (150), and in return won great blessings from Apollo and the Graces (147-8, 151). Likewise the victor himself, Argeios, has been granted this victory (and others) by Poseidon as 'reward for benefactions' (157). The parallel thus drawn then leads into the concluding series of generalizations, in which the themes of excellence, generosity to the gods, and moderation in life are again prominent (e.g. 163). (Interestingly, Pindar's allusion to the story (*Paian* 4.35f.) occurs in a context in which Euxantios refuses the wealth and power offered him by the Cretans, out of a very proper reverence for the gods and fear of excess. Clearly these qualities were characteristic of the family from the beginning.) The Telchines on the other hand illustrate the other side of the coin. They in their folly had abused the powers and privileges which they had been granted, and suffered a just retribution in consequence. Thus both parts of the myth are directly relevant to the present situation and to the purposes of the ode. If we are indeed correct in suggesting that the story was told here, the Telchines would stand as a negative *exemplum*, illustrating by contrast the character and behaviour of Argeios and his family, while Dexithea serves as a positive *exemplum*, illustrating by parallel the fortunes of the victor, who like her deservedly won honour from the gods. (For the terms 'positive' and 'negative' *exemplum*, see D.C. Young, *Pindar Isthmian 7, Myth and Exempla*, Leiden 1971, 37-8.) Thus the myth serves to enhance the praise of the victor in a complex way. Not only does it praise the victor's homeland by giving Ceos and its people a distinguished, even divine, ancestry, but the victor himself is included in that distinction as a descendant of Dexithea and Minos, while at the same time the positive and negative *exempla* in the myth enlarge our understanding of the character of Argeios and its rewards.

The poem

The fragmentary condition of the papyrus, resulting in the loss of more than half of this ode, makes it very difficult to determine the structure of the poem. In broad terms, however, it is fairly clear that the myth occupied the long central section of the ode and was framed by sections of more obviously programmatic material, that is, praise of the Games, the victor and his family. This simple tripartite structure is then completed by the final gnomic section (for the meaning of this term see the general introduction, n. 26) in which the lesson to be learned from Argeios' victory is extended to all men. In detail, however, much remains unclear, especially in the earlier part of the poem, and it will at once be obvious how much of what follows is speculative.

The poem opens with the typical invocation to the Muses, in which the poet seeks inspiration for his song. He invites the Muses to sing of the 'lord of the Isthmus' (6), that is, Poseidon, thus passing at once, *via* this reference to its patron god, to praise of the Isthmian festival and of the Games where the victory was won. This introduction leads naturally into the first section of praise of the victor, (cf. 9f.), where 'island' probably refers to Ceos, the victor's home. We might suppose a sequence of thought as follows: 'Sing, Muses, of Poseidon and his Games (5-6), of Ceos too (9), home of Argeios, who won at the Isthmus (13-14), descendant of Euxantios, whose mother welcomed Zeus when he came (19f.).' Thus the introduction and praise of the victor could provide a rapid and easy transition into the myth, by means of such a reference to the victor's ancestor, Euxantios. The myth then returns at its end to the birth of Euxantios (126-7), creating a typical ring-compositional frame within which the mythic narrative probably proceeded in a straightforward chronological sequence.

From the mention of Euxantios the poet passes to the second section of praise of Argeios, the victor (141f.), which picks up and balances the first (9f.), so that the ring-compositional structure becomes yet more elaborate. But this second section of victor-praise is interrupted by a brief but important digression (146-54) in praise of Pantheides, the victor's father, which is arranged in a little ring-composition of its own: 'the victory of Argeios enhanced the blessings of his father; among those blessings are five fine children, and one of these is the present victor Argeios'. In this way Bacchylides includes in his commission appropriate praise of the victor's family, before returning to his main subject – the victor himself, his prowess and the exemplary excellence of his character, for which the victory is seen as a reward. This then provides in turn a perfectly natural transition into the concluding sequence of *gnomes*, in which the value and the rewards of excellence are the major theme.

This final section of the ode (159-84) is itself very carefully constructed. There is again an overriding ring-compositional structure, within which the meaning is highlighted by the arrangement of key elements to create parallels and contrasts. The theme throughout is *areta* ('excellence') – a key word in the epinician poet's vocabulary. Bacch. uses the word 10 times, 11 if fr. 56 is correctly attributed to him; it is above all the quality displayed by the victors whom the poets celebrate, and it goes hand in hand with all those other qualities valued by the aristocratic society revealed in the poems, such as generosity, respect for one's fellow men and reverence for the gods. This theme, then, is announced without preamble – the best and only worthwhile honour comes from the pursuit and display of *areta* (159-60). This is at once contrasted with the vainglorious pursuit of wealth, which is no measure of a man's true worth (161-2), while an ancillary contrast is introduced between selfish greed and generosity; wealth is not all bad – if a man uses his wealth well, he may hope for reward (163-5). Thus Bacch. deprecates the pursuit of wealth for its own sake. This theme is then developed through a further contrast: better than the idle pursuit of wealth is a modest acceptance of one's station in life, whether rich or poor. This motif is stated twice (166-8 and 169-71), and summed up in 172-3; all levels of wealth have their own needs. But this is not the climax of Bacch.'s thought, nor a policy which he advocates above all else; rather the idea serves to reinforce the previous motif of the vanity and folly of greed. But human nature is such that men are never content with what they have (174-7); always they seek what eludes their grasp. So in the final Epode of the poem Bacch. returns to the theme of worthless ambition and the specious and ephemeral nature of the honour which it may bring (178-80), which leads in turn, again by way of contrast, into the final affirmation of the lasting value of *areta* (181-4). (See also note on 9.18.)

1 **daughters of Zeus** i.e. the Muses. Bacch. begins this ode, as he so often does, with the traditional appeal to the Muses to inspire his song. The Muses were daughters of Zeus and Memory (Hes. *Theog.* 53f.); memory is obviously a vital attribute for the early poet, composing orally, so that the Muses, as daughters of Memory, were naturally thought to inspire the poet, and from Homer on it became conventional to make such an appeal for inspiration. Sometimes the poet speaks as if it were the Muse herself who sings, and the poet regards himself merely as a vehicle for the transmission of the song – an intermediary between the divinities and man. See further on 3.1.

who rules on high The adjective (*hupsimedon*; repeated at 15.51) has a conventional ring, although it does not occur in *Iliad* or *Odyssey*.

Hesiod uses it at *Theog.* 529, from where Bacch. may have borrowed it. (For adjectives compounded with *hupsi-* see note on 13.71.)

2 Pierian maidens For this description of the Muses, cf. 16.3 and 19.3-4. At *Theog.* 53f. Hesiod tells the story of the birth of the Muses in Pieria, the region just to the north of Mt Olympus in Thessaly (cf. *Il.* 14.226, where Pieria is the first place over which Hera passes on her way from Olympus to Lemnos). Because of their proximity to the home of the gods on Olympus, the Muses are themselves often called Olympian (e.g. Hom. *Il.* 2.491; Hes. *Theog.* 25 and 52). Pieria was no doubt the original, and remained the principal, centre of their cult.

3 famed for the lyre The Muses had no original or special connection with the lyre; dance and song were rather their principal activities, as Hesiod describes them at *Theog.* 1-104. No doubt the description arises simply from their connection with Bacch.'s song, which was accompanied on the lyre (see e.g. frr. 20 B 1 and 20 C 1). Cf. also 4.8, where the Muse Urania is 'queen of the lyre', whereas at 6.10 she is 'queen of song'. However at *Theog.* 95 Hesiod says that it is because of the Muses that there are singers and lyre-players on the earth. On the nature and function of ancient lyres, see M.L. West, *Ancient Greek Music*, Oxford 1992, p. 48f.

4 weave If the text is correctly restored here, this would be an invitation to the Muses to create and sing the victory song, and would thus represent the poet as mouthpiece for the Muses (see note on 1 above, and for this attitude cf. also 3.1 and 9.3-4). The image of weaving is used again at 5.9-12 and 19.8; on both of these occasions, however, the poet speaks of himself as creator of the song.

6 lord of the Isthmus i.e. Poseidon, in whose honour the Isthmian Games were held. According to Paus. (2.1.6) Helios and Poseidon argued over possession of the Isthmus; Briareos gave judgment in favour of Poseidon, so that ever since that land has been sacred to him.

7-8 wise Nereus' daughter Amphitrite, cf. 17.110-11. When the sons of Kronos drew lots for influence in the universe, Poseidon won the sea (*Il.* 15.190-2); he thus displaced Nereus, an older, pre-Olympian sea-god (see Hes. *Theog.* 233-5) and took Nereus' daughter Amphitrite as his consort. Nereus himself was reduced to the status of 'the old man of the sea'.
wise Wisdom was traditionally the attribute of the old man of the sea; cf. Pind. *Pyth.* 3.92 (using the same adjective as Bacch. here: *euboulos*); Hesiod also (*Theog.* 232f.) describes his righteousness and good sense at length.

13-14 O god-built gates ... i.e. Corinth and the Isthmus; in a very natural metaphor, the Isthmus, which provides the only land access to the southern part of Greece, is described as the 'gateway to the Peloponnese'. Thuc. (1.9.1) relates how Pelops came to Mycenae from Asia, bringing great wealth, established the Pelopid dynasty through his son Atreus and became so powerful that the whole land was named after him (cf. Strabo, 7.7.1). The name Peloponnese in fact means 'the island of Pelops', which is exactly what Bacch. calls it (again at 12.39; cf. Soph. *OC* 696-7, also the Homeric *Cypria* fr. 11.3-4). For Pelops, see further on 5.181 and 8.32.

god-built This adjective (*theodmatos*) recurs at 13.163, where it is used, appropriately, of Troy (cf. *Il.* 8.519) in allusion to the story that the walls of Troy were built by Apollo and Poseidon for the king Laomedon (*Il.* 7.452-3). Bacch. uses it again at 11.58, of Tiryns, and relates at 11.77f. how the walls of that city were built by the Cyclopes, giants who were often regarded as craftsmen for the gods, and were credited with building the fortifications of many cities in the Argolid besides Tiryns. The massive walls which defend the citadel of Corinth are, like those of Tiryns, 'Cyclopean', and this may be the point of the description here. However the adjective is fairly common in the poets, and is used of various places (Delos, Pind. *Ol.* 6.59; Athens, Soph. *El.* 707; Aigina, Bacch. 12.7) where the divine connection is less obvious; it may have been reduced to a generalized honorific.

shining One of Bacch.'s favourite decorative adjectives (*liparos*); see note on 158, below.

19-20 the horses ... flew It would seem that someone starts out on a journey here. If this marks the beginning of the mythic narrative, the reference is perhaps to the journey of Zeus to Ceos for the visit during which he enjoyed the hospitality of the daughters of Damon. For a possible structure and sequence of thought, see intro., above.

49 ....]agora Probably the latter part of the name of one of the daughters of Damon, the 'maidens' mentioned in 48 (cf. 72). Blass suggests e.g. Lysagora.

50 from sleep The context suggests that the girls are warned in a dream (perhaps received by [Lys]agora, 49) of the imminent destruction of the Telchines, and are advised to save themselves by leaving home. The *scholia* on Ovid, *Ibis* (see intro., above) do not mention this dream or advice.

that soothes the mind This adjective (*meliphron*) recurs at fr. 4.76, again used of sleep. It is fairly common in the poets, e.g. Hom. *Il.* 2.34, *Od.* 7.182, Hes. *Shield* 428, etc. Curiously compounded of the words meaning 'honey' and 'mind', it should mean: 'having a mind with the quality of honey', and so Stanford understands it in his note on *Od.* 7.182, referring to Tennyson's 'honey-hearted'. But this is surely wrong; the word is normally applied to things like sleep and wine, which do not have a mind like honey, but which rather act upon the mind with the sweetness and soothing effect of honey.

54-5 a home ... in the light of the sun The girls are advised, it seems, to make a new home on the western shore of Ceos. This is no doubt the very place at which Euxantios later founds his splendid city. See note on 139, below.

72 ....]**sagora** cf. on line 49, above.

73 Makelo The restoration of this name is virtually certain. It would appear, therefore, that Makelo participated in the events described here, which perhaps related the removal from their home in order not to be involved in the destruction visited upon the Telchines, or perhaps the offer of hospitality to the gods, for which in fact the women were spared. Why then was she killed, as Ovid (and the *scholia*, following Nicander), relate, and as Pindar suggests? In fact Bacch. is probably following the version of the legend presented by Callimachos, in which both Makelo and Dexithea were spared (see intro., above). Maehler (vol. 2, p. 6) argues against this. It is true that Bacch. nowhere speaks of Makelo as the mother of Dexithea, as Callimachos does; rather he mentions 'maidens' (48) and daughters (138; the daughters of Damon?), but the ode is so fragmentary that this argument is not strong (as indeed Maehler concedes). On the other hand, Callimachos quotes as his source Xenomedes of Ceos, a fifth-century BC mythographer/historian, who wrote, according to Callimachos (*Aitia* 3, fr. 75.54-5) the entire history of that island. The work of Xenomedes would surely have been known to his fellow-Cean Bacchylides, who might well have used it as a source for the legend in his poem. Alternatively, Xenomedes may have used the poem of Bacch. in the compilation of his 'history'.

74 she who loves to spin See note on 9.1.

75 fair-flowing stream The same words are used at 9.42. The river referred to here is presumably the Elixos, mentioned by Strabo (10.5.6) as flowing to the sea at Koressia, on the northwest coast of Ceos. Cf. notes on 121 and 139, below.

76-7 addressed them – Perhaps in the preceding part of the ode (57-69) now lost, the destruction of the Telchines was related, and now, in this fragment, Makelo speaks to the others, lamenting their loss and comforting them. Others suppose that she is here addressing Zeus, offering hospitality and apologizing for its paucity (see intro.), but this is less likely. The hospitality for which the girls were saved will naturally precede, not follow, the dream which initiated their salvation.

comforting The word (*sainousa*) properly means 'fawning', 'flattering', and might be thought more appropriate to winning the goodwill of strangers (see previous note), but the verb also commonly means 'to gladden', 'to cheer up'; it is used in this sense at 164 below, which suggests that this is the meaning here. Perhaps there is a deliberate echo.

79 two-fold Properly = 'double-edged', used literally of a sword at 11.87 and fr. 4.72, and commonly in Homer (e.g. *Il.* 10.256) and other poets. Here metaphorical, it refers to the twin blows of misfortune suffered by Makelo, presumably the loss of her father and the loss of her home.

80 poverty Makelo perhaps presents her new-found poverty – no doubt resulting from the loss of home – as one part of the double misfortune which has overtaken her.

112-13 on the third day i.e. the third day after the destruction of the Telchines, if the order of events assumed above (see intro. and note on 76-7, above) is correct.

113 Minos The famous king who gave his name to the splendid 'Minoan' civilization of the Bronze Age which has been unearthed at Knossos and other centres in Crete, as well as in the Cycladic islands. The story of the marriage of Minos and Dexithea is clearly a reflection of a historical situation. There was in the Bronze Age a close connection between Crete and Ceos – excavations at Ayia Irini (adjacent to ancient Koressia; see also on 139, below) on the northwest coast of Ceos have revealed a fine bronze statuette of a youthful worshipper imported from Crete in the fifteenth century BC, as well as a large number of locally made female figures in Minoan dress (see E. Vermeule, *Greece in the Bronze Age*, Chicago 1964, p. 118, also pp. 217 and 285; further references in Maehler, vol. 2, p. 7, nn. 14 and 15). Likewise, the legend of the destruction of the Telchines perhaps reflects the major earthquake which destroyed the Bronze Age temple and its associated settlement at Koressia.

114 shimmering The word (*aiolos*) means 'quick-moving', and then, because rapid movement often produces a flickering effect of light, it comes to mean 'twinkling', 'flashing', etc., and is so used where there is no real or obvious movement. Cf. Soph. *Trach.* 94 (*aiola nux* = 'star-spangled night'). Cf. also 15.58, where the word is used metaphorically of 'profit' as an unworthy goal which flickers uncertainly before one's eyes. Here Bacch. may mean that the sterns of the ships reflect in some way the surface of the sea sparkling in the sunlight, but more probably it is merely a decorative word, somewhat imprecisely used. See also note on 9.36.

116 he took This word (*damasen*) has strong associations with violence. It means (of animals) 'to break in', (of men) 'to subdue by force', (of women) 'to rape'. But the word seems to have become a kind of heroic metaphor for the union between a hero (or a god) and his chosen woman; cf. 9.65 *edamesan* ('taken') and 5.167, where a related word *admeta* ('unwed') is used. Minos' behaviour to Dexithea, therefore, should not be considered reprehensible. But contrast Ode 17, where Minos tries actually to violate Eriboia, and is restrained by Theseus. There (17.43) the same verb (in the form *damaseias*) is used to describe Minos' action.
lovely This adjective (*bathuzonos*) literally means 'deep-girdled', a common poetic description of women and goddesses, beginning with Homer; Bacch. uses it also of the Graces (5.11), Leto (11.15), Theano (15.7) and perhaps the Muses (9.87). The word is clearly decorative and appeals to male perceptions of female beauty; it seems to indicate that the 'girdle' or 'sash' is drawn tight, so as to sit 'deeply recessed' in the folds of the robe, thus suggesting the meaning 'slim-waisted' (see W. Leaf on *Il.* 9.594; also D. Gerber, *Arethusa* 11 (1978), p. 211 n. 21).

Others understand the word as suggesting the practice of drawing the material of the robe up through the girdle so as to hang in a deep fold over it (e.g. W. Leaf, *The Iliad* (Hakkert, Amsterdam, 1971) vol. 2, p. 596. Note that in either case the description does not correspond to the Bronze Age style of women's dress, in which the breasts were left bare under a short open jacket above a narrow-waisted flared skirt (see e.g. E. Vermeule, *Greece in the Bronze Age*, p. 191 and plates XXVII and XXVIII).

118 Zeus ... willed it The preposition used here (*hekati* = 'by the will of') is always used by Bacch. of a divinity, especially the goddess of victory (Nike), who by her grace and goodwill confers the victory upon the athlete (5.35, 6.9, 10.15 and 11.10; see note on 6.9). So here the union with Minos is a mark of the favour of Zeus, designed to bring glory to Dexithea and her descendants. For this reason Zeus is here described as 'god of glory', an epithet nowhere else used of him. See also the following note.

119 half his people After the destruction of the Telchines, Minos re-populated the island with Cretan colonists, leaving Dexithea to become mother and founder of a distinguished line through her son Euxantios. The marriage to Minos, son of Zeus, naturally conferred great glory on Dexithea, as well as on her descendants, the Euxantidai, and the island of Ceos as a whole; thus the myth is not only thematic, in so far as the union with Minos is to be seen as part of her reward for piety; it is programmatic as well, in that it enhances the glory of the victor, his family and his home.

121 craggy Ceos is small and mostly mountainous. (This is indicated also in the description 'without horses' at 8.15 and Pind. *Paian* 4.24. Cf. *Od.* 4.601f., where Telemachos refuses a gift of horses because the hilly terrain of his homeland Ithaca is not suitable for these animals). On the other hand the vines for which Ceos was renowned (see note on 6.7) would grow well on the rocky hillsides. One of the four towns of Ceos mentioned by Strabo (10.5.6) was indeed called *Poieessa*, which is the Greek word for 'grassy', but the name may have been suggested by the fact that the town stood on the only moderately extensive grassy area in the island.

122 Europa's son i.e. Minos; see note on 113, above. Europa, daughter of Phoinix (cf. Bacch. 17.30-31; also *Il.* 14.321-2), was loved by Zeus, who, in the form of a bull, carried her off to Crete, where she bore him two sons, Rhadamanthys and Minos. These two, because of their unfailing reputation for justice, later became (along with Aiakos) judges of the souls of the dead in the Underworld (Hom. *Od.* 11.568-71; Verg. *Aen.* 6.566f.; Horace *Odes* IV 7.21).

125 the tenth month Cf. Hom. Hymn 4.11, where Maia gives birth to Hermes 'when the tenth month was established ...'; also Verg. *Ecl.* 4.61: 'ten months have brought long weariness to your mother'. These may be examples of inclusive counting (see note on 9.23) whereby a normal nine-month pregnancy (by our reckoning) becomes ten. Cf. also note on 11.92.

126 lovely-haired A typical honorific for females; cf. 3.34, where it is used of the daughters of Croesus.

127 Euxantios The legend of Dexithea and the Telchines was local to Ceos, and had no currency beyond that island, though the learned Alexandrians such as Callimachos knew of it (see intro. and note on 73, above; cf. also the intro. to Ode 11). The name Euxantios, therefore, given to the child of Minos and Dexithea, was almost certainly invented to provide the local clan of the Euxantidai with an illustrious and heroic ancestry. Since the victor Argeios belonged to this clan (141-2) the legend thus confers a reflected glory upon him (see also note on 119, above). See also Jebb, pp. 448-9, where he plausibly interprets 'Euxantidai' as the name of the local professional guild of 'wool-carders'.

128 glorious The word used here (*pherekudes*) more exactly means 'bringing glory' (cf. 13.59), and the sense is that the island of Ceos confers glory on its people through their descent from the illustrious Euxantios (and Minos). The adjective is used again at 13.183, of the island Aigina; it does not occur elsewhere in the surviving literature, and is clearly one of Bacch.'s many coinages. It is worth noting also, I think, that in both instances the context is markedly similar. In Ode 13 Bacch. is speaking of the value of *areta* ('excellence') which brings honour to Aigina, while here, having extolled the virtues of the victor Argeios, his father and his ancestor Euxantios (1.128-58), he turns abruptly to the long gnomic passage on the same theme ('excellence brings the greatest glory ...' 1.160f.) which concludes the poem.

139 a city ... This sounds very like the place on the western shore of Ceos referred to at 54-5. It would be natural for Euxantios to found his new city on the very spot at which his mother and her sisters had sought refuge. This city was presumably Koressia, the only one of the four cities of Ceos mentioned by Strabo (10.5.6) which corresponds to the indications given by Bacch., being on the western shore and adjacent to Ceos' only river, the Elixos (cf. note on 75, above). Koressia served as the seaport for Iulis – the major city in the island, which lay in the hills 5 km inland – and was later incorporated into it.

141 of his race i.e. the race of Euxantios. Thus Bacch. returns easily and naturally to his main subject, the praise of the victor Argeios (see intro., above).

142 strong] of hand Cf. 'bold of hand', 2.5. The restoration is virtually certain.

143 lion-hearted Lit. = 'having the spirit (*thumos*) of a lion', indicating the ferocity and courage of the fighter (cf. Hes. *Theog.* 833). Pindar (*Isth.* 4.46) compares the boldness and spirit (*thumos*) of the pankratiast

Melissos to that of roaring wild lions, but this need not suggest that the pankration was the event in question here (see intro., above).

144 the call to battle literally: 'whenever the need for fighting came upon him', i.e. on each occasion when he 'entered the ring'. There is an implied contrast between the spirit and aggression of Argeios in the contest (desirable qualities there), and his (presumably) peaceful and respectful demeanour otherwise.

146 mindful] of those blessings The 'blessings' (*kala*) bestowed upon Pantheides by Apollo are almost certainly successes in the Games. This is the normal meaning of *kala* in epinician poetry (cf. 2.6 and 3.96, although in 5.51 the meaning may be more general), and in such close connection with the victory of his son, it could hardly be otherwise here. Victory is always seen as a gift from the gods (cf. 155-6, below), and the fact that it is Apollo, Delphic god of wisdom, purity and order, who bestowed these blessings, suggests that Pantheides may have won at Delphi, in the Pythian Games, although there is no independent evidence of this. The translation 'mindful' is an unsupported guess, as the papyrus is broken at this point, but it seems at least plausible. The meaning then would be that Argeios keeps his father's victories in mind as inspiration for his own endeavours. (Cf., conversely, 2.6, where the present victory recalls the past.)

147 bow-[famed] a conventional poetic epithet (*klutotoxos*) for Apollo, cf. *Il.* 4.101, etc. Apollo (like his sister Artemis) was connected with the bow from earliest times. In the Homeric Hymn to Apollo the infant god cries: 'the lyre and the curving bow will always be dear to me' (Hom. Hymn 3.131), while the entire action of the *Iliad* is initiated by the prayer of Chryses to his god: 'Hear me, lord of the silver bow', and Apollo's lethal response (*Il.* 1.37f.). (See further W.F. Otto, *The Homeric Gods*, London 1955, p. 61f., esp. 75-7.) At 11.38 Artemis is described as *toxoklutos* ('famed for archery'), a simple variation of the adjective used here. (See notes on 11.37 and 38.)

149 healing art Pantheides evidently practised as a successful and respected doctor, recognized and rewarded by Apollo for placing his skill at the service of his fellows.

150 respect and love An elaborate expression of the quality of *philoxenia* (hospitality and respect for others) – a quality much valued by the aristocratic society of the poems. Cf. 3.16, 5.49 and 13.225 with the notes there.

151 the Graces' gifts This somewhat vague phrase perhaps refers to victory-songs celebrating the successes of Pantheides (see note on 146, above). For this aspect of the Graces' function, see notes on 5.11 and 9.2. It may, however, suggest that Pantheides himself was gifted with skill in poetry, cf. 10.39.

152 admired by many For the thought, cf. 10.48-9.

154 won great praise The adjective so translated (*megainetos*) occurs only in Bacch.; it is used again at 3.64, of Hieron.

155 to one of these Thus Bacch. returns finally to his main theme – praise of the victor Argeios – picking up at the same time the reference to Poseidon in the opening section (6-8). See intro., above, on the structure of the poem.

son of Kronos i.e. Poseidon. Among the children of Kronos and Rhea were Zeus, Poseidon and Hades (Hes. *Theog.* 453f.). In the distribution of spheres of influence, Zeus was allotted the sky, Poseidon the sea, and Hades the Underworld (*Il.* 15.187-93, and see notes on 6 and 7-8, above).

high-benched Elsewhere used only of Zeus (*Il.* 4.166, 7.69, etc., Hes. *Works and Days* 18, Bacch. 11.3 and fr. 20 D 8). The word (*hupsizugos*) derives from *zugos* ('bench' in nautical terminology) and is a metaphor for authority. Zeus rules the world from on high, just as the helmsman steers the ship from his high bench in the stern. See Fraenkel on Aisch. *Agam.* 182, Oxford 1950, vol. II, esp. pp. 109-10. Here it is transferred to Poseidon, appropriately, as the god who presides over the Isthmian Games.

157 reward for his benefactions Argeios was still competing as a boy, so that the benefactions are certainly those of his father Pantheides. It is not clear what form they took; for the thought, cf. 163-5, below.

158 other shining crowns Argeios must have won other victories at local Games, which, being of less importance, Bacch. does not take the trouble to detail. The Nemean victory recorded on the Cean inscription (*IG* XII 5 608; see intro., above) is not to be included here, since it was won in the 'youths' age class, i.e. later (provided that the Isthmian victory in the 'boys' class recorded there is indeed the one celebrated in this ode). The 'crown' at the panhellenic Games was a garland or wreath worn on the hair by the victor (cf. 2.7, 9.24, 13.197, etc.) and was the only prize awarded to the successful athlete (see the general introduction for details). Second-rank Games, such as those alluded to here, often used wreaths of palm leaves. Garlands of flowers appear also to have been worn by the friends and supporters of the victor and by the victor himself during the post-Games celebration (6.5f., 10.16, 13.69-70; cf. also fr. 53a: 'a crown ablaze with the buds of roses'), and similar wreaths were thrown at the feet of the triumphant athlete in a custom called *phullobolia* (= 'the throwing of leaves'), see 11.18-20 and Pind. *Pyth.* 9.123-4.

shining This word (*liparos*) originally meant 'oiled', 'anointed with oil'; from there it passed naturally into the meaning 'glistening', 'bright', 'radiant'. As a generalized metaphor, it then became part of the poet's honorific vocabulary. None of the contexts where it is used in Bacch. require, or indeed allow, any association with oil. (See 1.13, 5.169, 7.1, 11.39, 16.29, and perhaps 8.9.)

159 I say this now The strong, even abrupt, assertion leads into the final gnomic reflections on *areta* ('excellence') which the life of Argeios and his family illustrates. This is an example of what Mary Lefkowitz would call the 'bardic' first person, used by the poet in allusion to his own role as poet, and to introduce a new theme. See her article 'The First Person in Pindar', *HSCP* 67 (1963), pp. 177-253; also her book, *First Person Fictons – Pindar's Poetic 'I'*, Oxford 1991. On the sequence of thought in this final section, see intro., above.

161 wealth comes even to the unworthy For a similar notion, cf. 10.49-50.

162 to swell The meaning is probably not pejorative (as in 'to become swollen-headed'), but rather that the acquisition of wealth allows a man to take pride in his achievements, and to derive a certain degree of respect and honour from them. This sets up the contrast with what follows in the next line. For this meaning of *auxein* (lit. = 'to increase' or 'to enlarge') cf. 10.43; also *Il.* 17.225.

163 he who is generous to the gods i.e. the man who uses his wealth well and wisely (cf. note on 10.50). The phrase here echoes the 'benefactions' (157) of Pantheides, so that he (and his family) are included in this generalized praise of generosity.

164-5 can cheer his heart with hope on the use of the verb 'cheer' (*sainei*) see note on 76-7, above. For the expression cf. 13.220; also 10.38-41.

greater glory picks up 'greatest glory' (160, above); the contrast between the honour to be gained by the 'unworthy' and by those who display *areta* (which includes generosity to the gods) is developed more fully in the final epode, 178-84.

166-8 if a man There is a vague parallel to these ideas at 5.50f.

169f. every ... life This does not mean that every individual enjoys a delightful life; rather that there is the potential for pleasure at every grade and level of life. The rich and the poor alike have satisfactions commensurate with their status (172-3). In these lines, as far as 177, Bacch. seems to be drawing on Solon's discussion of the various activities and lifestyles of men (Solon 13.43f.). But whereas in Solon these are presented to underscore the vanity of human endeavour and the helplessness of mankind before the gods, in Bacch. the admonitory undertones are different, as well as much less prominent. Cf. 10.38, and the note there.

171 helpless poverty Cf. Hdt 8.111.3, where 'Poverty and Helplessness' are adduced as the 'gods' which prevented the people of Andros from paying an indemnity to Athens.

176-7 always the goal is The idea of the folly of spurning what one has to pursue what flees became a commonplace in the literature, e.g. Hes. fr. 61, Pind. *Pyth.* 3.22, Aisch. *Agam.* 394, etc.

179 worthless Lit. = 'very light', insubstantial' (*kouphotatai*). Cf. Soph.

Ant. 615-17: 'wandering hope ... deceives the light-minded (*kouphonoon*) desires of men'.

drive (*doneousi*, lit. = 'shake'); cf. 5.65, where the same verb is used, literally, of the wind that swirls the autumn leaves along the mountain ridges. So here, metaphorically, the mind of the man not focussed on true *areta* is blown hither and thither, like leaves in the wind, by frivolous ambitions.

180 may win The text is unreliable here, but the required meaning seems fairly certain.

181-2 excellence ... brought to its proper end As the reflections on *areta* arose directly (160, above) from the victories of Argeios, so Bacch. returns to that theme here, with typical ring-composition. The 'proper end' of *areta* is success in the Games (cf. 11.1-6: 'Goddess of Victory ... you determine the end of excellence'); it is this which 'brings the greatest glory' (160) and leaves a 'monument of renown' (184). Jebb (p. 248, note on 49-74) compares Bacch. unfavourably with Pindar here, suggesting that Bacch. rambles on with prolix generalizations, whereas Pindar 'would have brought in, before the close, some touch of allusion to the victory'. But this is unfair; behind these generalizations and driving them, it is impossible not to hear the prowess and achievements of Argeios. For the thought in these final lines, cf. esp. 13.59-66; also 9.78-87.

184 enviable Lit. = 'much-envied' (*poluzeloton*). For the desirability of being envied by one's peers, see 10.48, and notes on 5.53 and 7.10.

monument Elsewhere Bacch. always uses this word (*agalma*) to refer to his own victory poem, e.g. 5.4-5: 'this ornament, sweet gift from the Muses'; similarly 10.11-12 and fr. 20 B 5, and this must be the sense here (see note on 5.4). The 'monument', then, which brings posthumous honour to the victor is not merely the victory itself, but the song which celebrates it, and the song, no less than the victory, is part of the 'proper end' (182) of excellence. Thus Bacch. in concluding his poem not only returns to the praise of Argeios, but includes in this an oblique but unmistakeable reference to his own role as poet in the creation of undying fame. For this aspect of the poet's role, see esp. note on 9.2.

ODE 2
FOR ARGEIOS OF CEOS
Boys' Boxing, Isthmian Games, before 452 BC

This short ode bears the title 'For the same'; that is, it was composed in honour of the same athlete as the preceding Ode 1, and presumably to celebrate the same victory. (For a discussion of the event and its date, see intro. to Ode 1.) It was not unknown for the same poet to write two songs for the same victory (cf. Odes 6 and 7); the short Ode 2 would have been

Fig. 4. Competitors in the boxing. Attic black-figure amphora, *c.* 500 BC. Munich, Staatliche Antikensammlungen.

sung at the Isthmus, either at a celebratory party on the day of the victory itself, or during the festivities at the end of the Games, while the long and elaborate Ode 1 was presented after the return of Argeios to his home in Ceos. (See also note on 6.6.) For a contrary view see Jebb, p. 89, and notes on 2.2 and 2.11, below.

Like Ode 6, the poem is too brief to admit any mythic narrative, but otherwise contains all the usual elements of the epinician genre. The form is typically tripartite and ring-compositional. The strophe (1-5) announces the victory and introduces the praise of Argeios and his homeland, the antistrophe (6-10) develops both of these themes, and passes to praise of the Games themselves at the Isthmus, from which the epode (11-14) returns naturally and easily to the celebration there of the victory and the victor. There is also passing reference to the victor's family (13) and allusion to the poet's role in celebrating the victory (9 and 11). See also intro. to Ode 6, with which Ode 2 shows some remarkable similarities, both in form and content.

1 **Fame** Cf. 10.1, and for a generally similar expression, compare the invocation at 11.1: 'Victory, whose gifts are sweet'.

    giver of proud gifts The adjective (*semnodoteira*) occurs only here. Based on *semnos* = 'revered', otherwise used by Bacch. only of divinities (Artemis, 5.101; Zeus, 11.51; Athena, 13.193 and Amphitrite, 17.111), it should mean 'whose gifts are revered'. Fame is urged to hurry to Ceos to announce the victory of Argeios; her gift to him is widespread renown, but it seems extravagant to describe such a gift as 'revered'. The form is modelled on similar adjectives: *ainodoteira* (Orphic *Argonautica*, 352) used of the Furies, 'whose gifts are dreadful', and *barudoteira* (Aisch. *Seven* 975 and 987) of Destiny, 'whose gifts are burdensome', and it may be that Bacch. has simply coined a new and impressive-sounding poetic adjective without much concern for its precise reference.

2 **go quickly]** The papyrus is broken here, and the form of the verb is uncertain. There are, however, several victory poems which begin with an invocation to a god, a description of the characteristics or activities of that god, and a command, e.g. Pind. *Ol.* 12: 'O Saviour Fortune ... protect Himera ...'; Pind. *Ol.* 14: 'O Graces ... listen'; cf. Bacch. 12.1-3, and esp. 11.1-8: 'O Victory whose gifts are sweet ... be gracious ...'. There are sufficient of these to constitute a pattern, which suggests that this is the structure here in Ode 2 also. Thus the imperative (as translated) is the correct restoration, I believe. This in turn implies that Bacch. was at the Isthmus for the Games and that Ode 2 was written there. Jebb, on the other hand, restores the indicative: 'Fame ... has sped to sacred Ceos', which obliges him to believe that Bacch. was in Ceos when the news of the victory arrived, and that he then composed Ode 2, as well as Ode 1, on that island. Such a view is unnecessary and inherently unlikely – why would he write two odes for Argeios after his return home? Besides, Ode 2 has all the appearance of a rapid, on-the-spot composition. See also note on 11, below.

    sacred A purely decorative adjective; cf. 8, below, and see note on 5.12.

3 **glad news** A somewhat free translation of another difficult adjective. The 'news' is *charitonumos* (lit. = 'of gracious name') because it, and by implication the present ode which conveys that news, are both part of the 'grace' (*charis*) which the victory has bestowed upon Argeios. The word is another of Bacch.'s coinages; it occurs nowhere else, but cf. 17.31, where Europa, the daughter of Phoinix, is called *eratonumos* ('of lovely name').

5 **boxing** The name of the event does not actually appear here in the Greek. Bacch. merely says: 'victory in the battle', but boxing seems most probable. See the intro. to Ode 1, and cf. also 6.8, where boxing is named as one of the two events in which Ceans had previously won victories.

    bold of hand Cf. 1.142, where a similar adjective ('strong of hand') is used.

6 brought to mind Praise of the victor passes easily into praise of his homeland, and the two themes are neatly intertwined. Ceos has produced many successful competitors in the past, and Argeios continues this illustrious tradition. For similar reference to previous victories, not merely by the athlete himself but by his compatriots, see 12.36f. and 6.4-8, and notes on 6.8 and 6.9.

splendid deeds i.e. victories; for this meaning of *kala* (lit. = 'good things') cf. 3.96, and see note on 1.146.

7 seventy Bacch. is referring here specifically to victories won by athletes from Ceos (8) at the Isthmus (10). He claims that Cean athletes had already won 70 victories at the Isthmian Games since their inception in 582 BC. The Isthmia took place every second year, and the present victory was won earlier than 452 BC (see intro. to Ode 1), which means that these 70 victories were achieved in, at most, 65 festivals. This is a distinguished record, but by no means impossible. More than one Cean may have competed at the same Games, while a single athlete may have won more than one event in the same year. The number, 70, may be rounded off for poetic convenience (cf. 'thirty', 12.36), but must be close to the true figure. The inscription *IG* XII 5 608 (see intro. to Ode 1) has only thirteen names before that of Argeios, but the upper part of the stone is missing. As a Cean himself, Bacch. would have had access to official lists of victors, such as those on which this inscription was based.

8 Euxantios' holy island i.e. Ceos. For Euxantios see intro. to Ode 1, and notes on 1.119 and 1.127, and for 'holy' see note on 'sacred', line 2, above.

8-9 leaving … we have celebrated Bacch. includes himself – and the chorus celebrating the present victory – among those Ceans who went from Ceos to the Isthmus to support the competitors and celebrate the earlier victories (cf. 6.4-7, and note on 6.6), although he could not have been present at all of these, nor composed victory odes for all of them. Maehler, however (vol. 2, p. 30), comparing 3.93, where the same verb is used, argues that the phrase is a synonym for 'victories that we have *won*', i.e. 'that we Ceans have won'; if this is right, Bacch., as a Cean, is including himself among the victorious athletes, in the manner of team supporters everywhere.

10 far-famed a common honorific in the poems; cf. 8.32 (of Olympia).
neck a natural metaphor for this narrow strip of land; cf. 12.38-9: 'the throat of Pelops' holy island'; see also note on 1.13-14.

11 Muse On the role of the Muse (or Muses) in the creation of the song, see esp. note on 1.1.
of this place Lit. = 'born here', 'native'. Jebb takes this as further evidence that the song was composed in Ceos (see intro., and note on 2, above), but this is unnecessary. It may just as easily mean that the song 'was born' on the spot where the victory was won, i.e. at the Isthmus.

12 pipes The instrument in question is the *aulos*, often translated wrongly, especially in earlier works, as 'flute'. The *aulos* was in fact a woodwind instrument, consisting of a straight pipe with finger-holes and a double-reed mouthpiece. It was thus more akin to the modern oboe (apart from the fact that the oboe has a conical bore). It was normal practice for the performer to play two *auloi* at once, one in each hand. See M.L. West, *Ancient Greek Music*, Oxford 1992, ch. 4, esp. p. 81.

13 Pantheides Father of the victor Argeios (cf. 1.148), who unfortunately did not live to see his son's success (see 1.152).

ODE 3
FOR HIERON OF SYRACUSE
Chariot-Race, Olympic Games, 468 BC

The background

Hieron, tyrant of Syracuse in Sicily, was the most distinguished and best known of the patrons who commissioned victory odes from Bacchylides. Second of the four sons of Deinomenes of Gela, he belonged to a powerful, aristocratic and clearly ambitious family, which in the early decades of the fifth century spread its authority and influence over most of Sicily, or at least that part of it which had been colonized from Greece. His elder brother Gelon had begun the process in 491 BC, when he seized sole power in the city of Gela for himself, while supposedly helping the sons of the previous king to assert their claim to the throne. A few years later, in 485, he was invited by oligarchs exiled from Syracuse to assist them in securing their return to their native city. Gelon took up their cause, but again, when the city submitted to him, he quickly seized the opportunity to make himself tyrant of Syracuse also. He then transferred his court from Gela to Syracuse, and installed his younger brother Hieron as his regent in Gela. When Gelon died in 478, Hieron then succeeded him as tyrant of Syracuse, where he reigned for the next eleven years. He died, after a long and apparently painful illness, in 467, in the city of Aitna, and that city honoured him posthumously as its 'hero-founder' (Diod. 11.66.4).

Like his elder brother, Hieron seems to have been a capable military and political leader and strategist. He had already, in 480, shared in the glory of Gelon's victory over the Carthaginians at Himera – or at least had claimed a share in it, for the monuments dedicated at Delphi by Gelon and Hieron as thank-offerings for this victory stood side by side, although they were perhaps erected at different times (see note on 18, below). Later, in 474, he himself achieved a crushing victory over the Etruscans at Cumae. One of his more remarkable achievements, and perhaps the one of which he was most proud, was the establishment of the new city of Aitna. In 476 he removed the entire populations of Catana and Naxos to Leontini, and on the vacant site of Catana founded a new city, which he called Aitna,

88

populating it with settlers from Syracuse and the Peloponnese (Diod. 11.49.1) This bizarre and seemingly wanton relocation of populations was no doubt politically motivated, in an attempt to curb the growing power of his neighbour and rival, the tyrant of Rhegium.

Bacchylides and Pindar in their victory odes represent Hieron as a paragon of virtue, a fair-minded and just ruler, concerned for his people, hospitable to strangers, generous with his wealth and reverent towards the gods. It must be remembered, however, that the poets were writing on commission, and were not going to risk giving offence to their patron. A very different picture, more independent, and certainly more negative, emerges from the narrative of the historian Diodoros (see esp. Diod. 11.67.2-4; cf. also *CAH*, vol. V, pp. 150-1). Nevertheless, although we call these autocratic rulers, of whom there were many in Greek cities at this time, 'tyrants', it should be borne in mind that the word in this context merely represents the Greek *turannos* ('sole ruler'), and that it did not always or necessarily have the negative associations which the word 'tyrant' has in English today. In fact many of these tyrants served their citizens well, not least by their support for, and cultivation of, Greek art and literature.

Perhaps because they had seized power by force and unconstitutionally, the tyrants often sought to win over public support and reduce the opprobrium attaching to autocracy by turning their cities into centres of cultural splendour and renown. Hieron was no exception, and welcomed to his court, among others, the poets Simonides, Pindar, Bacchylides and the great tragedian Aischylos, whose *Persai* was performed at Syracuse and who wrote a play to celebrate Hieron's foundation of Aitna. Further, one of the most effective ways in which a tyrant might legitimize his rule in the eyes of Greece was by playing a prominent role in the great panhellenic religious festivals, by making lavish dedications to the gods, and by taking part in the Games attached to these festivals. This is why we find the names of tyrants so often on the lists of victors. Already Gelon had won the chariot-race at Olympia in 488 (Paus. 6.9.4), and Hieron followed in this tradition with conspicuous success.

Hieron's victories

Altogether Hieron won seven victories, four in the horse-race and three in the chariot-race. All but one of these are securely dated. From the *scholia* to Pindar *Pyth.* 1 and *Pyth.* 3 (ed. Drach. II, 5 and 62) we learn that he won the horse-race at the Pythian Games in 482 and again in 478, at least the second of these with his champion stallion Pherenikos. The list of Olympic victors (Pap. Oxy. II 222 Col. I 19 and Col. I 32) records his victories at Olympia in the horse-race in 476, again with Pherenikos, and in 472, this time with an unnamed horse. (See also intro. to Ode 5.) In 470 (*schol.* Pind. *Pyth.* 1, ed. Drach. II, 5) he won the chariot-race at Delphi, celebrated in

Bacch. Ode 4, while Pindar in *Pyth.* 2 celebrates another success in a chariot-race at an unidentified contest of unknown date (Jebb, p. 192, suggests a victory at Thebes in 475). Finally, in 468 (*schol.* Pind. *Ol.* 1, ed. Drach. I, 16) he won the chariot-race at Olympia, celebrated here in Bacch. Ode 3. (On the monument erected at Olympia after his death to commemorate all of his Olympic victories, see the intro. to Ode 5.)

With this last victory, only a year before his death, Hieron finally achieved what must have been the peak of his agonistic ambition. The Olympic Games were the oldest and most prestigious of them all, and the chariot-race the most glamorous and prestigious of all the events. This may be why the three odes which Bacch. wrote for Hieron, Odes 3, 4 and 5, are arranged as they are, not in chronological order, but perhaps in order of the importance of the event. It is interesting also to note, in light of the rivalry between Pindar and Bacchylides, and the commonly asserted superiority of Pindar, that although Hieron commissioned odes from both poets in 476 and 470, for this, his last and greatest triumph, only Bacchylides got the nod. Hieron's successes might be conveniently tabulated as follows:

Date	Games	Event	Celebration
482	Pythia	horse-race (perhaps Pherenikos)	
478	Pythia	horse-race (Pherenikos)	
476	Olympia	horse-race (Pherenikos)	Bacch. 5 Pind. *Ol.* 1
472	Olympia	horse-race (probably not Pherenikos)	
470	Pythia	chariot-race	Bacch. 4 Pind. *Pyth.* 1
		chariot-race	Pind. *Pyth.* 2
468	Olympia	chariot-race	Bacch. 3

The poem

It was remarked above that Hieron died in 467, only a year after the Olympic victory celebrated in Ode 3. He had evidently been seriously ill for a long time; in 470 Pindar had prayed that the time remaining to Hieron might allow him 'to forget his troubles' (Pind. *Pyth.* 1.46f.), and he goes on to compare Hieron directly with Philoktetes (*Pyth.* 1.50f.) Philoktetes, suffering from an agonising and incurable ulcer – the result of a snake-bite – had been abandoned on Lemnos by the Greeks on their way to Troy. But he won honour in the end, when the Greeks realized their need of him (see esp. Soph. *Phil.*), and Pindar prays for a similar fortune for Hieron (*Pyth.* 1.56-7). Similarly in *Pyth.* 3 (addressed to Hieron, but not a victory ode) Pindar prays for 'a healer against the burning sickness of great men' (*Pyth.* 3.65-6). It must have been common knowledge in 468 that Hieron had not long to live. Bacch. must have known it, and there can be little doubt that he offered Ode 3 to Hieron as a *consolatio* on his approaching death.

At the same time, the ode is primarily a victory ode, and Bacch. never loses sight of this purpose. All parts of the song are designed to glorify Hieron and his victory, and the function of the ode as consolation remains secondary. Nevertheless, it is integrated into the praise of Hieron closely and with considerable skill, especially through the close parallel which Bacch. creates between Hieron and Croesus, the subject of the myth. Because of his piety and generosity Croesus was honoured by the gods and rescued from an imminent death by Apollo, who transported him and his daughters to the 'Land of the Blessed'; so too Hieron may hope for immortality, not least through the undying fame conferred on him by Bacch.'s song. The major themes of the ode are the need for the wise and generous use of wealth and power, generosity and piety as the source of genuine honour, and the dependence of honour on the poet's song to celebrate and perpetuate it.

The structure of the ode is very similar to that of Odes 1 and 5 (see intros to those odes). It consists of four major sections, and again the chief organizational principle is ring-composition. The central mythic narrative, describing Croesus on the pyre and his rescue by Apollo (24-63) is framed by two sections devoted to the praise of Hieron (1-23 and 64-71), and the poem concludes with a gnomic section, which leads, through a priamel (for the meaning of this term see note on 86-92, below), to a renewed focus on Hieron, his merits, and the posthumous fame and honour which these will bring him.

The opening lines (1-8) contain the typical appeal to the Muse to sing of the victory, and reach their climax with the reference to Hieron himself (7-8). This leads into generalized praise of Hieron; the divine favour which he enjoys and of which the victory is a mark, is seen more broadly in the fact that Zeus upholds his regal authority, because he knows how to use his power and wealth wisely (10-14). Bacch. then proceeds to specific examples of Hieron's generosity and piety, both at Syracuse (15-16) and at Delphi (17-21), and the first victor-praise concludes with a *gnome*: 'the best kind of happiness lies in honouring the god' (22-3) – a truth which Hieron's success and fortune illustrate.

The *gnome* forms an easy transition to the myth. Not only does Hieron's fortune illustrate this truth; so too does the story of Croesus, and the explanatory function of the mythic story is made clear by the introductory 'For' (24). The narrative itself is clear and straightforward, while it too displays the typical ring-compositional structure. At its centre stands Croesus' appeal to the gods and the reminder of his piety (37-48); on either side (33-4 and 50-2) we see his terrified wife and daughters, whose hysteria is designed to contrast with the courage and calm resolve of Croesus, and the whole scene is framed by the gods, who alone control man's destiny. It was the will of Zeus that destroyed the city of Sardis (24-6), but Apollo rescued Croesus (26-8). At the end the gods appear again; Zeus quenches the flames (55-6) and Apollo carries Croesus off to the Land of the Blessed

(58-61). But now we are told the reason. Apollo saved Croesus because of his piety and generosity (62-3).

This allows Bacch. to return directly to the praise of Hieron, in a way which balances the first victor-praise (10-21) and at the same time makes the parallel between Hieron and Croesus unmistakeable (64f.). The elaboration of Hieron's merits here in the second victor-praise (64-71) again leads, as the first had done, to a gnomic climax: 'delight your heart with holy deeds, for this is the highest gain' (83-4), which mirrors the *gnome* at 22-3, and, again, can only be taken as a truth which Hieron's success illustrates. The last stanzas expand the victor-praise still further. Hieron displays true excellence (*areta*, 90f.), the only thing which will not fade with time; but even *areta* requires the Muse to sustain it. The twin functions of the ode, as praise and consolation, are thus combined. Hieron's merits are such that they deserve and will receive the poet's song, and so Bacch. ends with an allusion to his own role in the creation of immortality for the victor.

The myth

Croesus, whose name has become proverbial for wealth, was king of Lydia in western Asia Minor (modern Turkey) from 560 to 546 BC. Fearing the growing power of the Persians to the east under their king Cyrus, he resolved upon a pre-emptive strike, but first inquired of Apollo's oracle at Delphi if this was a good idea. (The whole story is told by Herodotos, 1.46f.) The oracle gave him the famous answer: 'If you attack the Persians, you will destroy a great empire' (Hdt. 1.53). Emboldened by this ambiguous advice, Croesus embarked on a campaign against Cyrus and the Persians. But the plan backfired; the Lydians were defeated, the capital Sardis was destroyed and Croesus himself was taken prisoner. Croesus had indeed destroyed a mighty empire; unfortunately it was his own (Hdt. 1.86). Herodotos goes on to describe the events which followed (1.86f.). Cyrus caused a great pyre to be built and on it he placed, in chains, his captive, Croesus, together with fourteen Lydian youths. The pyre was lit; then suddenly, in the face of death Croesus remembered the words spoken to him many years before by Solon, the Athenian wise man and law-giver: 'call no man truly happy until he is dead; the gods often give happiness to a man only later to destroy him' (Hdt. 1.32). This insight into the fragility of human fortune was communicated to Cyrus; impressed, and realizing that a similar reversal could as easily happen to himself, the Persian king ordered the pyre to be put out. But human efforts failed, whereupon Croesus with tears of despair appealed to Apollo to remember his gifts and rescue him. Storm-clouds appeared, rain quenched the fire, and Croesus' life was saved (Hdt. 1.87).

In Ode 3 Bacch. treats these same events, but there are significant differences from the version in Herodotos. In Bacch. Croesus does not wait for capture and enslavement. He takes charge of his own fate and faces his death with dignity and courage. It is Croesus who orders the pyre to be built, who climbs on to it, uncoerced, and who commands his servant to set fire to it (3.32f.). A similar picture is presented on an early red-figure amphora by Myson, now in the Louvre (Beazley, *ARV* 238) and dated to about 490-480 BC. This vase appears to depend on the same source material as Bacch., for there are interesting similarities. On the vase we see Croesus on the pyre, not in chains, but seated on his royal throne, a staff in one hand, a libation bowl in the other. In other words he is still the king; he is still in charge. He is attended by a single servant, just as in Bacch. (3.48-9), and most significantly, he is wearing a Greek style of dress. All of this is at variance with Herodotos. It differs also from the picture on an Attic hydria (water-pot) of about 475-450 BC (Beazley, *ARV* 571-4), which represents a scene from a Croesus-tragedy and seems to agree generally with Herodotos. This vase shows Croesus, wearing an oriental style of dress, standing on the pyre, which is attended by many servants, presumably belonging to Cyrus; they too are wearing oriental dress. There must have been two versions of the story current, and Ode 3 provides us with another fine example of the way in which Bacch. could adapt his sources, and change, add or omit elements to suit his purpose. For example, Bacch. makes it clear that Croesus' gifts to Apollo were made in genuine piety (3.62-3); in Herodotos on the other hand, they are offered only out of self-interest (Hdt. 1.50), to win Apollo over to his cause. Further, after his descent from the pyre, Croesus persuades Cyrus to allow him to lodge a formal complaint with the oracle at Delphi on the ground that Apollo had misled him (Hdt. 1.90). There is in Bacch. no trace of any such resentment or sense of betrayal. Again, the wife and daughters who accompany Croesus on to the pyre in Bacch. do not appear in any other source. This detail was probably invented by Bacch. himself, to provide a contrast between the hysterical women and the courageous king.

Bacch.'s purpose in all of this is clear. He hellenizes and heroizes the Lydian king, in order to be able to draw an unmistakeable parallel between Croesus and Hieron, and this parallel is the basis of the consolation. The story of Croesus is not in the ordinary sense of the word a 'myth', since it deals with a real historical person, but Bacch. grafts on to it the miraculous transportation of Croesus to the 'Land of the Blessed', which elevates the story to the mythological level, and at the same time allows the implication that Hieron too, whose piety and generosity to Apollo were no less, may likewise hope for immortality.

1 **Sing** The poet begins, typically, with an invocation to the Muse (cf. 1.1 and 1.4, and the notes there), inviting her to sing, first of Sicily, then of Demeter and Kore, its principal goddesses, and finally of Hieron, the victor. The narrowing focus is a common epinician device to concentrate attention on the last-mentioned (see Bundy, *Stud. Pind.*, esp. pp. 11-12).

Klio One of the nine Muses, named by Hesiod at *Theog.* 77f. Since Hesiod, they are traditionally the source of poetic inspiration (*Theog.* 22 and 31-2. Cf. Bacch. 5.4, 10.11, etc.). The Muses were not originally distinguished by function, and in the conventional appeal for inspiration Bacch. uses their names indifferently (e.g. Klio again at 12.1, 13.9 and 13.228; Kalliope 5.176, cf. 19.13; Urania 4.8, 5.10 and 6.10; cf. 'Pierian maidens' 1.2, and the general 'Muse' at 2.11 and 15.47). The allocation of individual spheres of influence was a much later development – cf. *Anth. Pal.* IX 505.12 – in which e.g. Klio became the Muse of History and Kalliope the Muse of Epic. (Even then the classification was fluid – cf. *Anth. Pal.* IX 504.2, where Klio's realm is given as Lyric Poetry.) The name Klio is probably derived from the Greek *kleiein*, meaning 'to make famous' (cf. Hes. *Theog.* 32 and 67). This would make her especially appropriate for the epinician poet, whose function was to celebrate the achievement of the victor.

whose gifts are sweet The adjective (*glukudoros*) recurs at 5.5, of the song itself, and at 11.1, of Victory. Since the song and the victory both confer glory on the victor, the sense here is probably similar. It is Hieron, not Bacchylides, who enjoys Klio's gift, in that her song bestows upon him undying fame. (Cf. 9.2, and the note there, but contrast e.g. 16.2f. and 19.3-4, where Bacch. himself is the recipient of the Muses' gifts.) The word appears not to occur outside Bacch. (except in the late Rufinus, *Anth. Pal.* V 22.1) and was probably coined by him.

2 **where the best grain grows** The fertility of Sicily was proverbial, cf. Pind. *Nem.* 1.14-15: 'the pride of the blossoming earth, Sicily, the rich', and *Pyth.* 1.30: 'the fruitful land'; Aisch. *Prom.* 369: 'the fertile plains of fruitful Sicily'; cf. also Diod. 5.2.4. The island became important early as a source of wheat, a position which it held even into the early Roman Empire (cf. Strabo 6.2.7; Pliny *Nat. Hist.* 18.21). Bacch.'s epithet thus has a conventional and ornamental quality, as praising the victor's homeland, (note that Pindar, Bacch. and Aischylos all visited the court of Hieron) but the poet reduces the conventionality of the description by coining a new word (*aristokarpos*) to express it. See also note on 7.7.

3 **Kore** Otherwise known as Persephone, and daughter of Demeter. The invocation to Demeter and Kore is triply appropriate. First, Demeter is the Greek 'corn-goddess', she who attends to the fruitfulness of the earth (cf. Hom. *Il.* 5.500). In the Homeric Hymn to Demeter (Hom. Hymn 2) this 'goddess of the splendid crops' (line 4), in grief for her daughter, abducted by Hades, causes a famine among men (305f.) by refusing to allow the seeds to sprout. As the goddesses responsible for the fertility of the earth, therefore, it is Demeter and Kore who give to Sicily one of the island's most conspicuous and renowned blessings (see note on 2, above). So the invocation of the gods is drawn into and enhances the praise of the victor's homeland. Second, the cult of Demeter and Kore in Sicily was ancient and widespread, and in Greek

tradition had existed, as it were, from the beginning (Diod. 5.2.3; cf. Pind. *Nem.* 1.13, where Sicily is 'the island which Zeus, lord of Olympus, gave to Persephone'; also *Pyth.* 12.2; 'Akragas, seat of Persephone'). Cicero (*Verr.* II, 4.48) speaks of the ancient tradition that Sicily was 'wholly given over to the worship of Demeter and Kore' (cf. also Diod. 5.1). The cult was brought from Greece to Sicily by the early colonists, where it soon absorbed or supplanted the worship of the local earth-goddess. Gelon had built temples to Demeter and Kore out of the spoils of Himera (Diod. 11.26.7) and Hieron himself was the priest of Demeter and Kore (cf. Pind. *Ol.* 6.95), since this office was hereditary in his family (Hdt. 7.153). (See further G. Zuntz, *Persephone*, Oxford 1971, esp. p. 70f.) Third, Demeter and Kore are at the heart of the Eleusinian Mysteries. Demeter, in the search for Kore, came to Eleusis, where a temple was built in her honour, and Zeus allowed Kore to return from the Underworld for a part of every year. The goddess herself then introduced her cult, teaching her secret rites to the people (the full story is told in Hom. Hymn 2). The ritual may have originally concerned the annual regrowth of the corn – the yearly return of Kore to the upper world is perhaps an image of this – but more importantly it satisfied that natural human hope for immortality. The Mysteries in some way offered to the Initiate the hope of survival beyond the grave, of happiness in the next world. This association, obliquely suggested by the invocation to Demeter and Kore, is thus appropriate in a *consolatio* to Hieron on his approaching death. See further G.E. Mylonas, *Eleusis and the Eleusinian Mysteries*, Princeton 1961.

violet-crowned (*iostephanos*) A word perhaps borrowed from the language of cult poetry (see Maehler, vol. 2, p. 272, note on 13.122). Compounds with 'violet-' are among Bacch.'s favourite colour and atmospheric adjectives. Here, as in 5.5 and 13.122, the reference is clearly to a garland of flowers; in 9.3, 19.5 and fr. 61.1 colour is obviously the important thing; in 3.71, 9.72 and 17.37 'violet-haired' may again suggest flowers braided in the hair, but is better understood, I think, as a colour word also, indicating the bluish sheen of deeply black hair. See also note on 11.83.

4 **mares** An inscription from Laconia (*IG* V 1 213) records a number of victories by Damonon in the four-horse chariot-race 'with his own mares', and the use of mares for this purpose seems to have been standard. Herodotos (6.103) tells us that Cimon won the chariot-race at three successive Olympics with the same team of mares, and there was a dedication by a certain Leon for a victory (440 BC) 'with his father's Venetian mares' (quoted by *schol.* Eur. *Hipp.* 231; cf. *schol.* Hom. *Il.* 2.852, who refers also to a belief that Venetian mares were best for chariot-racing). Maehler (vol. 2, p. 41, note on 3.3-4) refers to epic and tragic usage, which varies between masculine and feminine, but this is not relevant, as the horses there are fictional. Nor is vase painting useful, for

the same reason; besides, the vase painter may be following an epic scene. But when Bacch. represents Hieron's team as mares, we must accept the description as accurate. On the other hand, the horses used for the ridden horse-race seem regularly to have been stallions, as was Damonon's, and Hieron's own horse Pherenikos, celebrated in Ode 5. Pausanias, however, (6.13.9-10) tells the perhaps apocryphal story of the mare of Pheidolas, which, while racing at Olympia, threw her rider at the start, but finished the course at the head of the field and was declared the winner.

5 **beside the ... Alpheos** i.e. at Olympia. For the periphrasis cf. 6.3, 8.28, etc. The entire phrase is repeated verbatim at 5.40.
wide-swirling The adjective has a conventional and decorative tone (see note on 5.40). It is, however, an evocative and appropriate description of this great river, the largest in the Peloponnese.

6 **Victory** For the personification cf. 5.35, 11.1, etc. The goddess Victory is called 'pre-eminent' because it is she who gives pre-eminence to the successful athlete.
Splendour The word used here (*aglaia*) means 'beauty', 'magnificence', 'splendour', but it too is personified into a divinity attendant on the victory. In fact Aglaia was one of the three Graces (Hes. *Theog.* 907-9), who represented those aspects of human life which gave it charm and beauty (see esp. note on 5.11). Here there is in addition a more specific overtone. The combination of Victory and Splendour anticipates the splendid, munificent festivities with which Hieron will celebrate his success (15-16). It thus illustrates the generalization of 13-14, and initiates the important theme of wealth generously used.

7 **they brought good fortune** Lit. = 'they made him fortunate (*olbion*)'. The word means '(materially) prosperous', but includes the idea 'happy', 'blessed', 'favoured by the gods' (cf. 5.50, where it is used again of Hieron). Thus although the horses are the actual subject, the divinities Victory and Aglaia (Splendour) are included in the gift. Cf. 11.1: 'Goddess of Victory, whose gifts are sweet'.

9 **The people shouted** Reference to the presence of spectators and to their applause is a motif which goes back to Homer and the Funeral Games for Patroklos (*Il.* 23.766-7): 'and all the Achaians shouted out to him as he strained for victory and urged him on'. It is fairly common in Bacch. (cf. 5.48, 9.30-35, 10.23-4), who uses it not only to enliven the description of the event, but also to enhance the praise of the victor through the indication of popular support.

10 **thrice-blessed** Lit. = 'three times god-favoured' (*tris-eudaimon*). The word picks up the idea of divine favour already suggested in 'good fortune' (see note on 7, above); at the same time it can hardly fail to recall the central theme of Ode 5: 'no man is god-favoured (*eudaimon*) in all things' (see 5.50-5, and the intro. to Ode 5). Now, in contrast, Hieron is described as truly 'god-favoured'. These lines (10-14) are not

to be taken as depending on the previous line, as if they represented what the people shouted. Rather they are a direct apostrophe of Hieron by Bacch., and interpret not only his victory but all of his success and fortune as a gift from Zeus and a reward for his own merits.

12 **more than all others** i.e. Hieron, as lord of Syracuse and other parts of Sicily, held sway over more Greeks than any other sole ruler of his time. Cf. Hdt. 7.157, where the ambassadors to Gelon, seeking his help against the imminent Persian invasion, say: 'yours is not the smallest share of Greece, as lord of Sicily'.

13 **knows not to conceal** The motif recurs at the end of the ode: Hieron has displayed 'the finest flowering of wealth' (92-4), and just as he knows not to conceal it, so too Bacch. will not be silent, but will celebrate it in his song (94-8).

    towered The image is of great wealth piled up, but there is perhaps also a suggestion of the towers and fortifications of Syracuse, which that wealth has created and which in turn protect it.

14 **black shroud** The word (*melamphares*) occurs only here. As Maehler points out (vol. 2, p. 44, note on 13-14), it has nothing to do with death or funerals, in which in fact white shrouds were normally used. The metaphor is simply suggested by the noun 'darkness' – the darkness is itself the concealing shroud.

15-16 These two lines depict with broad strokes the celebration of the victory in Syracuse, continuing the victor-praise (10-14) with this specific example of Hieron's piety and liberality. Sacrifices and offerings of thanksgiving are made to the gods (15), while family and friends are lavishly entertained (16). Bacch. was perhaps at Syracuse for the festivities; these lines sound rather like an eyewitness account.

16 **guests made welcome** The quality of hospitality (*philoxenia*) was highly valued, and often forms an important part of the praise of the victor (cf. 5.49, also of Hieron, and 14.23).

17 **gold gleams** The short sentences (15-17), each with a simple and parallel construction, build the generosity-motif to its climax in the gifts of Hieron to Apollo at Delphi.

18 **tripods** According to Diodoros (11.26.7) Gelon dedicated a golden tripod to Apollo, as a thank-offering for his victory over the Carthaginians at Himera (480 BC). This is confirmed by Theopompos (a fourth-century BC historian), who is quoted by the late writer Athenaeus (6.231 E) as saying that Gelon erected a tripod and a victory-statue of gold. Theopompos then goes on at once to say that Hieron did the same. The French excavations at Delphi have revealed (see *BCH* XXI, p. 588f.) a large base of limestone, carrying two pedestals, clearly designed to support tripods, as each of them has three sockets to receive the feet. The pedestals carry inscriptions, one of which identifies it as dedicated by Gelon the Syracusan. The other inscription is mutilated, but enough remains to show that it was

Fig. 5. A bronze tripod. Olympia, Archaeological Museum. Tripods such as this were often given as prizes in the minor Games, and dedicated as thank-offerings for victory. See 3.18.

dedicated by a son of Deinomenes, who can only have been Hieron. This base and pedestals, then, are all that now remains of the magnificent golden tripods and Victory-statues to which the historians, and Bacch. here, allude. There may have been others as well. Two similar but smaller pedestals were also found; these may have held tripods associated in some way with Hieron's younger brothers Polyzalos and Thrasyboulos, as may be suggested by an epigram attributed to Simonides (*Anth. Pal.* VI 214, translated and discussed in J.H. Molyneux, *Simonides*, Illinois 1992, p. 221f.). At all events Bacch. allows the glow of Hieron's gold to be enhanced by an imprecise use of the plural 'tripods'. Gelon's dedication was made in 480, or 479, after Himera; although Hieron's tripod stood side by side with it on the same base, it was almost certainly added afterwards. The base seems to have been enlarged to receive the second pedestal, and besides, it is likely that Hieron would not have felt bold enough, while Gelon was still alive, to claim an equal share in the glory of Himera. (It is possible also that

Hieron's dedication celebrated his defeat of the Etruscans at Cumae in 474 BC.) See also Jebb's appendix, p. 452f.

standing high Bacch.'s description is both vivid and accurate. The plinth and tripods stood close to the entrance to the temple of Apollo, and just to the north of the Great Altar, at the top end of the Sacred Way. This was perhaps the most conspicuous position in the entire sanctuary, visible to everyone who ascended by the Sacred Way to the temple. Standing in the open air as they did, these golden offerings must have sparkled and shimmered in the summer sun, just as Bacch. describes.

21 **Kastalia** The name of the stream which breaks out from a spring on Mt Parnassos and flows down the mountainside to the sanctuary, and on to the plain below. Its water was used for ritual purposes by the priestess of the oracle.

22-3 **Glorify ... happiness** These two lines echo and balance the words used in lines 6-7. 'Glorify' (*aglaizeto*) recalls *aglaia* ('splendour'), while 'happiness' (*olbos*) echoes 'good fortune' (*olbion*; see notes on 6 and 7, above). Thus the *gnome* here underscores the close connection between generosity and divine favour – the underlying meaning is: 'honour the god with gifts, for that is the surest path to good fortune' – and at the same time creates a balanced ring-compositional structure for this first section of the ode.

24 **For once** The myth is designed as illustration of the preceding truth (see intro., above).

25 **Zeus** In the prose version of the story in Herodotos (see intro., above) Zeus is not present at all, while Apollo only appears to answer Croesus' urgent appeal for rescue. Bacch. has introduced Zeus into the story in order to enhance the parallel between Hieron and the Lydian king. Zeus honours Hieron (10-12) and upholds his power (and is the ultimate source of the present victory, for the Olympic Games are Zeus' festival); Apollo has welcomed his generous gifts (17-21). Similarly, it is Zeus who, although responsible for the destruction of Sardis, quenches the flames of the funeral pyre (55-6), and Apollo carries Croesus off (58-9). Thus both gods are emphatically involved with the fates of both Hieron and Croesus.

26 **fated judgment** We are not told here why Sardis was thus doomed, but Apollo, attempting to answer Croesus' complaint that he had been misled, claimed that the destruction of the city was ordained because of blood-guilt incurred by an ancestor of Croesus; he (Apollo) could not prevent it, but had in fact managed to postpone it for three years (Hdt. 1.91).

27 **lord of the golden sword** A Homeric epithet (*chrusaoros*) for Apollo (*Il.* 5.509, 15.526), also used by Pindar (*Pyth.* 5.104). The last part of the word is in fact missing in the papyrus here, but this seems the likeliest restoration. 'Of the golden chariot' (*chrusarmatos*) is also possible (cf.

13.194, of Athena). For adjectives compounded with 'golden', see note on 4.1.

Croesus too The implication is that Hieron also will certainly enjoy divine favour and protection.

28 **horse-breakers** Herodotos (1.79) describes the Lydians as courageous fighters and skilled horsemen.

30 **no longer** Maehler and Jebb understand: 'not to wait for slavery *as well*', i.e. in addition to the ruin of his city and the loss of wealth and power. But I think the temporal sense is preferable. Croesus can see slavery coming, and determines to avoid it without delay.

31 **tearful** A Homeric adjective (*poludakruos*). This and its variant *poludakrus* are used by Homer chiefly of war and fighting; Bacch. uses it also (16.24) of the god's plan which brought such sorrow to Deianeira (see intro. to Ode 5).

32 **bronze-walled** Bacch. imagines the walls of the palace of Croesus as decorated or faced with bronze plaques, a description which is conventional and Homeric, rather than historically accurate. Thus the palace of Alkinoos has 'walls of bronze' (*Od.* 7.86), as perhaps also the palace of Menelaos (*Od.* 4.72), and there are analogous descriptions elsewhere in Homer. The house of Hephaistos is 'built in bronze' (*Il.* 18.371), the palace of Zeus on Olympos is 'bronze-floored' (*Il.* 1.426, etc., a frequent formula), while the entire island on which Aiolos, god of the winds, lives, is surrounded by a 'rampart of bronze' (*Od.* 10.3-4). The image conveys magnificence, as well as strength and permanence; the descriptions may ultimately reflect the Bronze Age practice of decorating the tholos tombs with bronze plates. (See A.J.B. Wace, *Mycenae*, Princeton 1949, p. 32; also D.H.F. Gray, *JHS* 74 (1954), p. 3.)

33 **heaped up** Another Homeric word. The verb is used in a variety of contexts, which include, interestingly, the funeral pyre of Patroklos (*Il.* 23.139).

cherished The word (*kednos*) is only used by Bacch. in this sense (5.118 of Meleager's brothers, and 17.30 of Phoinix' daughter Europa), although it also means 'loyal', 'trusty'.

34 **lovely-haired** Cf. 1.126 and note there. If it seems odd that Bacch. draws attention to the loveliness of these terrified young women as they face an untimely death, the incongruity merely highlights the conventional nature of the epithet.

inconsolable The etymology of the word used here (*alaston*) is disputed, but it seems most likely to mean 'unforgettable'. All of its occurrences in Homer, where it is mostly used of grief, will allow this meaning. The source of the sorrow is something which cannot be forgotten. Thus Thetis grieves for the imminent death of her dear son Achilles (*Il.* 24.105), Penelope for her absent husband Odysseus (*Od.* 1.342) and Eumaios for the young Telemachos, long gone and in danger from the suitors (*Od.* 14.174). From there the meaning would pass naturally to 'inconsolable', which is the more appropriate emphasis here, for the cause of the young girls' sorrow is not something of long standing, not to be forgotten.

36 raising his hands For this gesture, in prayer, cf. 11.98-9. At 17.74 it is a gesture of gratitude for a positive response to prayer.

towering sky The same phrase is used at 9.33, of the throw of a javelin.

37 divinity i.e. Zeus, again included with Apollo in Bacch.'s version of the story of Croesus. See note on 25, above.

38 gratitude Beside genuine piety, where it existed, there was a strong undercurrent also of self-interest in Greek religious practice, based on a kind of mutual obligation. If a man honoured the gods with gifts and sacrifice, he felt entitled to expect divine support and protection in return, and this was recognized by the gods themselves. Examples are everywhere; see e.g. *Il.* 24.66f., where Zeus declares that he will honour Hektor and rescue his body from Achilles because 'he never failed of gifts to my liking. Never yet has my altar gone without fair sacrifice ... since that is our portion of honour' (24.68-70). It is entirely natural, then, for Croesus to expect, even demand, gratitude from the gods for his piety. Herodotos (1.87) and Bacch. agree on at least this detail of the story (see intro., above).

39 Leto's son For the birth of Apollo and Artemis to Leto see Hes. *Theog.* 918-20.

40 Alyattes Father of Croesus and king of Lydia *c.* 617-560 BC.

44 swirling waters ... rich in gold The translation represents the single word 'gold-swirling' (*chrusodinas*) which occurs nowhere else and must have been coined by Bacch. on the analogy of other adjectives of this type, applied to rivers; see note on 'wide-swirling' at 5.40, and cf. line 5, above. The first part of the compound 'gold-' is in fact missing from the papyrus, but is certainly to be restored here. The river Paktolos flowed through the Lydian capital, Sardis, beyond which it joined the Hermos, flowing westward to the sea near Smyrna (modern Izmir). It was renowned in antiquity for the alluvial gold which it brought down from its source on Mt Tmolos (Hdt. 5.101); cf. Soph. *Phil.* 394: 'Paktolos rich in gold', Verg. *Aen.* 10.142, etc. Vergil also described the Hermos as 'thick with gold' (*Georg.* 2.137). See also note on 'silver-swirling' at 8.28.

45-6 the women are taken Perhaps a reminiscence of *Il.* 9.591f., where Meleager's wife recounts the sorrows that come to men when their city is taken: 'and strangers lead the children away and the deep-girdled women'. Bacch. represents the destruction of Sardis as taking place before the very eyes of Croesus on the pyre; the direct speech of this eye-witness account intensifies the pathos, as it engages the audience more directly in the event.

46 well-built A conventional poetic epithet, cf. 5.149, etc. Herodotos

(5.101) tells us that the majority of the houses in Sardis were in fact built of reeds; even those built of brick had a reed-thatch roof.

48 to die is sweetest This climactic conclusion to the calamities which he sees unfold before him echoes his refusal to wait for 'tearful slavery' (30-1).

49 soft-stepping The Myson amphora (*ARV* 238, see intro., above) shows Croesus on the pyre with a single attendant. This is surely what Bacch. has in mind. The word used by Bacch. here (*habrobatas*) is found elsewhere only in Aisch. *Pers.* 1072, of the chorus of Persian elders mourning the defeat at Salamis. The *Persai* was produced at Athens in 472 and repeated at Hieron's request in Syracuse soon after; Bacch. would very probably have known the play, and could have taken this unusual word from it. The first part of the compound, *habro-* connotes grace or delicacy, from where the meaning moves towards effeminacy. So at Eur. *Med.* 1164, the princess 'steps delicately' (*habron*), as she admires herself in her new robe. As in Aisch., who uses a number of other words in *Persai* also compounded with *habro-* (*Pers.* 41, 541 and 543), the use of the word here perhaps reflects the Greek view of the voluptuous and self-indulgent life-style of the East, which was proverbial, but note that similar expressions were also used of Greeks. Bacch. himself speaks of Theseus as 'lord of soft-living (*habrobion*) Ionians' (18.2), and Euripides describes the Athenians 'stepping delicately (*habros*) always through the bright air' (*Med.* 830). See also note on 'the sweet voice', 13.73.

50 screamed Cf. 34; the contrast between the terrified daughters and the calm and resolute king is emphasized by the ring-composition; see intro., above.

53-4 the flashing force of the terrible fire An adaptation of the Homeric verse: 'breathing out the terrible force of blazing fire' (*Il.* 6.182).

55 Zeus Again associated with Apollo (58f.) to heighten the parallel between Croesus and Hieron; see notes on 25 and 37, above. Besides, although in Herodotos (1.87) it is Apollo who sends the rain, the intervention of Zeus in this way is more appropriate, for he is the Sky-god, in Homer the 'cloud-gatherer' (*Il.* 1.511, etc.).

56 yellow On the range of meaning of this colour word (*xanthos*) see note on 5.38. The phrase recurs at fr. 4.65.

57 Nothing is beyond belief Expressions of this type represent a conventional motif in epinician poetry, used to signal the end of the mythic narrative and the imminent return to the main subject – the praise of the victor. Cf. 17.117: 'nothing that the gods will is beyond belief' (not a victory poem, but the usage is analogous). For a discussion of the motif, and further examples, see Bundy, *Stud. Pind.*, pp. 2-3. According to Bundy, these passages 'intensify and signal the climax of a story by calling attention to the marvellous powers of the divinity that directs the events described'. So here, Bacch. concludes his narrative with the miraculous rescue of Croesus, and returns, *via* the transitional reference to the piety of Croesus, to praise of the piety of Hieron.

58 Delos-born Cf. 11.16. The Homeric Hymn to Apollo (Hom. Hymn 3) recounts at great length the birth of Apollo on Delos, and the island was a major cult-centre of the god from early times. Already by the date of the composition of the Hymn (eighth century BC?) the Delian festival of Apollo was well established (Hom. Hymn 3.147f.).

59 Hyperboreans The name means 'those who dwell beyond the North Wind', and they represent a distant, mythical Paradise, similar to the Elysian Fields (Hom. *Od.* 4.561f.) to which Menelaos will be transported after his death, or the Islands of the Blessed at the ends of the earth, where the heroes dwell, untouched by sorrow (Hes. *Works and Days* 168f.; cf. Pind. *Ol.* 2.71f.). Perseus went there (Pind. *Pyth.* 10.31f.) and Herakles (Pind. *Ol.* 3.13f.), but the land of the Hyperboreans was a paradise to which mere ordinary mortals could not aspire (Pind. *Pyth.* 10.29f.). The Hyperboreans were especially connected with Apollo; at Pind. *Ol.* 3.16 they are 'servants of Apollo', and Perseus finds them sacrificing to Apollo when he visits (*Pyth.* 10.31f.). Herodotos says that they were responsible for the earliest offerings made to Apollo on Delos (Hdt. 4.33f.).

60 set ... down A fairly uncommon poetic verb is used here (*katanaiein*), the same verb in fact as used by Hesiod of Zeus when he 'sets down' the heroes to dwell in the Islands of the Blessed (Hes. *Works and Days* 168; see previous note). Bacch. may have had the Hesiodic passage in mind here.

61 slender-ankled Cf. 5.59 (Persephone).

62 offerings The huge quantities of gold and other offerings sent by Croesus to Delphi are detailed in Hdt. 1.50f.; cf. also Hdt. 1.92 and 8.122.

63 holy Pytho The same words are used at 5.41. For the origin of the name Pytho as a synonym for Delphi, see note on 8.17.

65 who dwells in Greece As Jebb rightly points out (p. 262, note on 63), the limitation indicates only that Bacch. is 'not prepared to say that Hieron had surpassed Croesus'. As Croesus has given the greatest gifts of all men, so Hieron has been the most generous of all Greeks.

66 Loxias A common title for Apollo, cf. 13.147; Soph. *OT* 853, etc. The name most probably arose from a popular association with the word *loxos* ('slanting', 'oblique'), in reference to the oblique, ambiguous answers provided by the oracle.

more gold Picks up the gold of the tripods, 17, above. The ode has come full circle, and the repetition of this key word marks the return to the theme of the piety and generosity of Hieron.

67 feed on envy Cf. 13.199-202 and 5.188-90. These are examples of the so-called 'envy-motif', another rhetorical *topos* in epinician poetry designed to enhance the praise of the victor. The point is, essentially, that praise must be given to match the achievement, without stint and untrammelled by malice. See Bundy, *Stud. Pind.*, p. 59f.; see also notes on 5.188-97, and 5.189.

69 horse-loving man of war The second victor-praise is expanded to include Hieron's military prowess. See note on 'riders of ... chargers', 5.2.

70 the sceptre of ... Zeus The allusion is to Hieron's position as king of Syracuse, a position protected and upheld by Zeus. This, together with the foregoing praise of his gifts to Apollo (65-6), resumes, this time in reverse order, the elements of the first victor-praise (11-21), and completes, in typical ring-compositional style, the frame for the mythic narrative.

71 gifts of the Muses Jebb quotes Aelian (*Var. Hist.* 4.15) for the view that Hieron only became interested in the Muses (i.e. cultural pursuits, music, literature, etc.) after his illness enforced leisure, but this is probably not the point. Hieron's share in the Muses came to him through the songs with which Bacch. (and Pindar) celebrated his victories.
violet-haired Repeated at 9.72 (Aphrodite) and 17.37 (the Nereids). For compounds with 'violet-' see note on line 3, above, and for the meaning, see also note on 'hair shining black', 11.83.

72f.   The second victor-praise seems to pass, although the papyrus is badly damaged here, into a sequence of *gnomes* relating to the fragility and uncertainty of human life. This leads in turn, through the words of Apollo to Admetus, to the climactic advice of 83-4. On the general structure and sequence of thought in this final section of the ode, see intro., above.

75 fluttering hope The words are repeated almost verbatim at 9.18; see note there. The point here, as in Ode 9 and elsewhere, is the folly, given the brevity and uncertainty of human life, of worthless ambition, of seeking 'that which eludes the grasp', instead of focussing on the pursuit of true *areta*; see esp. 1.176f., and notes there.

77 son of Pheres i.e. Admetos, king of Pherai in Thessaly. Apollo and Admetos enjoyed a particularly close relationship. Apollo, as punishment for killing the Cyclopes, had been sentenced by Zeus to spend a year in servitude to the mortal Admetos, who won the god's favour and goodwill by his piety and generosity as a master. When it became known that Admetos was fated to die prematurely, Apollo tricked the Fates (Moirai) into allowing him to remain alive if he could find someone to die in his place. The only person to agree to take his place was his wife Alcestis. The story is related in full in Apollodoros (1.9.15 and 3.10.3-4), and it forms the background to Euripides' play *Alcestis* (see esp. Eur. *Alc.* 1-18). However, there is nothing to suggest that the advice given here by Apollo to Admetos has any connection with the Alcestis story. It is more probable that Bacch. is quoting from an early poem, or rather an early collection of gnomic and hortatory verses, which seems to have been in circulation under the title 'Sayings of Admetos', or perhaps 'Sayings relating to Admetos'. Athenaeus (15.693f.) quotes a number of Athenian drinking songs (*skolia*), one of which (no.14) is specifically described as a 'saying of Admetos', and may well have come from the same source (see Page, *PMG* 897, and Bowra, *Greek Lyric Poetry*, p. 377f.).

78-9 faith twofold The advice of Apollo is an elaborate variation of the theme: 'no-one knows what the future holds'; cf. Simonides (*PMG* 521.1): 'as a mortal, do not ever say what will happen tomorrow'. The same balanced form of expression as here in Bacch. is found again in Epicharmos (fr. 267, ed. Kaibel): 'keep in mind both that you will live for a long time, and for a short'.

81 live out your life For the phrase, cf. fr. 20A.9.

83-4 Delight your heart with holy deeds Almost an exact repetition of 22-3 ('glorify the god ... etc.'), and the parallel includes function, as well as form and meaning (see intro., above). These two lines represent the conclusion to be drawn from the preceding advice of Apollo – in view of the uncertainty of life, this is the only sensible mode of behaviour. Thus 83-4 provide the climax to the gnomic section arising out of the second victor-praise; this is a truth which the merits of Hieron illustrate, exactly as the truth in 22-3 formed the climax to, and was illustrated by, Hieron's generosity. The lines then lead easily into the final priamel (86f.), which intensifies the praise of Hieron and brings it to its proper conclusion.

holy deeds Given the closeness of the parallel with 22-3, this must include generous gifts and dedications to the gods.

85 He who has sense An example of oblique self-praise. Bacch. and Pindar are always conscious that they are writing for the educated, for the *cognoscenti*, who will understand and appreciate their work. See note on 5.9; also Pind. *Ol.* 2.83-5: 'there are many sharp shafts in the quiver under ... my arm. They speak to the understanding' (Lattimore's translation). At the same time, since the following priamel (86f.) is so strongly reminiscent of the opening of Pind. *Ol.* 1: 'Best of all things is water; but gold ... outshines all pride of wealth beside', which was also written for Hieron and was performed in Syracuse some years previously, in 476, there is probably also the suggestion that the erudite listener will pick up the reminiscence and appreciate Bacch.'s reworking of the Pindaric motifs. Pindar himself echoes his own words at *Ol.* 3.42-4: 'if water is best of all things, and of possessions gold is goodliest ...' (Lattimore's translation).

86-92 These lines constitute a clear and straightforward example of the device known as the priamel – as clear and straightforward, indeed, as any to be found in Bacch. The priamel (see Bundy, *Stud. Pind.*, p. 5f.) is a series of propositions with a common element, each of which stands as foil to the final and climactic proposition, so as to highlight and emphasize the truth of that climax. Here the common element is incorruptibility and permanence. The sky, the sea and gold are all adduced as elements impervious to decay, but the one thing above all else which will not fade or pass away is *areta* ('excellence'). Each of the terms of the priamel builds to this climax. In this instance, however, the climax is delayed further, this time by a negative proposition, which stands as foil by contrast: a man's youth will pass, his body fade and die (88-90), but the renown of his *areta* will not (90-2). This final proposition, then, is the gnomic 'cap' of the priamel, and it leads at once into the 'name-cap': 'you, Hieron' (92), introducing the concrete example which illustrates the truth of the gnomic climax. The final stanza of the poem (93-8) then elaborates this truth in concrete terms, in reference to Hieron.

86 **The deep sky** The same words are used at 5.19.

87 **gold brings delight** As a term of the priamel, Jebb (p. 264, note on 85-7) finds this expression 'tame'; his interpretation, however: 'gold is a joy for ever', is essentially correct. The meaning is, I believe, that one may always and at any time delight in gold, for gold is simply what it always is – elemental, pure and unadulterated. Thus the expression fits perfectly into the priamel. Maehler's interpretation, however, deserves notice (vol. 2, pp. 57-8). He refers to passages where 'gold' means, not the incorruptible element, but simply 'wealth', and especially 'wealth' as something impermanent and transient. Pointing to the echo of 22-3 in 83-4: 'delight your heart with holy deeds ...' (see note on 83-4, above) and to the gold of Hieron's gifts to Apollo (17f. and 66-7), as well as to his habitual generosity (13-14), Maehler understands 'wealth brings delight' to mean that it provides opportunity for delight through generous gifts to the gods and lavish victory celebrations. But wealth, and the joy that it can bring in this way, are ephemeral, and Maehler consequently attaches this to what follows (88-90) – wealth, like youth and physical vigour, will fade. He then interprets the entire passage as three pairs of contrasting ideas: the sky and the sea are incorruptible; wealth and youth are transient blessings, while *areta* and the song which celebrates it are truly permanent and enduring. Against all this it must be said that if Bacch. means that wealth brings only ephemeral delight, this is not what he actually says, and there is nothing in the text to suggest this meaning or to suggest that this proposition should be attached to the transience of youth which follows. The verbal echoes to which Maehler points are certainly present; it is Hieron who 'delights his heart with holy deeds' (83); it is Hieron's gold that shines out at Delphi (17, 67), but to highlight these as Maehler does produces in my view an unduly involved explanation which destroys the thrust of an otherwise perfectly clear priamel.

90 **a man's worth** *areta*; for the use of this concept in the climax of an ode, cf. 1.159f. and 13.175f., with the notes there. In Ode 1 the final gnomic reflections on *areta* illuminate the achievements of the victor Argeios, whereas here in Ode 3 the sequence is reversed: Hieron is the concrete example illustrating the truth of the *gnome*.

92 the Muse This picks up the opening appeal to Klio in line 1, and at the same time makes clear once again the essential interdependence of achievement and song. Success is insufficient by itself; it requires the poet's song to immortalize it; cf. 1.181-4, 9.78f., etc. and notes on e.g. 1.184, 5.191-4 and 9.2.

93 have displayed Bacch. returns here to the theme of generosity, picking up 13-14: 'not to conceal his towered wealth ... etc.' At the same time the meaning here certainly includes the idea: 'you have won splendid victories' (see note on 2.8-9), for it is in this area especially, as far as Bacch. is concerned, that Hieron has used his wealth, and it is this success especially that demands the poet's voice.

94f. silence brings no ornament Again echoing 13, above; see the note there.

96 in true report An example of the common assertion by Bacch. (and Pindar) that the praise is no less than the truth, no less than the merits of the victor demand. Cf. 5.188, 8.21, with the notes there; also 9.85.

achievement The word is *kala* (lit. = 'good things'); it is always used by Bacch., however, specifically of success in the Games. See note on 1.146. These lines closely echo the generalization of 90-2: as the Muse sustains a man's *areta*, so Bacch. will immortalize the achievements of Hieron.

97 will sing Echoes the imperative 'Sing' of line 1, thus completing the ring-compositional structure. For a similar structure, again involving Klio, cf. Ode 13, in which the reference to Klio in 9 is picked up in 228.

98 nightingale Bacch. ends with the not-too-veiled assertion that his own fame as poet will live on beside that of Hieron.

ODE 4
FOR HIERON OF SYRACUSE
Chariot-Race, Pythian Games, 470 BC

The background

The title of this ode in the papyrus is 'for the same, at the Pythia'. That is, it was written for the same victor as the preceding Ode 3, which was in honour of Hieron. (Cf. the title of Ode 2.) The name of the event is not given, but it is in any case abundantly clear from the poem itself that it celebrates a victory won by Hieron (3 and 13) in the chariot-race (7) at Delphi (4, 6 and 16). The date is therefore secure, for Hieron won only one such event, and that, as the *scholia* on Pind. *Pyth.* 1 tell us, was in the 29th Pythiad, i.e. 470 BC. This success was, like that in the Olympic horse-race of 476 BC, celebrated by both Bacch. and Pindar; Bacch.'s short Ode 4 was performed at Delphi, in the sanctuary of Apollo, as part of the concluding ceremonies at the end of the festival (4.4-5, and see note on 7.2), while Pindar's long and elaborate *Pyth.* 1 was composed for later performance in Sicily, in the new city of Aitna recently founded by Hieron. (For the practice of commissioning two odes for the same victory, compare also Odes 1 and 2, and Odes 6 and 7, and see the intros to Odes 1 and 6.)

A minor problem arises here. *Pyth.* 1 is addressed to Hieron as 'ruler of Aitna', and in the poem itself (*Pyth.* 1.31f.) Pindar uses words which can only mean that in the official proclamation of the winner at Delphi, the herald announced him as 'Hieron of Aitna'. Bacch. on the other hand, in Ode 4, does not mention Aitna at all, saying only (4.1-2) that the victory has brought glory to the city of Syracuse. But if Hieron's official designation as competitor was 'king of Aitna', why does Bacch. ignore this? Perhaps Bacch. did not go to Delphi for the Games, but sent his poem in advance, to be performed in the event that Hieron was successful. In this case he would not have known that Hieron entered as 'king of Aitna', and the poem could not be recast (by someone else) at the last minute to eliminate the reference to Syracuse. But one might well wonder whether the ode would have been presented at all under these circumstances (see Maehler, vol. 2, p. 64). On the other hand, if Bacch. was present at the Games, and Hieron did indeed compete and win as 'king of Syracuse', why did Pindar claim otherwise? The explanation may lie in the fact that victory at the Games conferred great honour on the victor, and was often used for political advantage (see intro. to Ode 3); Pindar's poem was written for performance in Aitna (see above), and Hieron may well have instructed Pindar to refer specifically to Aitna in this way, so as to suggest that his rule there was accepted and sanctioned by the Delphic authorities and even by Apollo himself. Thus he would impress the legitimacy of his kingship upon his subjects.

Bacch. tells us (4.6) that the present victory was Hieron's third at Delphi, and further (4.11-13) that it should have been his fourth. Unfortunately the papyrus is severely mutilated at this point, but the general sense seems clear: 'if justice had been done, Hieron would have a fourth victory to his credit'. In other words, there must have been a previous occasion on which Hieron, for whatever reason, was robbed of a victory which should have been his. Since Hieron had already won the horse-race at Delphi in 482 and 478, this must have been either the horse-race of 474, or the chariot-race of 482, 478, or 474.

We can only guess at the circumstances in which such a situation might have arisen. Perhaps Bacch. is referring to nothing more sinister than a very close finish in which the decision of the judges went against Hieron (cf. 11.34-5), but would the chagrin at such a loss still rankle after four, eight, or even twelve years? An entirely different and intriguing possibility is discussed by Maehler (vol. 2, pp. 66-7; see now also his article 'Bakchylides and the Polyzalos Inscription', *ZPE* 139 (2002), pp. 9-21).

Fig. 6. The Delphic Charioteer,
Delphi, Archaeological
Museum.

The famous bronze statue commonly known as the Delphic Charioteer was found in the sanctuary of Apollo, and was clearly part of an elaborate monument dedicated to the god as thank-offering for a victory in the Pythian chariot-race. Part of the limestone base on which the whole monument stood was also found, and the surviving block carries the right-hand part of the two-line dedicatory inscription. With plausible restoration of the left-hand part, the first line reads:

For victory in the chariot-race] Polyzalos dedicated me.

It would seem, then, that Polyzalos, younger brother of Hieron, won the Pythian chariot-race, and erected this statue to commemorate his success. But there is a problem. The statue-base was in fact reused; it originally bore an earlier inscription which was erased and the inscription referring to Polyzalos was engraved over it. The erasure, however, was not complete; traces of the original lettering remain, sufficient to allow the reading:

'..........] lord of Gela dedicated

If this is the correct reading, it cannot refer to anyone other than Hieron, who was 'lord of Gela' from 485 to 478. It cannot refer to his elder brother Gelon, for we know (*schol.* Pind. *Pyth.* 6 and 7, ed. Drach. II, 192 and 201) that during Gelon's rule at Gela (491-485) the Pythian chariot-race of 490 was won by Xenokrates of Akragas, and that of 486 by Megakles. Is it possible, then, that it was Hieron who, either in 482 or 478, while still 'lord of Gela', won the victory and dedicated the Delphic Charioteer, that Polyzalos somehow prevailed upon the authorities at Delphi to allow his own name instead to be listed as victor in the official record, and that he then appropriated the dedicatory monument already erected by Hieron and engraved his own name upon it? Could it be that this is what Bacch. has in mind when he refers to a fourth victory which eluded Hieron? This might seem an improbable sequence of events, but there is evidence of hostility between Hieron and Polyzalos (see note on 5.31), and we know that falsification of the official record for political reasons was a real possibility. Herodotos (6.103) tells the story of Cimon the Athenian, who, while in exile from Athens, won the chariot-race at Olympia for the second time, but allowed the victory to be credited to the tyrant Peisistratos, so that in gratitude (he hoped) Peisistratos would allow him to return to Athens from exile.

The poem

Ode 4, like the other short Odes 6, 7 and 8 (but not Ode 2) consists of a single pair of metrically corresponding stanzas. It begins with the confident assertion that Hieron enjoys the favour of Apollo (1-3) and returns to this idea at the end (18-20) in a rhetorical question which, although expressed as a generalization, has clear reference to Hieron. Within this circular frame are contained all the usual elements of the epinician – there is praise of the victor, his city and the place where the victory was won; the victor's honour is enhanced by reference to previous successes, this time with a regretful glance at what might have been (11-13), and Bacch. again alludes, as he often does, to his own role in the celebration of victory (cf. e.g. intro. to Ode 6). Maehler (vol. 2, p. 68) rightly draws attention to the careful balance between strophe and antistrophe, pointing out that to a remarkable extent metrically corresponding lines correspond in content also. For details, see the notes, below.

1 **still** because the present victory was Hieron's third success at Delphi (see 6, below, and intro. to Ode 3).
   golden-haired As gold is the most precious metal, so it becomes a metaphor for what is best (cf. Pind. *Ol.* 1.1-2: 'gold ... outshines all pride of wealth'). Thus adjectives compounded with 'gold-' (*chruso-*) naturally form a conspicuous part of the decorative and honorific vocabulary of the poets. There are 16 of them in Bacch. (3.27, 5.10, 9.1 etc.); this one, (*chrusokomas*) though occasionally used by other writers of other gods (e.g. of Dionysos, Hes. *Theog.* 947), is especially attached to Apollo. Cf. Pind. *Ol.* 6.41 and 7.32, where Pindar refers to Apollo simply as 'the golden-haired one'.

2-3 **loves ... and honours** As always (see e.g. 1.155-6, 6.9) the victory is seen as proof of the goodwill and favour shown to the victor by a god. On this occasion it is the gift of Apollo, patron god of Delphi, in whose honour the Pythian Games were held.

4 **navel-stone** The word (*omphalos*) properly means 'navel', and came to be used to mean 'the central point' of anything. Thus in Homer the island of Kalypso was 'at the navel of the sea' (*Od.* 1.50). In the sanctuary of Apollo at Delphi there was a stone which was believed to mark the exact centre of the earth – a later terracotta replica can still be seen in the museum at Delphi – and so this stone was naturally called the *omphalos*. The usage was extended to Delphi itself as 'navel of the earth' (Pind. *Pyth.* 11.9; cf. also Pind. *Pyth.* 4.74, Aisch. *Eum.* 40, etc.).

5 **for the third time** Hieron's two previous Pythian victories were in the horse-races of 482 and 478; see intro. to Ode 3.

6 **splendid ... mares** Lit. = 'he is celebrated ... together with the excellence (*areta*) of his ... mares'. For the importance of the concept of *areta* see intro. to Ode 1; this is the only occasion in Bacch. where the word is used in a more prosaic way, but cf. Pind. *Pyth.* 10. 23: 'prevailing through the *areta* of his feet', and Hom. *Il.* 20.411: 'displaying the *areta* of his feet'.
   mares For the use of mares in chariot-racing, see note on 3.4.

swift-running A Homeric adjective; *Il.* 5.296, etc.

8-10 Urania One of the Muses, cf. 5.10 and 6.10, and see the note on Klio, 3.1.

queen of the lyre (*anaxiphorminx*). The first part of the compound is restored here, but can be regarded as certain. Cf. 6.10, where Urania is 'queen of song' (*anaximolpos*), and see the note there for Bacch.'s use of compound adjectives with *anaxi-*.

rooster At 3.98 Bacch. describes himself as 'the honey-tongued nightingale of Ceos', at 10.10 he is 'the sweet-voiced honey-bee', and at 5.10 the 'servant of Urania'. So here 'Urania's rooster' can only refer to Bacch. himself. If 'rooster' seems a strange comparison, it is at least softened by 'sweet-voiced'; it is even appropriate, in that Bacch. sees himself as the herald, who announces or proclaims the victory, even as the rooster proclaims the coming day. In these lines then, Bacch. is clearly alluding to his own role as poet in the creation of victory songs, but further detail is very uncertain, given the fragmentary nature of the papyrus. Maehler (vol. 2, p. 70f.) argues for a contrast between past and present, suggesting a meaning such as: 'the rooster has sung for Hieron in the past' (alluding to the Olympic victory in the horse-race of 476, celebrated in Ode 5) 'but now again has willingly poured out his songs'. In support of this Maehler cites the very similar contrast between past and present in Ode 6 (see 6.4 and 6.9) and points out also that reference to an earlier Olympic victory here creates a parallel between these lines and line 17 below, which is typical of the structure of this ode.

9 with willing mind An example of the 'willingness-motif'; see note on 5.14.

10 showered with The image is drawn from the *phullobolia*, the practice of scattering flowers and garlands before the victorious athlete. See 11.18-20, and the note on 1.158.

11-13 For the probable general sense of these lines: 'This would be Hieron's fourth, not third, Pythian victory, if justice had been done', and for a discussion of the circumstances which might lie behind this failure, see intro., above.

rightly Only part of the word survives on the papyrus, but this seems the most likely restoration. There is a similar adverbial use of the same word at Soph. *OT* 419, and it gives here the simplest and best sense to the whole sentence. (See my article 'We wuz robbed', *LCM* 19 (1994), pp. 20-1.)

poised the scales of Justice In the *Iliad* Zeus weighs the fates of Greeks and Trojans (*Il.* 8.69f.) and of Achilles and Hector (*Il.* 19.223f.). Holding them by the middle, Zeus 'poised' the scales (i.e. lifted and held them still) to see which pan would fall, and the scales become an image of decision. Bacch. uses the same verb 'poised' (*heilke*) as was used by Homer, and no doubt had the Homeric image in mind. The 'scales of

Justice', then, suggest 'scales with which a just decision is made', so that the meaning of the whole clause, finally, is: 'if (someone) had made a fair and proper decision'. For a similar situation, very similarly expressed, see 11.27. Note also the echo in these lines of 1-3; Apollo honours Hieron, the just ruler (3), as the Chorus would now do (13) if justice were done (12). See intro., above.

13 **Deinomenes' son** With this reference to Hieron's father Bacch. completes the required salutation to the victor (3), his city (2) and his family.

14 **garlands** See note on 1.158. The phrase, together with 'sing' (17), picks up 'he is celebrated' (5).

15-17 **alone ... achieved this feat** i.e. no one else had ever won three Pythian victories (in equestrian events, although, in order not to diminish the praise of Hieron, Bacch. does not spell out this restriction). Cf. Hdt. 6.103.4, where we learn that Cimon's achievement of three Olympic chariot victories had once been equalled, but never surpassed. Reference to records of this kind is not uncommon in the epinician poems, and is naturally used to enhance the renown of the victor (cf. 8.22-5; Pind. *Nem.* 6.25-6).
that walk the earth The adjective (*epichthonios*) is used again of Hieron at 5.3; there, however, it has sombre thematic connotations which are not present here. (See note on 5.3, and intro. to Ode 5.)

16 **Kirrha's bay** Kirrha was the harbour town on the north shore of the Gulf of Corinth, just below Delphi. It was absorbed by conquest, around 590 BC, into Delphic (and Apollonian) territory. Here again there is an echo of the strophe (cf. notes on 13 and 14, above). The reference to the scene of the actual victory here (16) picks up and balances the reference to Delphi (4-6). The celebration of the victory, at which Bacch.'s ode was sung, took place in the sanctuary itself, which lay high above the sea on the slopes of Mt Parnassos, while the victory was won on the plain of Kirrha below.

18 **two Olympic prizes** These were Hieron's successes in the Olympic horse-races of 476 and 472; see intro. to Ode 3.

19-20 Mention of these Olympic prizes leads naturally into the final generalization which Hieron's life illustrates. 'Loved by gods' (19) echoes the love and honour which Apollo bestows upon Hieron (1-3), while the mark of the god's favour is now expanded to include 'blessings of every kind'. For the thought (again in relation to Hieron), cf. 5.50-3 and the notes there.

20 **one's share** Cf. 1.157-8, and esp. 5.51; the notion of one's proper share (*moira*) was important and deep-seated in ancient thought; one must not seek to go beyond it, for 'no man is god-favoured in all things' (5.54-5). See intro. to Ode 5.

ODE 5
FOR HIERON OF SYRACUSE
Horse-Race, Olympic Games, 476 BC

The event

Ode 5 was written to celebrate a victory in the horse-race at Olympia won by Hieron's famous stallion Pherenikos. This much can be deduced from the ode itself (e.g. Hieron 1 and 15; horse-race 43f.; Pherenikos 38; Olympia 40), but it is well supported by external evidence. After Hieron's death in 467, his son Deinomenes dedicated at Olympia an elaborate piece of statuary to commemorate his father's victories. The monument does not survive, but fortunately it was seen by that tireless tourist Pausanias, who described it for us (Paus. 6.12.1) and recorded the inscription which was engraved on its base (Paus. 8.42.9). The inscription reads:

> For victory at your holy Games, Olympian Zeus,
>   once with the team of four, twice with the single horse
> Hieron has given these gifts to you, and his son Deinomenes
>   erected this in memory of his father from Syracuse.

Thus Hieron won not merely one, but two, victories in the horse-race at Olympia.

According to Pausanias the statue had a centrepiece consisting of a bronze chariot complete with charioteer; on either side of this stood a bronze horse with a boy jockey; in other words all three of Hieron's Olympic victories were commemorated. Since the monument includes two race-horses, it seems likely that the two victories in the horse-race were won by different horses; one might think that some consideration of artistic symmetry could be involved, but really it seems improbable that if Pherenikos had won on both occasions, the feat would be immortalized by two separate statues, especially in a posthumous and 'inclusive' monument. The chances are strong then, that of Hieron's two Olympic victories in the horse-race, only one was won by Pherenikos, and the other by a different, unknown, horse. (If this is true, it means that Pind. *Ol.* 1, also written for a victory by Pherenikos (see *Ol.* 1.18) was composed for the same occasion as Bacch. Ode 5.)

The dates of these two victories are secure. We are fortunate in that parts of a copy of the official list of winners at Olympia has survived on papyrus, and from this we learn that Hieron was victorious in the horse-race in 476 BC and 472 BC (Pap. Oxy. II 222, Col. I.19 and I.32). Which of these was won by Pherenikos? Bacch. tells us (5.41, and cf. Pind. *Pyth.* 3.73-4) that Pherenikos had already been successful at Delphi, and the *scholia* on Pind. *Pyth.* 1 and *Pyth.* 3 in fact record two Pythian victories in the horse-race by Hieron, in 482 BC and 478 BC. Pherenikos therefore must

Fig. 7. Competitors in the horse-race (*keles*). Black-figure amphora, 500-480 BC. London, British Museum.

have won at least one of these, if not both. Bacch. also tells us (5.43f.) that Pherenikos was undefeated. It is hardly likely that this famous horse was successful at Delphi in 482, was not entered in 478, and then won at Olympia in 476. Nor is it likely that he won at Delphi in 478 or 482, or both, was not entered at Olympia in 476, and then won there in 472. The most natural and probable sequence, in terms of the career of a champion race-horse, is that Pherenikos was victorious at Delphi in 478, and again at Olympia in 476. He may also have won the earlier race at Delphi in 482 – a six-year racing career is by no means impossible, and Pindar's language at *Pyth*. 3.73-4 may be thought to suggest more than one success.

These arguments in favour of 476 BC for Ode 5 are admittedly speculative and subjective. Of greater weight is the fact that neither Bacch. in Ode 5 nor Pindar in *Ol*. 1 make any reference to an earlier Olympic victory. It was common practice in epinician poetry to enhance the praise of the victor by listing or referring to earlier successes (cf. 1.157-8; 8.17-18, etc.); if Bacch. and Pindar were writing in 472 BC, it is hard to imagine that they would fail to mention Hieron's Olympic victory of 476, even if it was not won by Pherenikos. We should bear in mind also that neither Bacch. nor Pindar make any mention of Hieron's great victory over the Etruscans at Cumae in 474, nor of the foundation by Hieron of the new city of Aitna (476-5 BC, see Diod. 11.49.1) of which he was immensely proud. On the other hand, in Ode 4, certainly composed in 470, Bacch. again makes no mention of Aitna, so that this part of the argument is perhaps less cogent (see intro. to Ode 4).

For a synopsis of Hieron's 'sporting' career in equestrian events, see the intro. to Ode 3.

The myth

The saga of the Twelve Labours of Herakles was already well entrenched in the mythological tradition. Homer (*Il.* 19.100-33) tells how, when Alcmena, the wife of Amphitryon, was about to give birth to Zeus' son, Zeus promised that the next man born of his blood would be a great king, but Hera, consistently hostile to Herakles, delayed his birth in favour of that of Eurystheus, so that the latter became king of Tiryns instead, and Herakles was obliged to be his subject. Later (according to Apollod. 2.4.12) Hera continued her persecution by sending a madness upon him, causing him to kill his children by his wife Megara, whereupon, as part of his purification for this outrage, he had to serve Eurystheus for twelve years and perform whatever tasks were set him. These were the Twelve Labours. One of these (traditionally no. 11) was to descend into the Underworld to bring back Cerberos, the monstrous dog that guarded its entrance (Hom. *Il.* 8.366-9; *Od.* 11.622-6, etc.). (See also Eur. *Herakles*, although Eur. represents the killing of Megara as taking place *after* the Labours, i.e. not as their cause.)

In the course of his visit to Hades, Herakles came face to face with the soul of the hero Meleager, son of Oineus of Calydon, king of the Aitolians, who, as Bacch. tells it, recounted to Herakles the circumstances of his death. The Calydonian boar-hunt, and the events which led in one way or another to the death of Meleager, were, like the descent of Herakles to the Underworld, an established part of the mythic tradition, but there appear to have been two versions of the story, as we can see from Homer and Bacch. In Homer (*Il.* 9.529f.) Artemis is angered by Oineus' disregard of her; she sends a wild boar to ravage the land; the Aitolians and their allies fight the boar until Meleager kills it, but a dispute arises between the Aitolians and the Kouretes over the hide. In the fighting which ensues, Meleager kills his mother's brother, who is on the other side, for his mother Althaia is the daughter of Thestios of Pleuron, king of the Kouretes. In anger Althaia curses Meleager, who then withdraws from the fighting in pique; the Kouretes gain the upper hand, until finally Meleager is prevailed upon by his wife Kleopatra to return to the fray. But now it is too late; although Meleager drives off the enemy and saves his people, he is not given the gifts and honour which had earlier been promised him. Homer makes no mention of the fate of Meleager, except to say that, in response to Althaia's prayer for her son's death, 'Erinys' (i.e. the spirit of vengeance) 'heard her out of the dark places' (Hom. *Il.* 9.571-2). (In Homer the story of Meleager is meant to serve as a warning to Achilles; if he does not return to the fighting, he too, like Meleager, will not be given the honour which is his due. Thus the manner of Meleager's death is irrelevant to Homer's purpose.)

Apart from a few unimportant details (the anger of Artemis is unexplained, 5.100f.; Meleager kills two, not one, of his mother's brothers, 5.127-9) Bacch. follows the Homeric story very closely, up to the point of Althaia's anger, but there the two significantly diverge. In Homer it is Althaia's curse which leads, through the agency of the Erinys, to the death of Meleager, in a way which Homer does not choose to describe; in Bacch. an entirely different motif is introduced. Here Althaia at once takes from its hiding-place the log which marks the term of Meleager's life, and burns it; thereupon Meleager dies. This is magic. The linking of a man's life to a physical object in this way – when the object is destroyed the life is ended – belongs to the realm of folklore, or fairytale. Nor can this version be reconciled with Homer's (despite the arguments of Jebb in his appendix on Ode 5, p. 471); the mother's curse delegates vengeance to the nether powers, and cannot be simply an incantation accompanying the burning of the log; besides, Homer certainly implies that Meleager's death lies in the future. There must therefore have been two separate traditions concerning the death of Meleager, and Bacch. has chosen that which better suits his purpose. (Note also that neither Homer nor Bacch. says anything of the role of Atalanta in the boar-hunt, although she is prominent in the painting of the scene on the famous 'François vase' of *c.* 570 BC (see e.g. J. Boardman, *Athenian Black-Figure Vases*, London 1974, pp. 33-4 and fig. 46.3) and plays a leading part in Euripides' play *Meleager*; this suggests yet another element in the tradition – a love story involving Meleager and Atalanta, which would again be as irrelevant to Bacchylides' purpose as to Homer's.)

According to Pausanias (10.31.4) the early tragedian Phrynichos, in his (now lost) play *The Women of Pleuron* (probably earlier than Ode 5), used the motif of the burning of the log; it is also mentioned in Aisch. *Libation Bearers* 603f. (458 BC) and it resurfaces in Apollod. 1.8.2-3. Pausanias however also says that Phrynichos merely alluded to the story in passing, as indeed does Aisch.; this suggests that the story was already established and well-known. It may therefore not have been invented by Phrynichos; Bacch. may have taken it from some earlier, perhaps epic, source. (Paus. also tells us (10.31.3) that in the epic poems *Minyas* and *Eoiai*, Meleager was killed by Apollo. Whether this was in response to Althaia's curse, and whether this form of the story was known to Homer, remains uncertain. Again, different versions appear to have been current.)

The story of the meeting between Meleager and Herakles in the Underworld appears, as far as our sources go, only here in Ode 5, and in Pindar. The Pindaric version does not survive, but we have a summary of it in the Homeric *scholia* on *Il.* 21.194. (The *scholia* refer the story only to Pindar, which suggests that they knew of no other source, but there must surely have been one, perhaps Stesichoros, or an earlier epic poem.) In both Pindar and Bacch., a marriage between Meleager's sister Deianeira and Herakles is foreshadowed, but again there is a significant difference in the treatment. In Pindar, according to the *scholia*, Meleager asks Herakles to marry Deianeira, to protect her from the monstrous river-god Acheloios who is pursuing her. Herakles agrees, and on leaving the Underworld hurries off to the palace of Oineus. (The fight between Herakles and Acheloios, alluded to in the *scholia*, is described at length in Soph. *Trach.* 497-530.) In Bacch., on the other hand, Herakles, moved by pity and admiration for the great hero, himself asks if Meleager has a sister whom he might marry. This pity and admiration, which lead to Herakles' question, are aroused by the account of Meleager's unhappy death, so that the whole story of the boar-hunt and its consequences, which in Pindar's version of the meeting would have no point, is essential to Bacch.'s narrative.

Thus Bacch. is the only writer who combines these two originally separate myths, using the meeting between Herakles and Meleager as a frame for the narrative of Meleager's death. Given the stated theme of the ode: 'No man is god-favoured in all things' (54-5), his purpose in adopting this structure is clear. He wishes to use both Meleager and Herakles as *exempla* to illustrate this theme. The fate of Meleager by itself would serve well as *exemplum*, but just as Bacch. chooses the story of the burning log to enhance the tragic pathos attaching to the death of Meleager, so he combines this with the meeting with Herakles, in order to lead into the question about Deianeira, which in turn reminds us of Herakles' future death at the hands of his innocent wife. For Deianeira killed her husband, although she was seeking only to regain his love with what she thought was a magic potion. (The full story is told in Soph. *Trach*; see also Ode 16.) Thus Herakles too becomes an *exemplum* illustrating this central theme. (See further below, and for the use of *exempla*, see also the intro. to Ode 1.) Ode 5, then, provides a fine example of the way in which Bacchylides could, like Homer, select and combine elements of the mythic tradition to suit his own purposes. (For similar creative treatment of the mythic material, see the intro. to Ode 11.)

The poem

The ode is constructed with great care and artistry, and exhibits yet again (see e.g. the intros to Odes 1 and 3) Bacch's favoured structure. It falls into four well-defined sections, connected by clearly marked and significant transitional passages. In the centre stands the myth (56-175) describing the meeting of Herakles and Meleager in the Underworld; on either side of this stands a section devoted to praise of the victor (1-49 and 178-87), and the whole poem is rounded off with a gnomic section, concluding with a prayer for the continued success and prosperity of Hieron (188-200).

Ode 5

The first victor-praise (1-49) is itself divided into three sections, with typical ring-composition. Bacch. begins (1-15) with specific (if sometimes oblique) praise of his patron on three counts – his victory, his kingship and his artistic sensibility; these opening lines are framed by the references to Hieron in 1 and 15, and summarized in 14-15. The theme of praise is then continued and developed in the eagle simile (16-30), illustrating the vast scope for praise offered by Hieron's talents (as well as Bacch.'s own ability to do justice to his achievements; see esp. notes on 9 and 17, below). Finally (31-49), Bacch. returns to praise of the victor, this time extended to Hieron's family in general; a brief prayer for continued success (see note on 36) then leads into specific praise of the horse Pherenikos and the glory which it has brought to Hieron. This section too is framed, this time by the repeated references to 'victory' (35 and 48), while the mention of Hieron's victory (48-9) picks up the 'fate-favoured leader' of line 1, thus completing the ring-compositional structure of this whole opening section of the poem.

The gnomic lines which follow (50-5) serve as transition to the myth, and at the same time present the major theme of the ode. The thought is expressed as a generalization, but in fact the immediate reference is to Hieron, as is clear from the fact that it arises directly out of the previous sentence: Pherenikos has striven to bring a new victory to Hieron (48-9); blessed is he who wins from god his share of good (50-1). It is impossible that this should not refer to Hieron. Besides, there are repetitions and verbal echoes in these lines which bring out the meaning and structure (and which in turn form part of the larger structure of the ode). 'Share of good' (*moiran kalon*, 51) recalls 'fate-favoured' (*eumoiros*, 1) which referred particularly to Hieron's victory (see note on line 1). It is Hieron, then, who enjoys his share of god's favour. In stark and immediate contrast to this, however, stands the proposition (54-5): 'no one is god-favoured in all things', and the myth which follows then illustrates this proposition – even the great heroes Meleager and Herakles (the latter a son of Zeus himself) did not enjoy their 'share of good' from god in all things, for Fate (*moira*) brought to Meleager a wretched and untimely death at the hands of a vengeful mother. Bacch. makes the point unmistakeable by using the word 'fate' three times in relation to Meleager (121, 142 and 158). Likewise Herakles was unwittingly killed by his wife Deianeira, and the reference to her (172) will at once recall this to the audience of the ode. Thus the myth serves as foil for the fate of Hieron – a negative *exemplum* which throws into high relief by contrast the success and good fortune of the victor, and this meaning is highlighted and emphasized by the repetition, after the myth (186-7), of the idea that the victory is a mark of god's favour (*eudaimonia*).

At the same time, while Hieron is unquestionably *eumoiros* ('fate-favoured', 1) no-one is *eudaimon* ('god-favoured', 55) in all things. These two words are similarly formed and virtually synonymous, and the latter is surely intended to recall the former. That there is here a reference to

119

Hieron is confirmed by a further repetition: he is one of those 'who walk the earth' (i.e. 'mortal', *epichthonios*, 3) but none of those who 'walk the earth' (the word is repeated at 54) is *eudaimon* all the time. It is difficult, then, not to hear an admonitory undertone in these lines; not even Hieron can expect to enjoy god's favour in all things or all the time, and in the midst of his praise Bacch. obliquely warns against complacency.

The mythic narrative itself is clear, linear and straightforward. A moderately lengthy introduction (56-77) describes the descent of Herakles to the Underworld, the reason for it, and the meeting with Meleager among the souls of the dead. The scene is strongly reminiscent of the confrontation of Homeric heroes on the battlefield (see note on line 56, below), and in true Homeric style it consists entirely, after the introduction, of direct speech. There are five speeches, symmetrically arranged. Meleager begins by pointing out to Herakles the absurdity of his belligerent attitude; Herakles responds by asking Meleager to identify himself, for he is clearly a great and worthy hero. The central and longest section is then occupied by Meleager's story of his own death, which in turn leads to Herakles' inquiry after a sister whom he could make his wife. Thus the central narrative is framed by questions from Herakles, inspired in each case by admiration for the courage and heroism of Meleager, and this whole is in turn framed by brief speeches from Meleager, in which allusion to the finality of death is echoed by the reference to Deianeira, who one day will inadvertently bring death to Herakles. There is no final section which might balance the introductory narrative of the descent to the Underworld, and the reason is clear. The name of Deianeira is left hanging, ominously, in the air; we are left to ponder its implications, and so we become aware that even the mighty Herakles illustrates Bacch.'s central theme.

After an abrupt transitional formula (176-7), the second victor-praise (178-87) follows immediately, in which the themes of the first are resumed. Bacch. sings of Zeus, of Pisa, Pelops and Olympia, of Pherenikos the horse and finally of Hieron himself, thus returning at the end to the praise of the victor with which the poem began. Likewise the final gnomic lines (188-200) pick up and balance themes made prominent in the opening section, such as Bacch.'s own role as servant of the Muse in sending the poem to Hieron, his willingness to praise him and the great scope for praise afforded by Hieron's achievements. The ode ends, appropriately, with a prayer, echoing the prayer of 36, for continued success and prosperity, but given the underlying theme of the poem, there is surely now an ironic undertone here.

1 **fate-favoured** The victory is, as always, regarded as a gift from the gods (cf. e.g. 6.1, and see also note on 1.118), and it is therefore a mark of their favour and goodwill. Thus Bacch. begins his song with praise of the victor, through an immediate, if oblique, reference to Hieron's success. But the word relates also to one of the major themes of the poem (see intro., above).

leader Hieron became king of Syracuse on the death of his elder brother Gelon in 478 BC, two years before the date of this ode.

2 **riders of … chargers** Jebb, in his note on this line (p. 269), approved by Maehler (vol. 2, p. 85) asserts that the reference 'is to the distinction of Syracuse in chariot-races'. This is most unlikely. It is true that Gelon had gained a victory in the chariot-race at Olympia in 488 BC (Paus. 6.9.4), but it would surely be tactless of Bacch. to allude to this when Hieron himself had not yet achieved this success. Besides, the word 'leader' in line 1 (*stratagos*, lit. = 'general') has military connotations, and the reference is more probably to the skill of the Syracusan cavalry. Gelon seems to have held the title *strategos autokrator* ('general with sole authority'), either taken on his assumption of power in Syracuse in 485 BC, or granted to him on his appointment as supreme commander against the Carthaginians in 480 (so Diod. 13.94.5; see also Jebb's appendix, pp. 465-7) and the title may well have become a euphemism for his monarchy. Whether the title passed to Hieron when he succeeded Gelon in 478 is uncertain; nor is there any evidence that Hieron achieved any significant military success, whether with cavalry or not, before this date, but he had at least shared in the glory won by Gelon in his victory over the Carthaginians (cf. note on 35, below). Bacch. may therefore be using the term simply as a generalized poetic reference to Hieron's position as commander of the Syracusan cavalry. Thus the praise of the victor implicit in 'fate-favoured' is at once broadened by reference to Hieron's distinction as king, in political and military affairs.

wide-wheeling This adjective, coined by Bacch. – it occurs only here in the surviving literature – is applied in fact to the Syracusans themselves; it literally means 'whirlers of horses', and could apply as well to cavalry in warfare as to chariot-racing (see previous note). Bacch., it seems, is more interested in the image of vigorous movement than in precise description.

3 **who … walk this earth** A common Homeric and poetic periphrasis for 'mortals', to distinguish them from gods, cf. e.g. 4.15 and 10.14. The word is significantly repeated at 54, below, and again at 96.

4 **will recognize** Bacch. expands the praise of the victor still further with a piece of blatant flattery. Not only does Hieron enjoy the favour of the gods; not only is he a great king; he is also a man of sensitivity and perception, whose victory gives him a special relationship with the Muses and who will thus appreciate this song. At the same time Bacch. foreshadows the theme of his own role in the celebration of the victory, which he will develop below, especially in the following antistrophe, where he compares his song to the flight of the soaring eagle. See further on 9, below.

ornament The word (*agalma*) indicates anything which confers honour on a person; in prosaic language it commonly means a statue or monument. Here, as in 1.184 and 10.12, it is used of the song itself, which immortalizes a man's achievements and brings renown.

5 **sweet gift** Cf. note on 3.1, where the same word is used. The song is a gift from the Muses to the victor, and the poet is intermediary between them. Cf. also note on 1.1.
violet-crowned See note on 3.3.

6 **Set aside your cares** The notion that song lightens care first appears in Hesiod's description of the birth of the Muses (*Theog.* 53f.). Bacch. uses words very closely related to those of Hesiod, and may be consciously recalling the earlier poet; cf. note on 10, below.
straight-judging The word occurs here for the first time as an adjective (and again at 24.7); previously it was a proper name (Euthudikos).

9 **guest-friend** i.e. Bacch. himself. This word (*xeinos*) marks a special relationship involving mutual respect, reciprocal hospitality, friendship and support. Bacchylides' uncle Simonides was in Sicily at some time during the years just before the composition of this ode (Timaios, *FGH* fr. 93b) and it was perhaps then that Bacch. was introduced to Hieron. By claiming guest-friendship, Bacch. places himself on a level of intimacy, even equality, with Hieron. Just as Hieron is blessed by the Muses (line 5), so too does Bacch. enjoy their favour and support in the creation of his song (10f.). Thus Bacch. passes from general praise of the victor to initiate another standard theme of the epinician. The song must be worthy of the occasion, and the poet must demonstrate that he has the status and the capacity to do justice to the prowess of the victor (cf. the intro. to Ode 6, and note on 8.19-21). Bacch. and Pindar both write in full consciousness of their own artistry and poetic skill (cf. Pind. *Nem.* 7.77-9, where he compares his song to a beautiful crown of gold, ivory and lilies). They are writing for the *cognoscenti*, for those who will understand. See also Bacch. 3.85, and cf. Pind. *Ol.* 2.83-5. Unabashed self-praise was therefore a common device in the victory ode, but this passage (9-30) is perhaps the most elaborate and extensive example of it in Bacchylides.

10 **famed servant** Cf. 192, below, where Bacch. calls the poet Hesiod 'the Muses' servant'. This is part of the elaborate structure of repetitions and echoes in this poem, whereby Bacch. represents himself as the equal of his distinguished predecessor. (Hesiod himself (*Theog.* 100) was the first to use this description of the poet's function; Bacch. may be recalling that passage.) Likewise 'famed' (a favourite honorific adjective in Bacch., cf. 8.32 and note there) forms part of the self-praise.
gold-garlanded Lit. = 'of the golden headband' (*chrusampux*), cf. fr. 65a.13. The word describes the band (*ampux*) worn over the forehead to confine long hair (see H.L. Lorimer, *Homer and the Monuments*, London 1950, pp. 386-7). Used by Homer of horses (*Il.* 5.358 etc.), it is later applied to the Muses (Hes. *Theog.* 916) and other semi-divine female figures. Cf. also *Il.* 22.468f., describing the elaborate headdress

of Andromache. For adjectives compounded with 'gold-' (*chruso-*), see note on 4.1.

Urania One of the Muses, cf. 4.10, 6.10, and see note on Klio at 3.1. Her name means 'the heavenly one'.

11 **lovely** Lit. = 'deep-girdled' (*bathuzonos*); cf. 90, below, and see note on 1.116.

Graces The Graces (*Charites*) are a personification of that quality of charm and grace inherent in all those activities which elevate and enhance human life and make it beautiful. For Bacch. that especially means athletic success and the songs which attend it, so that the Graces are often associated with the Muses in the creation of his song; cf. also 9.1 and 19.5-7. Interestingly, Pindar uses exactly the same phrase ('with the lovely Graces') – perhaps in direct imitation of Bacch. – at *Pyth.* 9.2-3, probably written in 474 BC, i.e. two years after this ode.

12 **weaves** For this image cf. 1.4 (with note) and 19.8. Here, in contrast to 1.4, Bacch. represents himself as creator of the song, with the help of the Muse and the Graces.

holy island i.e. Ceos, Bacch.'s home; so described also at 2.8. Unlike e.g. Delos, the birthplace of Apollo (Hom. Hymn 3), or Delphi (see on 41, below), there was no particular reason to describe Ceos as a 'holy' island; the adjective is simply honorific (cf. 'famed', 10, above), and, like all such adjectives, serves to contribute to the general aura of excellence and distinction which pervades the poems. Perhaps it was suggested to Bacch. by his own sense of intimacy with the Muses. The word is used also of Olympia at 11.45, where it is more appropriate.

13 **sends** Bacch. was evidently not present in Syracuse for the performance of the ode at the celebration of Hieron's victory. Contrast Ode 3, and see note on 3.15. Bacch. returns to this motif at 196, below.

14 **He wishes** An example of what Maehler (vol. 2, p. 123) calls the 'willingness-motif'. The victor's praise is enhanced, indirectly, when the poet asserts his readiness to praise him (cf. 4.9f. and 9.4; also frequently in Pindar). Again Bacch. resumes this motif at the end of the poem; see 195f.

17 **as the eagle** This is one of Bacch.'s finest and most elaborate similes. There are two points in the comparison. First, Bacch. equates the effortless soaring flight of the eagle with his own ability as a poet to sing the praises of Hieron (17-22); second, the achievements of Hieron provide unlimited scope for praise, as the eagle flies without restriction over sea and mountains (23-30). Thus the simile serves as transition from the 'willingness-motif' (see previous note) to the praise of the victor, while at the same time contributing to the poet's self-praise. Eagle similes were common in epic and early literature (e.g. *Il.* 21.252-3, 22.308f., etc.); Bacch.'s image is a composite of earlier usages. The major part of the simile goes back to Hom. Hymn 2.380-3, where the chariot carrying Persephone flies unchecked over sea, rivers, glens and

mountain peaks, 'cleaving the deep air' (cf. 19, below). For the image of little birds cowering before the mighty eagle, see Alkaios fr. 52 D, and Pind. *Pyth.* 5.111-12; Bacch. has added this to his simile, while changing the horses of the Hom. Hymn to the eagle. Since he uses the eagle to represent himself, it is probable that the other birds are intended to represent lesser poets; Pindar also uses the eagle as a metaphor for himself as poet at *Nem.* 5.22 (481 BC?) and *Nem.* 3.80 (*c.* 469-459 BC), the latter including a disparaging comparison of lesser poets to mere jackdaws, and a similar contrast appears again at Pind. *Ol.* 2.88, where he calls himself 'the divine bird of Zeus' (i.e. the eagle), while inferior poets are 'ravens'. *Ol.* 2 was written in 476 BC, the same year as Bacch. 5, but it is not likely that, in using the same image to express his superiority to other poets, either was responding to the other. Since Bacch. sent his ode from Ceos (cf. 13, above), and both were written to celebrate an Olympic victory (i.e. at around the same time) neither Pindar nor Bacch. will have seen the other's work.

messenger The phrase is probably taken from *Il.* 24.292f., where Hecuba urges Priam to pray to Zeus for an omen that he will return safely from his mission to Achilles. There the eagle is a 'messenger' because it conveys to Priam the message that he does indeed enjoy the protection of Zeus.

loud-thundering A literal and common description of Zeus (cf. 7.3 and note there), but also an intensifying compound, contributing to the heroic atmosphere of Bacch.'s poetry. See also esp. note on 7.7.

18 **whose realm spreads wide** The word (*euruanax*) is used only here. Bacch. is clearly fond of compound adjectives made from *eurus* (= 'wide'); he uses six such words and three of these are apparently coined by him, since they occur nowhere else. Interestingly, three of the six occur in Ode 5. For the sense cf. 11.52 (*eurubias*), and see also the previous note.

19 **deep sky** Cf. 3.86. For the reminiscence of the Hom. Hymn to Demeter, see on 17, above.

20 **pulsing** Jebb (p. 271), Maehler (vol. 2, p. 94) and other scholars understand this word (*xouthos*) as a colour word (= 'tawny', 'brownish-yellow') and many of its usages will allow this meaning. But cf. *xouthopteros* at Eur. *Herakles* 487, used of the honey-bee, where the buzz or hum produced by rapidly beating wings seems to be indicated. See also A.M. Dale on Eur. *Helen.* 1111 (Oxford, 1967), who argues that the common element in the usages is a 'quick throbbing vibrato of sound'. So here the image will combine the steady beat of the eagle's wings with the sound produced.

21 **mighty strength** Perhaps suggested by Homer's description of the eagle: 'and its strength is greatest', at *Il.* 24.293; see on 'messenger', 17, above. This may confirm that Bacch. had the Homeric passage in mind.

22 **screeching** The word used here (*liguphthongos*) is compounded from

the adjective *ligus*. This, and the related *liguros*, seem to have had two areas of meaning in relation to sound, viz. 'clear' and 'shrill'. (Perhaps a piercing clarity of pitch and timbre is the common element.) They are used, for example, of a 'howling' gale in Homer (*Il.* 5.526; *Od.* 3.176, etc.), and, esp. after Homer, are often associated with lament, suggesting the shrill, high-pitched keening of mourners (e.g. Aisch. *Pers.* 332; Eur. *Med.* 205). But they are also used of sweet, clear sounds, such as the song of the Sirens (*Od.* 12.44), the voice of the Muse (*Od.* 24.62, Alcman 14.1, etc.), and the lyre (*Il.* 9.186). Apart from the present passage, Bacch. uses these words only in this latter sense; so fr. 20 B 2 and fr. 20 C 1 (the lyre); 23.4 (the aulos); fr. 4.57 (songs); 14.13 (dances, alluding to the song which accompanied the dance); 5.73 (a bowstring; see note there). Most significantly, the same word as is used here (*liguphthongos*) recurs at 10.10, where Bacch. describes himself metaphorically as a 'sweet-voiced' honey-bee, suggesting the delightful quality of his song. Here, however, the word clearly suggests the harsh, raucous cries of frightened birds, and has no doubt been chosen precisely to point the contrast between Bacch. himself as the soaring eagle, and the screeching little birds (= lesser poets) who flee before it.

26 tireless In Homer the word (*akamatos*) is always used of fire; later the reference is much expanded. Here the image combines the ideas of the height and distance of the eagle's flight, as it conjures up a picture of an endless succession of huge storm-driven waves rolling across the sea's expanse. Sophocles, writing much later than Bacch., uses the word in a very similar context (*Trach.* 112-15; date uncertain, but probably in the 430s), where the hero Herakles is described metaphorically as buffeted by a succession of waves driven over the sea 'by the tireless south wind'.

28 endless (*atrutos*) Lit. = 'not worn away', i.e. 'lasting for ever', 'eternal'; cf. 9.81, where the same adjective is used of 'time'. But the secondary meaning: 'spatially endless', 'infinite', seems to be prominent also. The phrase seems to be a variation on that used by Homer at *Il.* 17.425, although the related adjective used there (*atrugetos*) was understood by some ancient commentators to mean 'barren'.

31 So now Although the simile had two parts (Bacch.'s skill and the scope for praise afforded by Hieron's achievements − see on 17, above), Bacch. appropriately resumes only the second of these, in returning to the motif of the praise of the victor.

children of Deinomenes i.e. Hieron and his brothers. Bacch. expands the praise of the victor, typically, to include the rest of his family. Hieron, believing that his younger brother Polyzalos was seeking to usurp the kingship of Syracuse, fell out with him, whereupon Polyzalos took refuge with Theron, king of Acragas. Hieron then began to prepare war against Theron, but Bacch.'s uncle Simonides, who was apparently in Sicily at the time (cf. note on 9, above), intervened and effected a reconciliation. Hieron then gave up his hostility to Theron and took Polyzalos back into favour. The circumstances are narrated by Diod. (11.48.3-5) and dated by him to 476-5 BC. Bacch.'s inclusive description here seems to indicate that he was aware that family harmony had been restored.

33 numberless pathways The same words are used at 19.1-2, and a very similar phrase at 9.47. Pindar also uses these words (*Isth.* 4.1) and a variation (*Isth.* 6.22). The expression is a common rhetorical device in epinician poetry, suggesting the copious material for praise which the victor's merits provide. Cf. Bundy, *Stud. Pind.*, pp. 14f. and 63f.

34 excellence On the importance of this concept (*areta*) to the poets and their patrons, see the intro. to Ode 1.

35 by the grace of See note on 6.9; cf. also 1.118 and the note there. In referring to Victory and Ares as sources for his song, Bacch. returns to the twin themes of praise established at the beginning of the ode. Hieron has enjoyed success in the Games and in war alike; see notes on 1 and 2, above. Thus the praise of the victor is resumed with typical ring-composition, before being developed in detail in the description of the race, 37f. The reference to Ares clearly points to the victory over the Carthaginians at Himera in 480 BC; this force was commanded by Gelon, but Hieron seems to have claimed a share in the success; see note on 3.18.

dark-haired The same word is used of the daughters of Proitos (11.83; see note there) and of Thebe (9.53). The personified goddess of Victory is 'dark-haired' only in the imagination of Bacch., so that the usage simply illustrates his fondness for striking visual detail. For the image, cf. 'violet-haired' (9.72), and see note on 'violet-crowned' at 3.3.

bronze-armoured i.e. Ares; the word (*chalkeosternos*) is another of Bacch.'s coinages; it seems to be a variation of the Homeric formula for warriors (*chalkeothorax* = 'with bronze breastplate', *Il.* 8.62, etc.); cf. also 'brazen Ares' (*Il.* 5.704 etc.).

36 I pray The prayer for the continuation of god's favour, which returns at the end of the ode (199-200), is perhaps an oblique anticipation of its major theme, viz. that no man is blessed in all things (cf. 54-5); in any case it serves as transition from the general praise of the victor Hieron to the specific praise of the horse Pherenikos which follows (37-48). Note how this is framed by the repetition of 'victory' in 35 and 48. Bacch. may well have seen Pherenikos run at Olympia; Maehler remarks on the vividness of the description (vol. 2, p. 98) and compares 13.46-9 and 9.27f.

37 the morning sun Apparently the equestrian events took place in the early morning; cf. Soph. *El.* 699, where the chariot-race is run 'at sunrise'; cf. also Xen. *Hell.* 7.4.29, which seems to suggest that the horse-race was the first event.

whose arms are golden Perhaps a variation on the Homeric epithet for Dawn, 'rose-fingered' (*Od.* 2.1, etc.). The image vividly suggests the slanting shafts of light characteristic of the early dawn. (Compare also 'rose-armed', used rather more literally at fr. 64.10, to suggest the delicate beauty of Deianeira.)

38 **watched** Cf. 11.22-3. This is an example of the 'witnessing-motif' (see esp. Bundy, *Stud. Pind.* , 60, with n. 66). Bacch. appeals to the sun as an independent witness to the prowess of the victorious Pherenikos; thus his glory is enhanced, for it does not depend on the testimony of the poet alone. This is one of the devices whereby the poet claims that he is doing justice to his theme. Cf. note on 9, above.

chestnut The word involved here (*xanthos*) is, like all colour words in Greek, notoriously imprecise. The dictionaries give 'yellow, often with a tinge of red', 'blond', 'auburn', 'brown'. Bacch. applies the word to horses, humans (and gods; cf. 92, below, where it is used of Athena) and fire; for horses, 'chestnut' seems the most appropriate translation. See J.K. Anderson, *Ancient Greek Horsemanship*, Cambridge 1961, p. 16 with n. 4.

colt Pherenikos was not a colt in the strict sense, but a mature horse; Bacch uses the word loosely. In fact races for colts were not introduced at Olympia until 256 BC. (Chariot-races for colts were introduced in 384 BC.)

39 **runs on the wind** (*aellodromas*) Lit. = 'storm-running', coined by Bacch. no doubt as a variation on the Homeric 'storm-footed' (*aellopos*) used of the messenger-goddess Iris (*Il.* 8.409, etc.). Cf. 'wind-footed' (*podanemos*, also used by Homer of Iris) at 6.13, with the note there, and for the comparison cf. *Il.* 10.437, where the horses of Rhesos could 'run like the wind'.

40 **beside the ... Alpheos** i.e. at Olympia, see on 6.3.

wide-swirling See note on 18, above. This word (*eurudinas*) occurs only here and at 3.5, on both occasions of the river Alpheos. The second element in the compound (*din-*) means 'eddy', and is much favoured by Bacch. in the creation of adjectives for rivers; cf. 8.28 and 12.42 (Alpheos), 3.44 (Paktolos) and 9.39 (Asopos). Compare also 'wide-wheeling' (*hippo-din-etos*), line 2, above.

41 **holy Delphi** A passing reference to Pherenikos' earlier victory at the Pythian Games; see intro. to this ode. For the description – appropriate, since Delphi was the major seat of Apollo – cf. 3.62.

42 **Calling the earth to witness** For the solemn asseveration, given the force of an oath, see note on 8.19-21, where the same phrase (in Greek) is used. Cf. also note on 'watched', 38, above.

46 **wind from the North** The north wind, in the northern hemisphere, was notoriously wild and wintry; see esp. *Il.* 15.170-1 and Hes. *Works and Days* 505-6. Thus the phrase picks up 'storm-running', 39, above. See also note on 13.124.

47 **responsive** Pherenikos is described as an active participant in the

victory, appropriately, since the victor-praise here belongs rather to the horse than to Hieron himself. At the same time the word probably includes the sense 'keeping safe'.

48 bring again Because this was not Hieron's or Pherenikos' first victory; they had already won at Delphi in 478 (see intro. and note on 41, above).

applause A reminder of the presence of spectators, cf. 3.9, 9.35 and 10.23. The applause and admiration of the audience serve at the same time to enliven the description of the event and to enhance the victor's praise. Cf. Pind. *Ol.* 9.93, where the victorious wrestler 'walked through the ring to loud acclamation in the pride of his youth' (Lattimore's translation).

49 for Hieron Thus Bacch. makes the transition from the prowess of the horse to Hieron himself, returning easily and naturally to his main subject, and rounding off this section of the poem before the introduction of the myth. As well, the phrase is picked up at the end (186-7), thus balancing the first and second sections of victor-praise and providing a frame for the theme of the ode as a whole.

friend of guests A compliment to his patron, which at the same time echoes 'guest-friend' at 9, above. See also note on 1.150.

50-5 Blessed is he ... For the importance of these lines to the structure and theme of the ode, see intro., above.

51 share of good Jebb (pp. 275-6) refers this specifically to Hieron's success in the Games, and the following phrase ('a life ... of good fortune') to his wealth and status as ruler of Syracuse. This is probably right; there is certainly a reference to Hieron in these lines (see intro.), and the word translated here as 'good' (*kala*) is used as a synonym for athletic success at 1.146, 2.6 and 3.96. For the thought in general, cf. 4.18-20.

53 coveted This and related words are common in Bacch. (1.184, 7.10, 10.48, etc.). Curiously, however, Pindar avoids them. Hesiod (*Works and Days* 195-6) speaks of Envy as a foul-mouthed evil thing, and Pindar may have shared this attitude, but for Bacch. envy was a legitimate part of the reward of success. Cf. note on 7.10.

54 walks this earth The word is repeated from line 3, and points the contrast between the good fortune of Hieron and the ill-fated Meleager and Herakles in the myth which follows. See also intro. to this ode and note on 94, below.

56 Hear now The text is a little uncertain here, but the transition into the myth as an explanation of the preceding *gnome* seems abrupt. The narrative of the meeting of Herakles and Meleager recalls similar confrontations between heroes on the battlefield in Homer, and there are in fact a number of Homeric reminiscences and Homeric features in Bacch.'s language throughout, as the following notes will indicate. One thinks especially of the meeting of Diomedes and the Trojan Glaukos

(*Il.* 6.119f.), where the heroes exchange gifts and agree not to fight after discovering a bond of guest-friendship between them. The same elements – initial hostility, proud self-identification, and the discovery of a bond (Herakles' admiration for Meleager sparks his desire to marry Meleager's sister) – are all present here in Bacch., which makes it likely that the Homeric passage served as his model. (See also note on 65, below.)

57 never-conquered The same word (*anikatos*) is used at 103, below, of the anger of Artemis. This is probably deliberate, intended to suggest a contrast between goddess and hero, and to raise the question: which of them is really 'invincible'? The anger of Artemis leads indirectly to the death of Meleager, which in turn leads, even more indirectly, through his marriage to Deianeira, to the death of Herakles. Artemis prevails, in the end, over both. Thus *anikatos* used of Herakles becomes ironic, for even he, as any mortal might be, was brought low by divine disfavour.

destroyer of cities The word occurs only here, invented by Bacch. for the sake of variety; cf. 13.167, where a similar coinage is used. The allusion is to exploits such as the sack of Troy in the time of king Laomedon (*Il.* 5.638-42), the conquest of Pylos (*Il.* 11.689f.) and the destruction of Oichalia in Euboea, ostensibly in revenge, but really to win the king's daughter as his bride. This last exploit forms the background to Sophocles' *Trach.*

58 son of Zeus Cf. 79, below. Remarkably, Herakles is not named in this entire narrative, but the reference in these opening lines (58-61) to the Cerberos adventure would be more than enough to identify him. At 71 he is 'son of Alcmena', at 86 and 156 he is 'Amphitryon's son'. For the birth of Herakles see *Il.* 19.98f.

bright-thundering A conventional Homeric epithet for Zeus, lord of the thunderbolt (*Il.* 19.121, etc.), also borrowed by Pindar (*Ol.* 8.4). The image combines thunder and lightning, sound and light.

59 halls of … Persephone A simple and common poetic periphrasis for the Underworld, alluding to the abduction of Persephone, daughter of Demeter, by Hades. See note on 3.3.

slender-ankled A variation of the Homeric 'lovely-ankled' (*Il.* 9.560, 14.319, etc.), not invented by Bacch., however, for Persephone is already 'slender-ankled' in Hom. Hymn 2.2 and 77. Bacch. uses the word again at 3.61, of the daughters of Kroisos; it is yet another of the many conventional decorative adjectives (cf. 'lovely', 90, below) which, in the Homeric manner, cumulatively impart an aura of grace, beauty and splendour to the world of the poems. Cf. note on 7.7.

61 saw-toothed (*karcharodonta*) An epithet for dogs in Homer (*Il.* 10.360, 13.198), intended to convey the idea of savagery. The root of the word survives into the Modern Greek word for 'shark' (*karcharias*).

62 child An unusual word to use of an animal, especially a monster.

Soph. more appropriately calls Cerberos 'Echidna's nursling' (*Trach.* 1099). As Maehler points out (vol. 2, p. 103) the use of the word 'humanizes' and so 'heroizes' Cerberos, thus presenting him as a worthy opponent for Herakles.

Echidna A monster, half lovely nymph, half dreadful serpent, consigned by the gods to dwell for ever in a hollow cave beneath the earth (Hes. *Theog.* 295f.). The union of Echidna and Typhaon (another monster, conceived by Hera in vengeful anger when Zeus gave birth independently to Athena – Hom. Hymn 3.306f.) produced, among others, Cerberos, the hound of Hell (Hes. *Theog.* 306f.).

63 Kokytos One of the rivers of the Underworld; the name, derived from *kokuein* = 'to lament', suggests 'the river of lamentation'; the other rivers in Hades were Styx ('the hateful river'; cf. Hes. *Theog.* 775-7, and see notes on 11.4 and 11.9), Pyriphlegethon ('the river of fire') and Acheron, whose name seems to have no specific meaning. As one might expect, the geography of Hades was variously imagined and not consistently described; in Homer (*Od.* 10.513-14) Kokytos is a branch of Styx, which, together with Pyriphlegethon, flows into Acheron. Vergil on the other hand (*Aen.* 6.296) makes Acheron debouch into Kokytos, while at 6.323 Kokytos and the marsh of Styx are together visible to Aeneas. Contrast also Verg. *Georg.* 4.478-80 (the descent of Orpheus to the Underworld), where the description is clearly more atmospheric than 'factual': '(the dead) whom all around the black ooze and squalid reeds of Cocytos, and the marsh unlovely with its sluggish wave, enchain, and Styx confines with the nine circles of his stream'. At Eur. *Alc.* 439-44 the dead are conveyed across the lake of Acheron by the ferryman Charon; Aristophanes, in *Frogs*, does not name the lake which Dionysos must cross to enter Hades, but there is comic play with the names of the rivers later (*Frogs* 470-2).

65 like the leaves The image recalls *Il.* 6.146f., where Glaukos compares the generations of men to the leaves which every year fall and are renewed; Glaukos is proud of his place in this cycle. Here, however, regeneration is not part of the image; the souls of the dead lie fallen, finished, helplessly blown on the wind. Thus Bacch. imparts a tone of melancholy to the narrative, and underscores the sadness attaching to the death of Meleager. In spite of this difference, the parallel is close enough to suggest that Bacch. had the Homeric passage in mind; cf. note on 56, above.

67 Ida Two mountains bore this name, one in central Crete, the other near Troy, from where Zeus looks out over Troy and the Achaians (*Il.* 8.47f.; cf. also *Il.* 22.171). Given the Homeric tone of the whole narrative, it seems probable that Bacch. had the Trojan Ida in mind.

69 Porthaon's son Bacch. here uses a 'papponymic' adjective to describe Meleager (i.e. an adjective formed on the name of the grandfather, although he slightly changes the form of the name; in Homer (*Il.*

4.115-17) Meleager's father Oineus is the son of Portheus). Such pap-
ponymics are uncommon (cf. *Od.* 11.471); Homer, and later poets,
normally use the patronymic, based on the father's name, e.g. 86, below,
6.12, etc.
  bold-spirited The word is borrowed from Homer (*Il.* 5.639, *Od.*
11.267).

70 **spear-fighter** Another Homeric word (*Il.* 2.131, 14.449, etc.).

71 **son of Alcmena** Here, most unusually, Bacch. uses a 'metronymic'
adjective (lit. = 'the Alcmenian hero') based on the name of Herakles'
mother Alcmena; cf. note on 69, above.

72 **shining in his armour** A Homeric formula, cf. *Il.* 17.214, 18.510 and
20.46.

73 **sweet-sounding** This word (*liguklanges*) occurs only here and at
14.13; it was clearly coined by Bacch., and is here designed to suggest
the sweetly satisfying twang of a tight bowstring. (For words com-
pounded with *ligu-*, see note on 22, above.) The description brings to
mind the stringing and testing of his bow by Odysseus (*Od.* 21.404f.,
esp. 410-11): 'then plucking it in his right hand he tested the bowstring,
and it gave him back an excellent sound like the voice of a swallow'. No
doubt Bacch. was thinking also of the Homeric picture of the ghost of
Herakles in the Underworld: 'holding the bow bare with an arrow laid
on the bowstring' (*Od.* 11.607).

76 **bronze-head** (*chalkeokranon*) occurs only here, invented by Bacch.
for variation from the standard Homeric 'fitted with bronze' (*chalkeres*,
i.e. 'bronze-tipped', *Il.* 13.650, *Od.* 1.262) and 'heavy with bronze' (*chalk-
obares*, *Il.* 15.465, *Od.* 21.423). Bacch. has modelled his description on
Il. 4.116, where much of the same vocabulary is used. There Pandaros
'stripped away the lid of the quiver, and took out an arrow ...'.

78 **knowing well the truth** A Homeric phrase (*Il.* 1.385, 13.665, *Od.*
2.170), used especially to describe a superior, often prophetic, knowl-
edge; so Meleager, being dead, has an insight not given to Herakles. He
knows that he is beyond the reach of further harm. See 83, below.

79 **son of great Zeus** Meleager evidently recognizes Herakles at once.
Although this is not implausible – the hero was such a renowned and
well-known figure – the reason here is probably to avoid interruption
to the flow of the narrative by stopping to make an unnecessary
identification. Cf. Hom. *Od.* 11.615, where the ghost of Herakles imme-
diately recognizes Odysseus, and see note on 94, below.

82 **tearing** Cf. 13.111, where the same word (*trachus*) is used metaphori-
cally of the anger of Achilles.

83 **to no purpose** Explained in the following words; Herakles can hurt
Meleager no further. So too Aeneas in the Underworld vainly confronts
the phantom shapes there with a show of heroic violence, and must be
restrained by his companion, the Sibyl (Verg. *Aen.* 6.290-4).

86 **Amphitryon's son** Here Bacch. uses the standard patronymic adjec-

tive, formed on the name of Herakles' father Amphitryon; cf. note on 69, above, and cf. 6.12.

was amazed A Homeric word (*Il.* 8.77, etc.) borrowed by Bacch. and later poets.

87 Who of immortals ...? Herakles' questions are an elaborate variation on the standard Homeric formula: 'What man are you and from where?' (*Od.* 1.170 etc.). Cf. also Ode 18.31.

90 lovely Lit. = 'with a lovely girdle' (*kallizonos*), a conventional decorative epithet for women (Hom. *Il.* 7.139, etc.), here used, no doubt, for the sake of variation from line 11 above, where 'deep-girdled' (*bathuzonos*) is used. See note on 1.116.

Hera The hostility of Hera to Herakles is perhaps surprising, since he bears the goddess' name (Herakles must have originally meant something like 'the glory of Hera'), but she was always, and naturally, jealous of her husband Zeus' lovers and their children. See intro., above, and 9.7-9, with notes there. Cf. also Pind. *Nem.* 1.35f., which describes how Hera sent (unsuccessfully) two snakes to destroy the new-born Herakles.

that man There is a fine poetic touch here, as Jebb points out (p. 279, note on 89f.). Herakles has been at once impressed by the appearance and demeanour of Meleager, and naturally assumes that it must have been a great warrior who killed him. He is about to learn that Meleager's death was brought about by a woman, his own mother Althaia.

91 fair-haired For the meaning of this word (*xanthos*) see on 38, above. It is used of Hera at 11.51, and Pindar applies it to Athena at *Nem.* 10.7. For the decorative quality of such adjectives, see notes above on 'dark-haired' (35) and 'slender-ankled' (59).

Athena will ... take care The expression is reminiscent of Hom. *Il.* 17.515 and 23.724, where the meaning is: 'Zeus will determine the outcome'. Here however, protection is implied; if Hera should assail Herakles, Athena will look after him. Athena was always his protector; in the *Iliad* (8.363f.) she says to Hera: 'often I used to rescue ... Herakles, beaten down by the tasks of Eurystheus' (for which see intro., above), and Herakles himself, speaking of his return to the upper world from Hades, says that Athena, with Hermes, escorted him (*Od.* 11.626). The exploits of Herakles were popular as subject matter for Athenian vase painting, and Athena and Herakles often appear together. See J. Boardman, *Athenian Black-Figure Vases*, p. 221f. and illustr. 161 and 165.

93 addressed him Meleager does not directly answer Herakles' questions, identifying himself only through the reference to his father Oineus (97). Cf. note on 79, above. Bacch. prefers to introduce Meleager's narrative with a *gnome* which the fates of both Meleager and Herakles will illustrate: 'the gods can be implacable, if they so choose'. This in turn obliquely reflects on Hieron, and the reference is made unmistakeable by the repetition of the phrase 'men that walk the earth' (*epichthonios*, 96), already used of Hieron (3). See the intro., above, and notes on 3 and 54. Bacch. may have had the Homeric passage in mind here, in which Nestor describes Agamemnon's desire to appease Athena's anger with sacrifice: 'Fool! He did not know that he was not going to persuade her' (*Od.* 3.146).

97 rider of horses Lit. = 'horse-striker', perhaps referring more exactly to the use of a whip from a chariot. The word itself (*plaxippos*) is Homeric, used of Pelops (*Il.* 2.104), Menestheus (*Il.* 4.327) and Orestes (*Il.* 5.705), but not of Oineus, whom Homer describes as 'horse-driver' (*hippelata*, *Il.* 9.581) and 'horseman' (*hippota*, *Il.* 14.117). Meleager's narrative follows the Homeric version of the story very closely, at least up to 135 (see intro., above), but Bacch. likes to vary the details of its expression.

99 blood-red Lit. = 'red-backed' (*phoinikonotos*), cf. 'red-haired' (*phoinikothrix*, also used of cattle, 11.105). On Bacch.'s use of compound adjectives with *phoiniko-* (all of which he seems to have created) see note on 9.10.

100 anger Homer relates how Oineus had incurred the wrath of Artemis for his failure to offer to the goddess the first-fruits of the harvest (*Il.* 9.534-5), but Bacch. does not trouble to explain background details which would have been familiar to his audience already. Cf. note on 79, above.

102 white-armed Used again at 176 of Kalliope; see also note on 9.7.
  flower-crowned Another conventional poetic epithet, used also of the daughters of Proitos (11.108). Cf. fr. 53a: 'a crown ablaze with the buds of roses', and see note on 'violet-crowned', 3.3. Jebb (p. 280, note on 98f.) draws attention to the fact that the three adjectives here describe divine status ('holy'), a personal quality ('white-armed') and a conventional attribute ('flower-crowned') and he compares 13.193-4 (of Athena). For an even more elaborate accumulation of adjectives attached to Artemis, see 11.36-8.

103 the Maiden Artemis was always the virgin goddess, an attribute which relates naturally to her role as goddess of the wild, protector of the purity and inviolability of nature. See W. Otto, *The Homeric Gods*, p. 82f.; also note on 11.37.

104 lovely dancing-grounds The same adjective (*kallichoros*) is used at 11.31 of Olympia, and cf. 'the broad dancing-grounds' (*euruchoron*, 10.31, of Argos). Jebb (p. 281, note on 106f.) rightly remarks that the epithet 'suggests civic life and festivals', and 'depicts a city at peace'. Its use thus intensifies by contrast our sense of the devastation caused by Artemis.

105 wild wide-ranging Bacch.'s adjective (*eurubias*, lit. = 'of wide-ranging power') is perhaps intended to recall the Homeric *eurukreion* ('wide-ruling'), one of the formulaic descriptions of Agamemnon (*Il.*

1.102, etc.). Maehler suggests that this is deliberate, in order to 'heroize' the boar as a worthy opponent. Cf. note on 62, above.

106 implacable in fight Lit. = 'without a sense of shame in the fight', i.e. 'shameless', 'not to be deterred by any consideration'. The word occurs only here, and is another of Bacch.'s creations. See also note on 157, below.

107 with ... force of flood Lit. = 'overflowing with strength', a variation of the Homeric phrase 'exulting in strength' (*Il.* 12.42, used there in a simile of 'boar or lion'; see note on 115, below).

108f. Observe the climactic arrangement of the boar's victims – crops, animals and men. In Homer the boar destroys Oineus' orchard (*Il.* 9.541-2); Bacch. changes this to a vineyard, no doubt in allusion to the belief that the name Oineus was derived from *oinos* ('wine'), and to the story that he had received the vine as a gift from Dionysos (Apollod. 1.8.1).

111 we, greatest of Greek heroes Homer tells us that 'Meleager gathered hunters and dogs from many cities ...' (*Il.* 9.544-5) but he does not name these allies. Similarly, although unnamed allies may be implied in the phrase 'greatest of Greek heroes', Bacch. mentions only the Kouretes, because he too, like Homer, wishes to concentrate attention on the ensuing fight over the hide, and its consequences. (See intro., above, for the difference in purpose and treatment between Bacch. and Homer.) The Calydonian boar-hunt became immensely popular as a subject for literature and art, not least because of Atalanta's role in it; the story was much expanded and sources from Stesichoros to Ovid mention many participants. (For the treatment by Stesichoros see the convenient discussion in Bowra's *Greek Lyric Poetry*, p. 95f.; Ovid (*Metamorph.* 8. 262f.) treats the story at length and takes 23 lines (298-320) to name all the major hunters.)

114 the god Probably not Artemis, whose anger after all continues. The word used here is *daimon*, which must be understood in a very general sense as virtually equivalent to 'Fate' (*moira*), so that there is an oblique reference to the central theme of the poem. The *daimon* has given victory over the boar to Meleager, but this leads in the end only to his untimely death at the hands of his mother. Thus by means of a verbal echo, Bacch. underscores the fact that Meleager's fate illustrates the central proposition: 'no mortal is *eudaimon* ('god-favoured') all the time' (55). See also intro., above.

Aitolians Homer represents the conflict as between Aitolians and Kouretes (*Il.* 9.529-32 and 549), using the term 'Aitolian' to refer only to the Calydonians, although the Kouretes were themselves Aitolian (*schol. Il.* 9.529). Here, however, the term must be inclusive, embracing both the Calydonians and the Kouretes.

115 loud-roaring Hardly an accurate description of the sound made by a wild boar. But in Homer, the furious courage of the heroes is often highlighted by a simile, and in these lion and boar are commonly mentioned together. Thus Hektor 'fought on like a whirlwind. As when .... a wild boar or lion turns at bay in the strength of his fury ...' (*Il.* 12.40-2; cf. *Il.* 5.782-3 and 17.20-2). It is likely, then, that familiarity with these passages led Bacch. to colour his description of the boar with elements more appropriate to a lion.

117 Ankaios One of the major figures in the boar-hunt. He appears in the representation of it by Scopas on the pediment of the temple of Athena at Tegea, described by Pausanias (8.45.7), and his corpse is featured on the François vase (see intro., above). Nestor, recounting his youthful participation in Funeral Games (*Il.* 23.626f.) mentions (636) Ankaios of Pleuron (i.e. one of the Kouretes). This must surely be the same person.

119 far-famed A conventional decorative epithet, cf. 2.10, etc.

121 deadly Fate (*moira oloa*) A Homeric expression (*Il.* 16.849, etc.). For the importance of *moira* to Meleager's story, see note on 114, above.

122 daughter of Leto i.e. Artemis; see Hes. *Theog.* 918-20.

123 fierce-hearted Repeated at 138 below, of Althaia, thus emphasizing her joint responsibility with Artemis for the death of Meleager.
huntress the word (*agrotera*), already used of Artemis by Homer (*Il.* 21.471), recurs at 11.36; see note there, and notes on 103, above, and 11.37. Observe that a picture of Artemis now emerges very different from that presented at 101-2 above.

124 stay her anger The words are repeated from 100, emphasizing the helplessness of mankind before the gods.

125 steadfast The word (*meneptolemos*) is repeated at 171 below, and is a variation of the word which Homer (*Il.* 9.529) applies to the Aitolians (*menecharmes*).

126 lurid Lit. = 'blazing' (*aithon*). As a colour word it suggests the reddish-yellow of flames, and is thus more appropriate to a lion-skin than to a boar (see note on 115, above). Cf. also 13.50, where the adjective is applied to the flash of a bronze sword.

127 Iphiklos Bacch. is drawing on well-established tradition here. The Funeral Games described by Nestor (*Il.* 23.626f.) included Aitolians (633), and Nestor goes on at once to mention Ankaios and Iphiklos (see note on 117, above). Iphiklos is not specifically described by Nestor as Aitolian (as Ankaios is), but surely Bacch. is referring to the same person. Aphares, however, as a son of Thestios, is otherwise unknown.

129 swift-running Perhaps a traditional epithet for Iphiklos, since Nestor claims to have defeated him in the foot-race (*Il.* 23.636).

130-5 These sad lines are based on the truism that in the melee of war it is often impossible to distinguish friend from foe. (Cf. *Od.* 11.537: 'the war-god rages without discrimination', and Soph. fr. 838: 'for Ares is blind and confuses everything'.) It is true that Aphares and Iphiklos were now on the other side, as Kouretes; they were of 'the enemy' (133), but the use of the words 'friend' (131) and 'blind' (132) implies that Meleager would not knowingly have killed them.

130 staunch-hearted i.e. 'resolute', 'unyielding'; the word belongs properly to the warriors themselves (cf. *Il.* 13.050, 14.512, etc.) rather than to their god.

135 god wills it Meleager here returns to the gnomic idea with which he began: 'men cannot turn aside the will of gods' (95f.). The 'god' here is again *daimon*; see note on 114, above.

138 fierce-hearted daughter Echoes the description of Artemis, 123, above; see the note there.

139 reckless (*atarbaktos*) Found only here and at Pind. *Pyth.* 4.84. The word seems to be related to *tarbos* ('fear'); i.e. Althaia is without fear or concern for the consequences of her action. (In Pindar, however, 'fearless' seems less appropriate.)

140 ornate chest Exactly the same words are used by Simonides (*PMG* 543, 1-2), to describe the casket in which Danae and her infant son Perseus were cast adrift at sea by her father Akrisios. Bacch. was probably imitating his uncle, rather than the reverse; although Simonides' poem is undated, he was 80 years old when Bacch. composed Ode 5.

141 my sudden doom An Epic word (*okumoros*), applied by Homer either to persons, in the sense 'destined to die soon' (so esp. Achilles, *Il.* 1.417, etc.; also the suitors, *Od.* 1.266) or to arrows, as bringing an early death (*Il.* 15.441, *Od.* 22.75). So here the log is *okumoros*, as it brings to Meleager an untimely end.

142 Klotho The notion of Fate in early Greek thought was personified as not one, but three divinities (Hes. *Theog.* 218 and 905). The 'Three Fates' (*Moirai*) were Klotho (she who spins the thread of a man's life), Lachesis (she who determines its length) and Atropos (she who cannot be turned aside). Bacch. does not actually use the name Klotho here; rather he says: '*Moira* spun ...', using the verb from which Klotho's name is derived. The translation obscures this important reference to *moira*. See notes on 114 and 121.

146 stripping It was standard practice for the epic heroes to strip the armour from a slain foe, as spoils of war (cf. e.g. *Il.* 13.619, where the same verb is used). (Sometimes, however, the verb means simply 'to kill', as at *Il.* 4.448 and 6.30; cf. also Ode 13.153.) Klymenos is otherwise unknown.

148 in front of the ... walls i.e. the walls of Pleuron, as is evident from the following lines. The fighting took place around Calydon, naturally (*Il.* 9.529-32); we must suppose therefore that the Calydonians had succeeded in driving the Kouretes back to their own city. Similar success is implied in Homer (*Il.* 9.550-52), up to the point of Meleager's withdrawal.

149 well-built A conventional Homeric epithet (*Il.* 2.501, etc.); cf. also 11.122.

151f. The death of Meleager is closely modelled on the two famous death scenes of the *Iliad*, those of Patroklos (16.855-7) and Hector (22.361-3), in both of which identical language is used (Lattimore's translation):

> He spoke, and as he spoke the end of death closed in upon him,
> and the soul fluttering free of his limbs went down into Death's house
> mourning her destiny, leaving youth and manhood behind her.

151 the sweet life ... ebbed away Echoes Homer's 'the soul went down'. Bacch. in fact uses the same word as Homer (*psucha* = 'life'); Lattimore's translation ('soul') is anachronistic. In Homer *psucha* was the life force, that property of breath or blood which made a man alive; it was only much later conceptualised into the meaning 'soul'. See Julian Jaynes, *The Origin of Consciousness in the Breakdown of the Bicameral Mind*, (Penguin Books, 1976), p. 270f., esp. p. 288f. The usage in 64 and 170 is closer to the post-Homeric meaning.
sweet Bacch. adds the emotive adjective to heighten the pathos and the sense of loss. For the phrase 'sweet life', cf. Simonides, *PMG* 553.
ebbed away Cf. 3.90-1, where the same word is used.

152 my strength was gone Bacch. has created a word here (*oligostheneon*, not found elsewhere) for the sake of variation. Homer uses *oligodraneon* of the dying Hektor (*Il.* 22.337). The meaning is the same.

154 splendid youth Again (cf. 'sweet', 151, above) the adjective is added, for pathos, to the Homeric phrase. The same words are used at Hes. *Theog.* 985.

155 the only time The pathetic effect is heightened yet again by drawing attention to the unprecedented nature of the great hero's response. Here he weeps in sympathy for Meleager, killed by his mother; in Sophocles (*Trach.* 1070-5) he weeps for his own agony, as the poison on the robe given him by his wife consumes his burning flesh. There too (*Trach.* 1072-3) he claims: 'no man could say he has ever seen me weep before'. There may have been a tradition that Herakles never wept, which could have given rise to these effective variations. Cf. also Soph. *Aias* 317-18.

156 Amphitryon's son The standard patronymic; see note on 86, above.

157 fearless warrior Lit. = 'not fearing the war-cry'. Found only here and at 11.59, the word is another of Bacch,'s inventions. Compounds of this type, involving a negative prefix and two descriptive elements, are much favoured by Bacch. Cf. 106 and 180; also 11.67 and 16.27.

160 Not to be born ... This was a very common *topos*, or theme, esp. in early Greek poetry. It finds its fullest expression in Theognis 425-8, whom Bacch. virtually quotes, with only minor verbal alterations. The *topos* expressed the helplessness of man before the will of gods; here however, Herakles seeks to console Meleager with his sympathetic understanding that human life was born to suffering. Note that Herakles does not continue with the second half of the *topos*: 'but the next best thing, once born, is to die as soon as possible' (so Theognis 427-8; cf. Soph. *OC* 1225-8). This would be small consolation to Meleager, who is already dead and lamenting his loss of life.

162 there is no profit This too (see previous note) was something of a commonplace, cf. *Od.* 10.202, *Il.* 24.524, etc. It is likely that Bacch. had this Iliadic passage in mind; Achilles there tells Priam that he will achieve nothing by lamentation; he will not succeed in bringing Hektor back to life. Herakles draws from the truism its positive corollary.

166 lover of war A common heroic epithet, cf. 1.120, 11.113, 15.50.

167 unwed The word (*admeta*) is derived from *damazein* (= 'to subdue', 'to overpower'); it literally means 'unsubdued', but is here used without any suggestion of violence. See note on 1.116. It is used again, similarly, of the daughters of Proitos, 11.83.

169 shining See note on 1.158.

171 steadfast A conventional Homeric epithet (*Il.* 2.749, 19.48, etc.). Cf. 125, above, and 17.73.

173 the pale skin glowing Bacch. uses a word here (*chlorauchen*) which literally means 'green-necked', and at first sight appears hardly appropriate to the lovely Deianeira. The first part of the compound, from the adjective *chloros*, is derived from *chloe*, which means 'the new shoots of plants in spring'. The general sense is thus 'green', but as with all colour words in Greek, there is a wide variation. In Soph. *OC* 673 it refers to the dark green of shaded woodlands, and from there it can move through pale green to greenish-yellow to the colour of honey (*Il.* 11.631, *Od.* 10.234) and sand (Soph. *Aias* 1064). The word is also used of the pallor produced by fear (*Il.* 10.376, etc.) and this is certainly what Sappho means when she describes herself, looking at her beloved talking to another, as 'more *chloros* than grass (fr. 31.14). The meaning here must be at the very bottom end of this spectrum, simply 'pale', with little if any suggestion of colour. Pale skin was a part of the ideal of feminine beauty (cf. the frequent adjective 'white-armed', 102, above, 176, below, 9.7, etc., and women's skin in black-figure vase painting was regularly represented in white). At the same time the word describes the freshness and vigour of new growth; the tender skin of Deianeira's neck is vibrant with youth and life.

174 innocent i.e. still virginal, picking up 'unwed', 167.

176 Kalliope The renewed invocation of the Muse (cf. 10, above) signals the end of the myth and the transition to renewed praise of Hieron (cf. 10.51 and note). Note how this is arranged in narrowing focus – Zeus, Olympia, the Games, the horse, the victor's city – climaxing in the 'name-cap' Hieron in 186. Thus each of the previous terms acts as foil to enhance the praise of Hieron himself. Cf. 3.1, and the note there.

177 chariot The 'Muses' chariot' is a metaphor for the song itself; with the conventional epithet for a chariot (cf. Hes. *Shield* 64) Bacch. implies that his song too is 'well-made'.

180 Alpheos i.e. Olympia, see note on 6.3.

tireless Lit. = 'not tiring in the flow'; for the form of the adjective see note on 157, above. Cf., also 26, above, where a closely related word is used.

81 Pelops For the legendary association of Pelops with the Olympic Games, see notes on 7.5 and 8.32.

182 Pisa The poets often used the name Pisa as a synonym for Olympia. Pisa was the chief city of Elis – the area which included Olympia – where Pelops established himself after defeating its king Oinomaos in a chariot-race, thus winning his daughter Hippodameia as his wife. The story is told in some detail by Pindar, *Ol.* 1.67f. (There was, however, another widespread version of this story, in which Pelops won by cheating (cf. Soph. *El.* 505f., Eur. *Or.* 985f., *Helen* 386f.) and so brought down a curse upon himself and his descendants, but this more disreputable version, not appropriate to encomiastic poetry, is naturally not alluded to by either Bacch. or Pindar.)

184 and came For the importance of the return home as climax to the triumph, see note on 9.39.

185 Hieron Cf. note on 49, above.

187 the garland A reference not only to the crown of olive which was the prize of victory, but also, metaphorically, to the song of praise which accompanied that victory and was no less the mark of success.

god's favour (*eudaimonia*) The contrast between the fortunes of Meleager and Herakles on the one hand, and of Hieron on the other, highlights the good fortune of the latter, and thus enhances the praise. Hieron is *eudaimon* as Herakles and Meleager were not. See note on 114, and the intro., above.

188-97 This passage is well discussed by Bundy (*Stud. Pind.*, pp. 60-1), who points out the rhetorical conventions for praise which it illustrates. The main motifs are the need for praise without stint, and the need for the poet to do justice to the victor's merits.

188 as truth requires i.e. the poet must not understate the achievements of the victor. For the emphasis on truth, cf. 3.96, 9.82-87, 13.203-4, and see esp. note on 8.19-21.

189 malice Envy is acceptable (see note on 53, above), but malicious jealousy is not; cf. 13.199: 'if a man is not overmastered by envy'; many of the motifs of the present passage are restated there.

192 Muses' servant Cf. 10, above, where Bacch. himself is 'famed servant of Urania'.

191-4 The gnomic generalization (193-4) quoted from Hesiod, although it does not in fact appear in the surviving works of that poet, explains why it is necessary to praise Hieron without stint (188-90). The explanation is put, as Bundy notes (*Stud. Pind.*, p. 60) 'in the mouth of an ancient authoritative witness', so that the claim does not depend on the authority of Bacch. alone. It is thus a variation of the 'witnessing-motif', see note on 38, above. For other examples of the interdependence of success and fame through song, cf. e.g. 1.181-4, 3.94-7, 13.61-6. This is the only occasion on which Bacch. mentions another poet by name. (Pindar also (*Isth.* 6.67-8) refers to Hesiod by name when he paraphrases the earlier poet's dictum (*Works and Days* 410) on the value of hard work and practice.)

195 I am easily persuaded Bacch. here picks up the 'willingness-motif' with which he began (see notes on 13 and 14, above). Hieron's achievements are so great that they virtually demand celebration.

197 the path of what is proper This echoes 'as truth requires' (188). The song will be no more than what is appropriate to the merits of the victor Hieron.

198 the stock The image is that of a tree or plant. The 'blessings' (i.e. good fortune, success, cf. 4.20) of a family are the rootstock which the song waters and makes bloom and grow strong.

200 them i.e. the blessings.

in peace Despite the fact that Bacch. refers to Hieron's military stature and prowess (see notes on 2 and 35, above) he concludes the ode with a prayer for peace. The poet's personal attitude to the destructive power of strife can be discerned, I believe, in the description of the quarrel between Proitos and Akrisios at 11.64-76.

ODE 6
FOR LACHON OF CEOS
Stadion, Olympic Games, 452 BC

Odes 6 and 7 were written in celebration of the same victory (compare Odes 1 and 2, for Argeios, also of Ceos). Ode 7 was performed at Olympia (see note on 7.2), at the time of the victory, while Ode 6 was sung in Ceos (cf. line 14 and note, below).

These two odes are among the few which can be securely dated. Part of an ancient copy of the official list of Olympic victors survives on a papyrus fragment found in Egypt (Pap. Oxy. II 222), which lists the winners at the Olympic Games from Olympiad 75 (480 BC) to 83 (448 BC). Here, under Olympiad 82 (452 BC) we read: 'Lakon of Ceos, boys' stadion'. Despite the spelling of the name, this surely refers to the subject of Ode 6. Lachon, son of Aristomenes of Ceos, was clearly a talented and successful athlete. In addition to the present Olympic victory, his name appears twice in the inscription recording victories by Cean athletes (*IG* XII 5 608, lines 27-8) where he is credited with two victories in unidentified boys' events at the Nemean Games. (See also the introduction to Ode 1.) It is highly unlikely that there were two successful young athletes from Ceos at around the

140

Fig. 8. The stadium at Olympia, looking east. Part of the starting line can be seen at the lower right.

same time with such similar names, and the spelling on the Olympic record is surely a simple engraver's error. If this is indeed the case, we then have a certain date of 452 BC.

Ode 6, although short, is complete, and structured with great care. It falls into three sections. Beginning with a brief celebration of Lachon's victory (1-3), Bacch. passes to a reminiscence of earlier victories by Ceans (4-8) and concludes with a restatement of Lachon's distinction (9-16). Each of the three sections is longer than the one before; the rising, climactic structure and the ring-composition draw attention to, and enhance, the praise of the victor. (See also the notes on 9 and 16, below.) The ode contains no mythic narrative, but includes all the major elements of the epinician programme: praise of the victor, proclamation of the event and the place of victory, reference to the city and parentage of the victor and praise of the victor's homeland. In addition, in the reference to the Muse, Urania, as the source of his song (line 10), Bacch. makes an oblique allusion to his own function and standing as the poet celebrating the event. Self-reference of this kind was frequent in the genre (cf. 3.96-8, 4.8-10, 5.10 etc.).

1 **Lachon** The spelling of the name (see above) is confirmed also by the form of the verb 'has won', which in Greek is *lache*; there is a word-play here between subject and verb which emphasizes the meaning of the latter ('to obtain as one's lot'), drawing attention to the fact that the victory is, as always, the gift of the gods.

2 renown unparalleled The adjective may perhaps be suggested by the fact that the Olympic Games carried the greatest prestige, but this is less likely; at 1.159 the phrase 'greatest glory' occurs in a generalization, while the word translated as 'unparalleled' here (*phertatos*) is otherwise applied mostly to persons or to Zeus.

3 where the Alpheos runs to the sea A common type of periphrasis for Olympia, cf. 3.5, 5.40, etc. Bacch. actually says: 'at the outflow of the Alpheos', which is not strictly accurate, but is acceptable in a broadly general sense. Olympia is in fact about 14 km from the coast, but it lies on the plain where the river, having descended from the Arcadian mountains, begins its final meander to the sea.

4 for which The relative needs an antecedent, which presumably stood at the end of line 3, where a word is missing. The following lines refer to earlier victories by Ceans at Olympia, a tradition which Lachon's present victory enhances, so that a supplement such as that suggested by Jebb (p. 295, note on 3) 'adding to the successes for which ...' seems required. Cf. 2.6f.

5 victory-garlands On the use of garlands of flowers, see on 1.158.

6 have sung The songs to which Bacch. alludes here are perhaps formal, commissioned victory odes sung on site, on the last day of the festival, when the victors were honoured and the prizes given out; Ode 7 certainly, and Ode 2 probably, are of this kind. It is also possible however, that they were informal, impromptu songs sung by the victor's friends during the *komos* (the festive procession to the celebratory feast), and the passage need not bear on the question whether the commissioned songs were sung solo or by a chorus. Cf. Pindar *Nem.* 3.3f., where likewise 'young men are waiting, makers of the sweet-voiced *komos*'. See M. Lefkowitz, 'Who sang Pindar's victory odes?' *AJPh* 109 (1988), pp. 1-11; also M. Heath, 'Receiving the *komos*: the context and performance of epinician', *AJPh* 109 (1988), pp. 180-95.

7 rich in vines Coins from Ceos often show amphorae, bunches of grapes, or Dionysos himself; wine was clearly one of this small island's major products (cf. also 8.12 and Pindar, *Paian* 4.21-6). The adjective is thus both ornamental and part of the 'programme', praising the victor's home, but Bacch. gives novelty to the description by coining a new word for it (*ampelotrophos*). Cf. the note on 3.2 ('where the best grain grows').

8 success in boxing and the foot-race Bacch. refers here to earlier victories by Ceans, otherwise unknown to us, but perhaps including that of Argeios, celebrated in Odes 1 and 2. For his access to an official list of Cean victors, see note on 2.7. (Cf. also 12.36.)

9 and now Stands in strong contrast to 'in the past' (line 4). So too 'at Olympia ... young men have sung' (4-6) corresponds to 'with songs before your house' (14), while 'for her success in boxing and the foot-race' (8) is picked up by 'successful in the foot-race' (15). The strophe alludes to previous victories by athletes from Ceos, the antistrophe to

Lachon's present victory, so that the careful placement of these key ideas (the contrasting phrases in 4-6/14 and 8/15 are placed at the same position in strophe and antistrophe, although the translation obscures this), and the emphatic contrast thus created between past and present, mark Lachon's victory as a climax, the culmination of a long series of earlier victories, and thus enhance its distinction. Cf. also the note on 10.9.

by the grace of Victory's goddess The victory is personified, and success attributed directly to the will and favour of the divinity. Bacch. uses this expression four times (5.35, 10.15, 11.10, and here). Cf. also 1.118, and note.

10 **Urania** One of the nine Muses, source of poetic inspiration. See the note on 'Klio', 3.1. As the victory comes from god (lines 1 and 9) , and the song which honours that victory comes *via* the poet from the Muse, so the poet is intermediary between man and god.

queen of song (*anaximolpos*) Cf. 4.8, where Urania is called 'queen of the lyre' (*anaxiphorminx*); altogether Bacch. uses six words compounded with *anaxi-* ('lord of ...' or 'queen of ...'). In addition to these two there are *anaxippos* (14B.10, 'master of horses'), *anaxibrentas* (17.65, 'lord of the thunder'), *anaxialos* (20.8, 'lord of the sea') and *anaxichoros* (fr. 65a.11, 'queen of the dance'). Of these six, all but one (*anaxiphorminx*, which is used also by Pindar, *Ol.* 2.1) do not occur outside Bacch., and were presumably coined by him. Compare also 12.1, where Klio is again called 'queen of song' (*hymnoanassa*) in another of Bacch.'s coinages. (On the impact of compound adjectives of this kind, see note on 7.7.)

12 **child of Aristomenes** Bacch. uses a patronymic adjective here (literally = 'Aristomenian child'), which is especially a feature of Homeric poetic language. See note on 5.69.

13 **swift-footed as the wind** The word (*podanemos*) is borrowed by Bacch. from Homer, who uses it frequently of the messenger-goddess Iris; it does not occur elsewhere except perhaps in a fragment of Simonides (Pap. Oxy. 25.2430). See also note on 5.39.

14 **before your house** This indicates that Ode 6 was sung in Ceos, presumably on the arrival of the *komos* at Lachon's house (see intro., above). For the circumstances of presentation of the victory song, see Heath's article, referred to above in the note on line 6, esp. p. 193.

16 **brought fame to Ceos** The concluding words echo line 7 'in praise of Ceos'; again present is set against past. At the same time the words pick up the first line of the poem. Just as Lachon has won great glory for himself, so too does his homeland derive glory from that same victory. A victory always confers honour upon the athlete's home as well as upon the athlete himself, and the sharing of the victory enlarges its scope and value. Thus the ode is rounded off structurally by the ring-compositional use of this theme.

ODE 7
FOR LACHON OF CEOS
Stadion, Olympic Games, 452 BC

On the date of this ode, sung at Olympia on the occasion of the victory, see intro. to Ode 6 and note on line 2, below.

Line 3 of Ode 7 is the last line of column 16. At that point the papyrus is broken vertically down the right edge of column 16, and the next surviving column does not fit at the break. Two questions then arise: (1) how many columns are missing? And (2) are the poems printed as Odes 7 and 8 in fact the beginning and end of a single ode whose central section has been lost in the break?

The next surviving column shows, on the upper part of its left edge, a few letters and syllables which are clearly the ends of long lines written in the previous column. In addition, Blass (p. 66) has identified some fragments which the appearance of the papyrus, the continuity of sense and the similarity of metre suggest belong to the early part of Ode 7, and in fact the surviving letters at the left of the next column fit perfectly into these fragments. It would appear then, that only one column (*c.* 35 lines) is missing. This means that between the beginning of Ode 7 and the end of Ode 8 (as printed) there are 54 verses: 3 at the bottom of column 16, 35 in the lost column 17, and the first 16 lines of column 18. Is this enough for two odes?

Some scholars (e.g. Blass, followed by Jebb) have supposed that Odes 7 and 8 are in fact the beginning and end of the same ode. This is not in itself impossible, but it would be very unusual that the official celebratory ode, presented on the victor's return to his home (Ode 6, 16 lines) should be so much shorter than the more or less impromptu song offered at the victory party at Olympia (Ode 7+8, 54 lines). Odes 1 and 2 (for Argeios) illustrate the usual practice; the short Ode 2 was sung at the Isthmus in the immediate celebration after the victory, while the long and complex Ode 1 was the formal epinician composed for the victor's return to Ceos.

If Odes 7 and 8 are indeed a single poem, then the whole is in honour of Lachon's Olympic victory in the stadion for boys in 452 BC. But there are difficulties with this theory. At 8.17 the poet refers to previous successes, at the Pythian, Nemean and Isthmian Games. Lachon did indeed win at Nemea (but probably in 451 BC, i.e. after this Olympic victory; see intro. to Ode 1); if he won as a boy at the Isthmus as well, it must have been in 452 or earlier, to be mentioned in this ode, yet no Isthmian victories are credited to Lachon in the Cean victory-list (*IG* XII 5 608). Further, extolling the athlete's prowess, the poet says (8.22f.): 'no one competing in his age-group, as boy and man, has won more victories', which seems to indicate (see note on 8.22) that the athlete being honoured was already competing in the men's age class, whereas Lachon was still a boy. The surviving text should therefore be separated into two poems, Odes 7 and 8, each consisting of a single pair of corresponding stanzas (cf. Ode 6).

Only the strophe of Ode 7 survives in anything like a coherent form, so that the structure of the ode is uncertain. But the invocation of the personified 'Day' with which the song opens occupies the whole of the strophe. It appears to celebrate the time and place of the contest, the Olympic festival and the Games themselves, and it climaxes with a reference to Lachon's victory (see further note on line 8). The antistrophe may well have developed the praise of the victor and his achievement (cf. the note on line 17), in which case the ode will fall into well-balanced halves, praise of the Games and praise of the athlete, with the mention of the victor's name and family serving as a bridge between the two.

1 **O shining daughter** The invocation of this divinity is picked up by 'you' in lines 5, 8 and 12, and she dominates the whole of the strophe, being involved somehow in the assignment of victory and so in the bestowal of honour upon Lachon. Who is she? Some words are missing in lines 3-5; the grammar of the sentence is not certain, and it is not obligatory to take 'you' (*se*) as in apposition to 'day' (*hameran*), but this seems the most natural interpretation. It is then the 'sixteenth day' who judges, who grants victory, and who adorns Lachon with the crown. 'Day' is daughter of 'Night' at Hes. *Theog.* 124, and daughter of 'Time' at Eur. *Supp.* 787-8. Cf. also Soph. *Trach.* 94-6, where 'sparkling night gives birth to the sun'. Other candidates are (1) Nemesis, whose name means 'she who allots to each his due'; the verb 'you grant' (8), in Greek *neimeis*, is related to her name, while Nemesis also is daughter of Night at Hes. *Theog.* 223. But already in Hesiod Nemesis is a deity of vengeance and punishment, inappropriate for the gift of prizes and honour. (2) Selene (the moon) or Hecate-Selene, cf. Bacch. fr. 1 B, where Hecate is daughter of Night. But one could hardly say that Selene, the moon, bestowed the victory, when the Games were held in broad daylight. For the personification of the giver of victory as a deity, cf. the note on 'Victory's goddess', 6.9.

shining For the word used here (*liparos*), see note on 1.158.

2 **sixteenth day** According to *schol.* Pind. *Ol.* 4.14, the Olympic Games were held from the 11th to the 16th of the month. On the last day the prizes were awarded, and processions, banquets and celebrations held in honour of the victors. The personified 'Day' is thus identified with the particular day of the prize-giving at the end of the festival; this suggests very strongly that this ode was intended to be sung in the celebrations at Olympia itself.

fiftieth month Ancient calendars were commonly organized according to the rotation of the moon around the earth (approx. 29½ days). But a year of 12 such lunar months contains only 354 days, so that the lunar year would soon become seriously out of step with the 'real' or solar year

(365¼ days). An early attempt to keep the two aligned was the development of an 8-year cycle, which involved the insertion of an extra month in each of three of the eight years. The Olympic Games were scheduled according to this eight-year cycle of 99 lunar months (8 x 12 + 3); the Games took place therefore alternately after periods of 49 and 50 months (confirmed by *schol.* Pind. *Ol.* 3.5). See also E.J. Bickerman, *Chronology of the Ancient World*, London 1968, p. 22f., esp. p. 29. Thus when Bacch. speaks of the 'fiftieth month', he simply means the period elapsed since the previous Games; the time for the festival has come around again. This enhances the sense of immediacy in this ode, and strengthens the view that it was presented at Olympia (see above).

3　**by the grace of** For the expression, cf. 6.9 and note there; also 1.118. **loud-[thundering Zeus** This restoration is virtually certain. Bacch.'s epithet begins with *baru-* (lit. = 'heavy', but also 'oppressive', 'burdensome'), and this is frequently used to form compound adjectives denoting 'loud' or 'deep' sound, cf. 9.8 'deep-throated' (lit. = 'deep-voiced', *baruphthongos*); 16.18 'deep-bellowing' (*baruakhes*); 17.77 'deep-roaring' (*barubromos*). Besides, such a description of Zeus is common; cf. Hom. *Il.* 5.672, Hom. Hymn 2.3, Pind. *Ol.* 8.44, and Soph. *Ant.* 1117, the last three all using *baru-* compounds for the meaning 'loud-thundering'. A reference to Zeus (father of Herakles) would be entirely in place here; note that at Pind. *Ol.* 6.68 Herakles founds the Olympic Games 'for his father'.

5　**[Alcmena's son]** i.e. Herakles (cf. 5.71). The restoration is for example only. These lines appear, esp. in view of the generalization in 6-7, and the reference to the supervision of Zeus in 3, to relate to the foundation and organization of the Games, traditionally by Herakles (cf. e.g. Pind. *Ol.* 2.3-4 and 6.68), although local Elean tradition associated the event with Pelops. The general sense required is something like: 'the founder of the Games appointed you, the 16th day of the month, to judge ...'; hence the restoration. Maehler in his translation (vol. 1, p. 89), following a suggestion by Snell, restores 'Pelops', but there seems to be no reason for Bacch. to follow local, rather than 'mainstream' legend here (see further note on 8.32).

6　**to judge** The day of the prize-giving, the 16th day, did not determine the results; the victors' names were known at the time of competition on the previous days, but the expression is not too extravagant. The presentation of the prizes on the last day made the judgments and the results official. It was the day which, in Jebb's words (p. 204) 'set the wreath on the brows of Lachon'.

6-7　**speed of ... feet and ... strength of ... limbs** This is a generalization, embracing the Games as a whole. The two spheres of athletic prowess, speed of foot and strength of limb, encompass all the events of the Games.

7　**heroic strength** The translation attempts to render the Greek *aris-*

talkes. Besides this word, Bacch. uses three others compounded with *aristos* ('best') – *aristokarpos* (3.2, 'where the best grain grows'), *aristopatra* (11.106, 'whose father is supreme'), and *aristarkhos* (13.58, 'whose rule is supreme'). All of these, except perhaps the last (quoted also from Simonides, fr. 231, Bergk), occur only in Bacch., and have been coined by him. Bacch. is very fond of compound adjectives in the Homeric manner; often these epithets are non-specific and purely decorative (e.g. 'violet-eyed', used of the Muses, 9.3, and of the Graces, 19.6), but frequently also the compound intensifies the meaning (cf. 'loud-thundering', above, 3). They are not literally Homeric, in that many of them do not even occur in Homer, being coined by Bacch. himself (cf. the note on 'queen of song', 6.10), nor are they formulaic, as Homer's epithets are, yet they are 'Homeric' in the sense that, cumulatively, they impart to the poems a feeling that the world inhabited by the athletes is in some way bigger, better, more lordly, than the world of ordinary mortals, so that in the end the athlete and the prowess of his victory are elevated into the world of gods and heroes. On the use of epithets, see also C.P. Segal, 'Bacchylides Reconsidered', *Quaderni Urbinati* 22 (1976), pp. 99-130.

8 **He to whom** The whole of the strophe is predicated on the invocation to 'Day', and appears to build to a climax in the manner of a priamel (for which see esp. note on 3.86-92, and Bundy, *Stud. Pind.*, p. 5f.). The priamel closes with this generalization, or *gnome*, leading into the praise of the victor Lachon (the 'name-cap', in Bundy's terminology; see esp. note on 9.26). The climax of the name-cap is enhanced by the asyndeton, i.e. the lack of connective particle between this sentence and the preceding; this serves to isolate the sentence and thus focus attention more sharply on the name.

10 **envied** Lit. = 'much-envied' (*poluzelotos*); note the intensification in the compound. This is a favourite word of Bacch. (also at 1.184, 9.45 and 10.48, and cf. *poluzelos*, 11.63). Cf. 5.53 and the note there. The envy of one's fellows is a proper and desirable part of the rewards of success. For the general sense of 6-10, Jebb compares Pind. *Ol.* 1.95f.

11 **Aristomenes' son** Bacch. again (cf. 6.12) employs the patronymic adjective to refer to the victor Lachon. Thus the praise of the victor is extended to include his father, a common device in the epinician poems; cf. e.g. 1.146-54 and 13.224f.

12 **the victor's crown** On the use of crowns, i.e. garlands, see notes on 1.158 and 8.31.

17 **newly-judged** Probably refers to the victory which Lachon has just won, which suggests that the antistrophe developed the praise of the victor himself after a strophe in praise of the Games and their founder (see intro., above). The adjective picks up the verb 'to judge' in line 6; there was probably a pattern of verbal echoes through this ode, as there is in many others, but it is impossible now to discern its extent.

ODE 8
FOR LIPARION OF CEOS (?)

In the introduction to Ode 7 it was argued that Odes 7 and 8 were separate poems. If this is indeed the case, then Ode 8 is not in honour of Lachon of Ceos. Can we discover for whom it was composed? The place name in 14, although not fully preserved on the papyrus, may well have been Ceos; this is perhaps confirmed by the adjective 'rich in vines' (12), which is elsewhere applied to this island (cf. 6.7). The victor, then, probably came from Ceos. Lines 17-18 indicate that he had already won victories at the Pythia, at Nemea and at the Isthmus, and from 24 we learn that at least some of these victories were gained in the 'men's' age class. If he is indeed from Ceos, we should expect to find his name in the Cean victory-list (*IG* XII 5 608; see intro. to Ode 1). This inscription contains only two names of athletes who won at both the Isthmian and the Nemean Games: Argeios son of Pantheides, and Liparion son of Liparos, who won three victories at the Isthmia in unidentified men's events, and one at Nemea (lines 4, 5, 8 and 22). Argeios' Isthmian victory has already been celebrated in Odes 1 and 2; this leaves Liparion as the most likely candidate for Ode 8.

The date of the victory, the event and the Games in which it was gained, are not recoverable, but since Liparion was active earlier than Argeios – there are four entries between them in the Isthmian list, not counting Liparion's brother, who won in the same year as Liparion himself, and three in the Nemean list – the present victory, even if it is not one of those recorded on the inscription, (e.g. a Pythian victory), will have been earlier than those of Argeios. This is not helpful, however, as the date of Argeios' victory is itself uncertain.

Lines 8-16 were originally treated as a separate fragment (fr. 7, Kenyon), but the metrical correspondence with lines 24-32 shows that they must belong to the strophe of this ode. Since there is only one column of the papyrus missing (see intro. to Ode 7), there is only room for the restoration of this one stanza in Ode 8, which therefore consisted, like Odes 6 and 7, of a single pair of responding stanzas.

Like the other short odes, Ode 8 contains no mythic narrative, but includes all the usual elements of the epinician. The structure appears to be straightforward, simple and linear. The ode probably began with praise of the victor himself (cf. Ode 6), leading into a reference to the event and praise of the Games. It was standard practice also to include praise of the victor's family and homeland, and this may be what is indicated in the surviving fragment, cf. Liparos (9) and Ceos rich in vines (12-14). Note also the reference to 'song' (line 13); the poet probably included here some indication of his own role in the celebration of the victory (cf. intro. to Ode 6). The antistrophe then passes to the previous victories won by this athlete at the three great panhellenic Games other than the Olympic, combining this with emphatic praise of the victor and his record-breaking achievements, and the poem concludes with a prayer (as seems most likely) for the ultimate success, at the Olympic Games themselves.

9 Liparos (?) The papyrus shows the letters *lipa*[; this may be part of the name of the athlete's father Liparos, see intro., above. (The metre will not admit the athlete's name, Liparion.) However the letters may equally well be part of the ordinary adjective *liparos* ('shining'), which is one of Bacch.'s favourite words (cf. 1.14, 1.158, 5.169, 7.1, 11.38, and 16.29; see esp. the note on 1.158). If this were the case, Bacch. may be using the adjective in word play here, but the text is too fragmentary to allow discovery of the intended effect.

12 rich in vines Evidently a common description of Ceos, cf. 6.7 and note. Here Bacch. uses a different word (*poluampelos*) from that used in 6.7, but again it is a word which he has coined himself. (Homer, however, uses the similar *polustaphelos* with the same meaning.)

15 without horses This description also (cf. previous note, and the note on 6.7) was applied to Ceos (Pindar, *Paian* 4.24) and strengthens the view that the ode was composed for a Cean. Cf. 'craggy', 1.121, and the note there.

17 singing The verb-form in Greek is singular, and probably refers to the poet himself, and to his role in celebrating this and previous victories; there may, however, be a reference to the choral performance of songs by the *komos*, cf. 2.9 and 6.6, with the notes there. With the phrase 'singing in praise of ...', Bacch. means 'celebrating victories at ...', since it was standard practice in the epinician to include praise of the place of victory (cf. e.g. 6.6-7 and 9.3-6).

Pytho A standard poetical synonym for the region surrounding Delphi, or for Delphi itself; the derivation of the name relates to one of Apollo's earliest adventures. After laying out the foundations of his temple at Delphi, Apollo slew a monstrous dragon or serpent, which had been terrorizing the people of the area. (The story is told in Hom. Hymn 3, 300f.) The monster's body was then left to rot upon the ground. The Greek for 'to rot' is *puthesthai*, 'whence', as the writer of the Hymn relates (372-3), 'the place is called Pytho'. Likewise Apollo himself became known as the Pythian god. Later writers and mythographers (e.g. Plut. *Moral.* 293C) gave the name 'Python' to the serpent itself (which is the origin of the English word), but this does not occur in the Hymn.

where sheep are sacrificed Pindar (*Pyth.* 3.27) uses a similar epithet for Delphi. It was customary for those who would consult the Delphic oracle to sacrifice a sheep before entering the inner shrine, but since there is no allusion to the oracle either here or in Pindar, the description has clearly become ornamental.

19-21 laying my hand upon the earth The same phrase recurs at 5.42

(where I have translated it: 'calling the earth to witness'). For the gesture cf. also Hom. *Il.* 14.271f., where Sleep demands that Hera clasp the earth in affirmation of her promise (further references in Maehler, vol. 2, p. 00). These lines illustrate some of the most common recurrent motifs of the epinician: the gesture of touching the ground solemnizes and strengthens the assertion which follows, giving it the force of an oath. So here again the earth is called to witness the truth of the assertion. The debt is the debt of praise owed by the poet to the victor, and represents an acknowledgment by the poet that the victor deserves and requires to be adequately praised, while at the same time he proclaims his own skill in doing so; finally, in claiming that 'truth attends it (cf. 3.96, 5.188 and 9.85) Bacch. means that the praise is just and proper and worthy of the victor's merits. These elements – the witness, the oath, the solemn asseveration, the acknowledgment of debt and the need for praise – build to a climax and herald an especially emphatic praise of the victor, introduced by the negative 'no man ...' in 22. The structure at 5.42 is similar, if less elaborate. (See further Bundy, *Stud. Pind.*, pp. 60-1, with notes 66 and 69; also my note on 11.24.)

22 competing in his age group If this means 'competing in his own age group', the expression is redundant, for the athlete must always do so; besides, it would mean that the present victor (Liparion?) held the all-time record for the number of victories in a career. If this were the case, why have we not heard more of such a distinguished athlete? Rather the meaning appears to be quite specific: the recipient of this ode has won more victories than any of the individuals against whom he competed as a boy, and more likewise than any of his fellow-competitors in the men's age class. Jebb (and others) understand: 'no one has won more victories *in equal time*, whether as boy or man', but it is not likely that the Greek will bear this meaning. See also intro. to Ode 7.

26 whose spear is the thunderbolt The adjective (*keraunegkhes*) occurs only here, and was evidently coined by Bacch., but Pindar twice (*Ol.* 13.77 and *Pyth.* 4.194, both dating from the mid-460s) uses *egkheikeraunos*, making a compound with the same meaning out of the same elements in reverse order. Who was imitating whom? This illustrates the close attention which each of the rival lyric poets clearly paid to the work of the other.

27 may you bring There are breaks in the papyrus at crucial points here, and it is not certain whether the verb represents a wish (as translated) or a statement ('you have brought'). Likewise in line 30 'give' might be 'you have given'. Those who regard Odes 7 and 8 as a single poem take the latter view, understanding a reference to Lachon's Olympic victory, which in their view is the subject of the combined Ode. See intro. to Ode 7. But Maehler argues, rightly, I think (vol. 2, pp. 137 and 141), that after the elaborate and emphatic praise of previous victories in 18-25, such a reference to the athlete's present victory would be a grievous anticlimax. It is much more plausible, surely, that the ode should end with a climactic prayer for future success, not yet achieved, at the most important of all the festivals.

28 by the banks of Alpheos i.e. at Olympia; cf. 3.5, 6.3, etc.

silver-swirling Not to be understood literally; this fairly common adjective (*argurodinas*) is used by the poets of several rivers, such as Peneios (Thessaly, Hom. *Il.* 2.753), Acheloios (northwest Greece, Hes. *Theog.* 340), and Scamander (Troy, Hom. *Il.* 21.8); none of these is especially renowned for alluvial silver. The reference is more probably to the silvery colour of water and foam in an eddying river, and the word is probably used simply for the sake of variation from 'wide-swirling' of 3.5 and 5.40, where see note. Contrast the literal use of *chrusodinas* ('gold-swirling') at 3.44, and see the note there.

31 the Aitolian olive i.e. the crown or garland of olive leaves which was the victor's prize. Pindar (*Ol.* 3.13f.) relates how Herakles brought the wild olive from 'the shadowy springs of Ister' (the Danube, i.e. the remote far north) to be the prize at Olympia; Paus. 5.7.7, has Herakles bring it from 'the land of the Hyperboreans' (for whom see note on 3.59). The Eleans, who lived in the area around Olympia and had control of the Games, traced their descent from the Aitolian Oxylos, who came with the children of Herakles when they entered the Peloponnese to reclaim their inheritance, and received Elis as his reward; consequently anything related to Elis, and especially to the Games, might be called Aitolian (cf. Hdt. 8.73; also Pind. *Ol.* 3.12, where the judge is 'Aitolian'). The legend of 'the return of the Herakleidai' (i.e. the children of Herakles; see Strabo 8.3.30; Diod. 4.57.8) is probably a reflection of the historical so-called 'Dorian Invasion' (the second major migration of Greek-speakers into the Greek mainland, *c.* 1100 BC, see Thuc. 1.12). But there is some evidence which may cast doubt on the reality of this 'invasion'; for example, the major break in pottery style at Sparta occurs *c.* 900 BC, which seems too late. See also G. Horrocks, *Greece: A History of the Language and its Speakers*, London 1997, pp. 11-13; also J. Chadwick, 'The Dorian Invasions', in Diana Bowder (ed.), *Who was Who in the Greek World*, Oxford 1982, pp. 15-16.

silvery Cf. 11.29. This colour word (*glaukos*) is commonly applied to the olive (e.g. Soph. *OC* 701). According to Plato (*Tim.* 68C) it denotes blue mixed with white; in fact its range is wide, covering light blue through green to grey. It is thus particularly apposite for olive leaves, which combine green with a silvery grey.

32 far-famed One of Bacch.'s favourite decorative and honorific adjectives; cf. 2.10, etc.

games of Phrygian Pelops Cf. 'the courses of Pelops', Pind. *Ol.* 1.95. These and similar references need not be taken to mean that Pelops was believed to have founded the Games; they show merely the antiquity of the connection between Pelops and Olympia. The Games were traditionally founded by Herakles, the great hero, son of Zeus and Alcmena (cf. Pind. *Ol.* 2.3-4 and 6.68), but Paus. (5.7.6f.) quotes ancient Elean tradition for the view that the founder was a different Herakles, one of the Curetes or Idaean Dactyls, from Mt Ida in Crete (for whom see Paus. 8.31.3). This story reappears in Diod. 5.64.6 and Strabo 8.3.30, although Strabo specifically denies it. To this latter Herakles was attached a succession of other legendary heroes who 're-established' or 'renewed' the Games, among them Pelops (Paus. 5.8.2), and a confused version of the foundation appears in Favorinus (*On Exile* IV.46-50) who speaks of 'Pelops or some Idaean Dactyl'. It is true, however, that the cult of Pelops was of great importance at Olympia; the hero had his own sanctuary there, and a black ram was sacrificed to him every year (Paus. 5.13.1-3). Further, all those who would sacrifice to Zeus were obliged to sacrifice to Pelops first (*schol.* Pind. *Ol.* 1.149a). Paus. claims that the cult of Pelops was established by Herakles son of Alcmena (so also the *schol.* Pind.), and no doubt the mainstream tradition was that the Games were founded, not by Pelops, but by Herakles in honour of Pelops (cf. Dion. Hal. V.17). On the connection of Pelops with Olympia, see also 5.181, and note on 7.5.

Phrygian For this description of Pelops, cf. Hdt. 7.11.4 and Soph. *Aias* 1292. Pelops was properly a Lydian (e.g. Pind. *Ol.* 1.24 and 9.9) since his father Tantalos was ruler around Sipylos in Lydia. Phrygia was a separate part of Asia Minor, but the name was often used in a larger sense, to include Lydia (and even Troy; cf. Eur. *Or.* 1381-2). Cf. Soph. *Ant.* 824, where Pelops' sister Niobe is also called Phrygian.

ODE 9
FOR AUTOMEDES OF PHLEIUS
Pentathlon, Nemean Games

The event

This ode was composed to honour Automedes, son of Timoxenos, of Phleius, for his victory in the pentathlon in the Nemean Games. This much we learn from the poem itself (Automedes, 26; Timoxenos, 102; pentathlon, 27; Nemea, 22), but beyond that nothing is known of the victor, his family, or the date of his victory.

His home town, Phleius, was a generally unremarkable settlement in the northeastern corner of the Peloponnese. It lay nestled in a fertile valley in the hill country between the coastal plains of Argos to the south and Sicyon and Corinth to the north. On its western side were the mountains of Arcadia, while immediately to the east lay the valley of Nemea, home of the Games and the scene of Automedes' victory. The town drew its livelihood largely from the production of wine and corn, and although it was

Fig. 9. The fourth-century stadium at Nemea. Halfway down on the left, a passage-way led through a tunnel to the athletes' changing rooms.

large enough to provide a contingent of 200 to fight the Persians at Thermopylae (480 BC; Hdt. 7.202; Paus. 10.20.1) and 1,000 at Plataea (479 BC; Hdt. 9.28), it never played a major part in Greek history, nor acquired any great distinction. It was the home of Pratinas, a writer of satyr-plays and contemporary of Aischylos in the early fifth century BC, but the only athlete from Phleius other than Automedes to achieve success at any of the major panhellenic Games was one Timainetos, who won the *hoplitodromos* (a foot-race in full armour) at the Pythian Games in 498 BC (Paus. 10.7.7). No doubt, therefore, the victory of Automedes was a very special occasion for civic pride. For an extensive account of the 'history' and mythology of Phleius, see Paus. 2.12.3 to 2.13.8.

The myths

(a) *The foundation of the Nemean Games*
The foundation legend of the Nemean Games involves the early part of the saga of the so-called 'Seven against Thebes'. When Oedipus went into voluntary exile from Thebes, his two sons Polyneikes and Eteokles disputed the kingship. Polyneikes went off to Argos, where he prevailed upon the king, Adrastos, to help him raise a great army (in seven contingents, each with its own commander, hence the 'Seven against Thebes') to march against Thebes and install him on the throne. But there was a problem to be overcome first. The prophet Amphiaraos could foretell the future; knowing that no one would return alive from this ill-fated enterprise

153

except Adrastos, he tried to dissuade them (Apollod. 3.6.2). But Amphiaraos had sworn that in any dispute between himself and Adrastos he would defer to the judgment of his wife Eriphyle. Knowing this, Polyneikes bribed Eriphyle, with the necklace of Harmonia, to use this oath to compel her husband to take part, against his better judgment, and so the great expedition finally set out. (The story was widely known already from the epic poem *Thebais* (see note on 54, below), and episodes from it appear on sixth-century vase paintings).

On the way north from Argos the army came to Nemea, where (as Eur. relates in his *Hypsipyle* – see T.B.L. Webster, *The Tragedies of Euripides*, London 1967, pp. 211-15), they found Opheltes, the infant son of the king Lykurgos and Eurydike, in the care of his nurse Hypsipyle. While Hypsipyle's attention was distracted by the need to attend to the visitors, the child was killed by a serpent. The heroes thereupon buried Opheltes and, before continuing on their way to Thebes, held Funeral Games in his honour – the legendary origin of the historical Nemean Games. It seems to have been Euripides who introduced the nurse Hypsipyle into the story – she does not appear in earlier versions, nor is she necessary to the allusive treatment of the legend by Bacch. here. Bacch. uses the story in this ode (10-20) primarily to honour Nemea and the Games through their association with the heroes, but interestingly, he selects, in a very oblique and allusive manner, only those parts of the story which contribute to his poetic purposes.

(b) *The daughters of Asopos*

The river Asopos flows north through the territory of Phleius and Sicyon into the Corinthian Gulf, and the many tributaries of that river were, naturally enough, regarded as the daughters of Asopos. Personified as nymphs and minor goddesses, they became the eponymous heroines of cities spread far and wide throughout the Greek world, including Corcyra in the west, and Sinope in the east, on the southern shore of the Black Sea. As brides of various gods, they became also the mothers of many of the great heroes of legend. The names of those whom we know from the ancient writers as 'daughters of Asopos' are very numerous – Diod. (4.72.1) names 12; Apollod. (3.12.6) speaks of as many as 20, although he names only Aigina – and the reason is that there were in fact two rivers called Asopos, each, originally, with its own list of 'daughters'. The other Asopos was in Boeotia, and it is evident that for the most part the names of the daughters fall into two groups, clustered around either the Phleiasian Asopos (e.g. Nemea, Cleonai, Aigina, Peirene) or the Boeotian (e.g. Thebe, Tanagra, Thespia). But in practice the two lists were always combined. Thus the statue group representing Asopos and his daughters, dedicated at Olympia by the city of Phleius, included Thebe as well as (*inter alias*) Nemea and Aigina (Paus. 5.22.6), while the poetess Corinna, who was herself a Boeotian and seems largely to have confined herself to Boeotian subjects, when she describes Asopos lamenting the loss of his daughters, mentions Aigina, Corcyra and Sinope as well as the Boeotian Thespia (*PMG* 654, Col. III; see D.A. Campbell, *Greek Lyric Poetry*, London 1967, p. 412, note on line 12). It is no surprise then, that Bacch. himself, who devotes the central mythic section of the ode to honouring Phleius through its association with the daughters of Asopos and the heroic exploits of their descendants, should highlight Thebe as well as Aigina (see lines 54-5).

The poem

Ode 9 displays the typical structure familiar from many of the other longer odes (see esp. Odes 1, 3 and 5, and the introductions to those odes). The central mythic narrative (40-65) is framed, as usual, by two sections of victor-praise (1-39 and 66-82), of which the second leads through a gnomic sequence (82-96) to a renewed focus on the victor (97-end), exactly as in Ode 3. (Ode 1 is analogous, but there is at the end of Ode 1 no return to specific victor-praise.)

The opening section itself shows the same ring-compositional arrangement. The prayer to the Graces to 'grant renown' (1-2) leads to the praise of Phleius, the victor's home, and of Nemea, the seat of the Games, honoured by its association with the first of the Labours of the mighty Herakles. This is balanced by the renown which the athletes win at those famous Games in Nemea (21f.), and in between stands the story of the foundation of the Games by the 'Seven against Thebes'. But the balance is not merely structural; it is thematic as well. The killing of the Nemean lion was a great victory, and the exploit of Herakles sheds its lustre on the victories won in the Games at Nemea; the frame thus created highlights the contrast between the deluded ambition of Polyneikes and the 'Seven', and the worthwhile ambition of the athletes. (See also notes on 19 and 26, below.) The general reference to Nemea and the fame to be won there (21-4) then leads naturally to specific praise of the present victor, and the first section of the poem concludes with a detailed description of Automedes' prowess in the pentathlon (27-38).

The return of Automedes to his home provides an easy transition into the myth, in which Bacch. extols the fame of Asopos and his descendants, who include great heroes such as Telamon, Aias and Achilles (40-7) and more specifically the daughters of Asopos (48-65). The function of the myth is simply to praise the victor's homeland of Phleius through its local association with the divinities and heroes of legend, in much the same way that the local legend of the Euxantidai is used in Ode 1 to praise the family of the victor Argeios, who claimed descent from Euxantios.

The papyrus is badly damaged around the end of the mythic narrative, and the nature of the transition to the second victor-praise cannot be discerned, but the scene clearly, if abruptly, changes to the victory celebration in Phleius. This final section of the poem also has a ring-compositional structure of its own. Beginning (as it seems) with the festivities in Phleius (66f.), a reference to the song of celebration (78) leads into gnomic reflections on the dependence of success on song for genuine immortality, and the uncertainty of human endeavour. Only the gods know what will be the end result of human effort, which brings us back to the victor, for Zeus has granted his favour to Automedes, and the ode ends, as did Ode 3, with specific praise of the victor, his family and his victory.

1 **Graces** On the role of the Graces in the creation of the poem, see note on 5.11.

   of the golden distaff The distaff (*alakata*) was a split wooden rod on which a bundle of wool or flax was held, whence it was drawn off to a rotating spindle, where it was spun into thread. Thus the word belonged to the sphere of women's work, so that adjectives such as that used here (*chrusalakatos* = 'of the golden distaff') could be applied as a generalized decorative honorific to any female, whether human or divine. Pindar uses the word several times, of Leto, Artemis' mother, *Nem.* 6.36; Amphitrite, *Ol.* 6.104; and the Nereids, *Nem.* 5.36; and cf. Bacch. 1.74, where Makelo is called *philalakatos* ('she who loves to spin'). But see also note on 11.37.

2 **grant renown** i.e. to the victor. Automedes has won glory by his success in the Games, but this is not enough; the victory requires the poet's song to celebrate it and make it truly immortal (a common motif, cf. esp. 9.78f., below; also 1.181-4), while the poem itself requires the help of the Graces (and the Muses). Thus the Graces are here regarded as the ultimate source of the fame which will flow to Automedes. Others take the view that Bacch. means 'grant to me'; i.e. he prays for the skill to compose a song which will persuade its audience of the merits of Automedes. If he succeeds, the song will bring fame to Bacch. himself as well as to the victor, so that the renown of the poet will further enhance that of the victorious athlete. This would then be a version of the common epinician motif that the poet and the poem must be worthy of, and do justice to, the victor and his victory (see esp. notes on 5.9 and 8.19-21), but is much less likely. Not only is the expression, on this view, unduly compressed and obscure, but the structural balance between the prayer for Automedes here, and the answer to that prayer in 25-6, would be entirely lost. Further, the word 'renown' is the very first word of the poem; in this emphatic position, in a victory ode, it could hardly do other than refer to the victor.

   that sways mankind If the above interpretation is correct, this will simply mean that Automedes' victory will make him respected and influential among his peers.

3 **voice of the Muses** i.e. the poet himself. For the inspirational role of the Muses and for the poet as conduit for the Muses' song, see notes on 1.1 and 1.4.

violet-eyed See note on 'violet-crowned', 3.3.

4 **ready** An example of the 'willingness-motif'; see note on 5.14.

5 **verdant** (*euthales*). Alluding in a general way to the fertility of Nemea and the surrounding area (see intro., above), but also more specifically to the victor's crown, made of the leaves of the local wild parsley (cf. *panthales* = 'all in bloom', 13.70). Thus in praising Phleius Bacch. praises the victor and his homeland, while the reference to Nemea includes the Games and the victory won there. (Bacch. in fact fulfils this promise in reverse order, first glorifying Nemea through the stories of the Nemean lion and the legendary foundation of the Games, before turning to a description of the victory and the stories of the daughters of Asopos). All of these motifs are resumed at the end of the introductory triad (21-6).

7 **where** The fame of Nemea, and its Games, is enhanced by association with the exploits of Herakles, as the scene of his first Labour. Further, the word conventionally translated 'labours' (*aethloi*, 9) actually means 'contests'; it was from Homer on (*Il.* 8.363) the ordinary word for the Labours of Herakles, but it was also the ordinary word for the 'events' or 'competitions' in the Games, or collectively, for the Games as a whole (cf. Soph. *El.* 49). The idea is picked up in 21, below: 'from those renowned Games in Nemea'; just as Herakles won fame in his 'contest' there, so too do the victors in theirs. The parallel thus elevates the victorious athletes generally, and Automedes in particular, to the level of the great hero.

Hera ... reared Bacch. is following Hesiod closely here: 'the Nemean lion, which Hera ... reared and set down in the hills of Nemea, a bane to men' (Hes. *Theog.* 327-9), and 'the Lernaean Hydra, which the white-armed goddess Hera reared, angry beyond measure with the mighty Herakles' (*Theog.* 313-5). For the hostility of Hera to Herakles, and her role in the imposition of the Twelve Labours, see intro. to Ode 5, and the note on 5.90.

white-armed The Homeric formulaic epithet for Hera (*Il.* 1.55 etc.), thereafter widely used of other goddesses as well as mortal women. Bacch. uses it of Artemis (5.102), Kalliope (5.176), Iole (16.28) and Europa (17.53). See also note on 5.173.

8 **deep-throated** A somewhat free translation of *baruphthongos*, referring to the deep growling roar of the lion. Adjectives compounded with *baru-* (lit. = 'heavy') are frequent in Bacch. See note on 7.3.

9 **first** The killing of the Nemean lion was traditionally, and naturally, the first of the Labours, as it was from this exploit that Herakles furnished himself with the lion-skin which thereafter became his 'trademark' attire (see e.g. Pind. *Isth.* 6.48 and Eur. *Herakles* 359; also Arist. *Frogs* 46; on the dress and equipment of Herakles generally, see Preller-Robert, *Griechische Mythologie* (4th edn, Berlin, 1894) pp. 441-2). The Labours are narrated in detail in Apollod. 2.5.1f.; for a

convenient summary see H.J. Rose, *A Handbook of Greek Mythology*, 6th edn, London 1958, p. 211f.

far-famed Cf. 5.119, 10.19 etc., and note on 8.32.

10 There i.e. at Nemea, through which the 'Seven' passed on their way to Thebes. For details of the legend, see intro., above.

blood-red The adjective (*phoinikaspis*, lit. = 'crimson-shielded') occurs only here. In tragedy the Argive warriors are consistently described as carrying white shields (Aisch. *Seven* 89, Soph. *Ant.* 106, Eur. *Phoin.* 1099); the adjective used in these passages (*leukaspis* = 'white-shielded') is borrowed from Homer (*Il.* 22.294) and probably means 'burnished', 'shining', 'bright'. In any case it is certainly decorative rather than literal. The variation here again shows Bacch.'s fondness for vivid colour, especially red. As well as the simple adjective 'crimson' (*phoinikeos*, 13.92 and *phoinissos*, 18.54) and the verb *phoinissein* ('to stain red', 13.164 and 27.36), Bacch. has five adjectives compounded with *phoinik-*, of which four are not found elsewhere, and the fifth (*phoinikosteropas*, 12.40) is shared only with Pindar (*Ol.* 9.6). All five were probably coined by Bacch. himself. See also note on 5.99.

12 first Because the Games held to honour Archemoros were regarded as the legendary origin of the historical Nemean Games.

Archemoros The name means 'beginning of doom', as Bacch. explains in 14: 'token of death to come'. It was given to the slain infant by the prophet Amphiaraos, who (rightly) saw the death of the child as an omen of imminent disaster, and prophesied that the expedition of the Seven against Thebes was doomed. Bacch. varies the standard version of the legend on this point. As outlined above in the introduction, the reluctance of Amphiaraos to take part in the expedition, his attempt to dissuade the others, and his coercion by his wife Eriphyle, all took place in Argos, before the expedition set out – and this seems to have been known to Homer already, who twice (*Od.* 11.326-7 and 15.244-7) alludes to the venality of Eriphyle. For Bacch. on the other hand, the reluctance of Amphiaraos is the direct consequence of the death of Opheltes, and Eriphyle plays no part. The reason perhaps is to concentrate attention on the foolish determination of Adrastos by avoiding reference to the other aspects of greed and corruption involved in the story. The defeat of the Argives and its consequences (from the Theban point of view) are treated in Aischylos' tragedy *Seven against Thebes* and Sophocles' *Antigone*.

14 yellow-eyed (*xanthoderkes*) For the meaning of the first element in this compound (*xanthos*) see the note on 'chestnut' at 5.38. Here a baleful yellow glare seems indicated.

15 O Destiny A variation of the common Homeric phrase 'powerful destiny' (*Il.* 5.83. etc.). The direct invocation is intended to heighten the pathos; cf. 16.30, and perhaps 5.139.

16 son of Oikles i.e. Amphiaraos, who through his father was descended from a long line of seers, beginning with Melampous (see Homer, *Od.* 15.225-46).

17 **streets of heroes** i.e. back to Argos. The word 'streets' is used by a simple metonymy for 'city', as again in 52, below, and perhaps 14B.2. Pindar uses the same figure at *Pyth.* 8.55, also in a prophecy by Amphiaraos regarding Adrastos; *Pyth.* 8 probably belongs to 446 BC, so that this may be a reminiscence or imitation of Bacch. The description of Argos as 'city of heroes' is a general honorific, but it carries also an oblique and ominous reference to these specific heroes who have left Argos and will not return.

18 **Hope steals away** The expedition of the Seven against Thebes was driven by lust for power, greed and corrupt ambition (see intro., above). If it seems strange that Bacch. chooses to glorify the Nemean Games and their foundation through a legend with such negative associations – and these are only reinforced by the death of the infant Opheltes/Archemoros, the interpretation of this omen by Amphiaraos, and the refusal of the Seven to heed the seer's good advice and abandon the enterprise – at least he turns it to his advantage. The papyrus is mutilated at the end of line 20 and the connection of thought is not certain, but there seems to be an implicit contrast between the vanity of foolish ambition on the one hand (16-20) and the athletes' legitimate quest for glory through the display of prowess on the other (21-6). This is a point which Bacch. has made elsewhere, and more explicitly; see 3.75-6, also 1.176f., with the notes there. The idea is taken up also by Soph.: 'wandering hope ... deceives the light-minded desires of many men' (*Ant.* 616-18).

21 **From those renowned Games** Picks up and balances the renown attaching to the Games through their association with Herakles (6-9); see intro., above.

23 **each second year** Bacch. uses an expression which literally means 'the three-year crown', i.e. the crown awarded every third year. The reason is that Greek counting was 'inclusive', in the sense that it included the point from which counting began, so that in reckoning the number of years from one Nemean festival to the next – e.g. 475 to 473 – the year of the first was included. Or to put it another way, the ancient Greeks counted the fence-posts, whereas we count the spaces in between. Cf. Pind. *Nem.* 6.40; also *Ol.* 3.21, where the Olympic Games, which took place as we would say every four years, are called a 'five-year festival'; so also the festival of Apollo on Delos, Thuc. 3.104.2.

24 **fair hair** For the colour word used here (*xanthos*) see note on 5.38. It is hardly likely that all the successful athletes had blond hair, and the word must be understood as a general decorative epithet. Contrast 10.16, and see the note there. The usage here does indicate, however, that fair hair was regarded as attractive for men, no less than for women.

25 god has given it i.e. the crown. The idea that victory is a gift of the gods is frequent in Bacch., cf. 1.155-6, 4.1-3, 6.9, etc.

26 Automedes At last Bacch. arrives at the name of the victor. All that has gone before – the victory of Herakles over the lion, the disaster implicit in the expedition of the Seven, and the contrasting glory to be won at Nemea – is foil for the achievement of Automedes, and the reference to the victor constitutes the 'name-cap' (for this term see note on 3.86-92) which climaxes the whole sequence and leads into the detail of the first victor-praise. (Cf. also the note on 7.8.)

28 Selene The moon-goddess, i.e. the moon itself. Bacch. probably uses the word here without personification. For the comparison cf. Sappho 34: 'the stars around the lovely moon conceal their bright light, when she shines full upon the earth'; also Sappho 96.6-9: 'and now she stands out among the women of Lydia, as the ... moon, when the sun sets, surpasses all the stars'. Bacch. is probably imitating Sappho directly.

31 displayed his awesome form i.e. his body, the splendour of his physical perfection; cf. Homer, *Od.* 18.67f., where Odysseus, preparing to fight Iros, 'displayed his splendid thighs, his broad shoulders ...'. Also, less literally, in Bacch. 13.75-6: 'you displayed all-mastering strength'.

  Much is unclear about the organization and judging of the pentathlon, but it is generally agreed that an athlete who won three of the five events was declared the overall winner (see general introduction). Bacch. here describes only three events – the discus, the javelin and the wrestling – which naturally suggests that these were the three events which Automedes won, and that he was unsuccessful in the long-jump and the footrace. Bacch's description of the events is lively and enthusiastic, bringing the scene vividly to the imagination of his audience and allowing them to share the excitement; cf. 5.43-47 (the undefeated Pherenikos) and 10.21-25 (the unnamed runner standing panting and sweating on the finishing line). Maehler (vol. 2, p. 158) rightly points out that this marks a significant difference between Bacch. and Pindar, who very rarely describes details of the contest, preferring to concentrate on the achievement of renown and ignoring the sweat and effort required to achieve it.

33 the towering sky Cf. 3.36, where the same words are used.

34 dark-leaved elder The branches of the elder (*Sambucus nigra*) are long, straight and with few knots, making it especially suitable for javelins (see Theophrastos, *Hist. Plant.* II, 4.4). The same adjective 'dark-leaved' (*melamphullos*) is used by Pindar of the wooded peaks of Aitna (*Pyth.* 1.27).

35 the roar of the crowd Bacch. likes to draw our attention to the presence of the spectators at the event, to enliven the description and draw his listeners into the scene, as well as to enhance the praise of the victor. See note on 31, above, and notes on 3.9 and 5.48.

36 glittering dance The word used here (*amarugma*) properly means 'twinkle' or 'sparkle', but carries also the suggestion of rapid movement, since this commonly produces a sparkling effect; cf. Arist. *Birds* 925, where a closely related word (*amaruga*) is used: 'swift as the glancing flash of horses' feet'. Here the reference is to the rapid interchange of foot positions as the wrestlers strive to make a throw. Cf. also the note on 'shimmering', 1.114, for the same association in reverse.

38 strong-limbed The same word (*guialkes*) is used at 12.8. It was probably coined by Bacch., as it occurs otherwise only in very late writers, who may have been imitating him. Cf. also 11.12, where the related *euguios* (lit. = 'well-limbed') is used, and 13.137 (*himeroguios* = 'desire in her lovely limbs'); both of these also are unique to Bacch.

39 then came The return of the victorious athlete to his home is the culmination of his achievement, and signals the end of the victor-praise; cf. 5.184 and 11.30. Here the mention of Asopos – the river of the victor's homeland – provides the peg on which to hang the narrative of the daughters of Asopos and their descendants. See intro., above.

dark swirling waters (*porphurodinas*). For adjectives compounded from -*din*- (= 'eddy') see note on 5.40. The first part of the word here (*porphuro*-) has two areas of meaning: (1) 'heaving', 'surging', often used of a heavy swell at sea, e.g. Hom. *Il.* 16.391, *Il.* 14.16, etc., and (2) 'purple', 'dark-red', commonly used of clothing dyed that colour, e.g. *Il.* 8.221 etc., Bacch. 17.112 and 18.52; also of wine, Theocr. 5.125, and of blood, *Il.* 17.361. This colour seems inappropriate here, but perhaps simply 'dark' is meant.

41 distant Nile This may simply emphasize the previous line, suggesting that the fame of Asopos reaches 'even to the ends of the earth'; cf. Pind. *Isth.* 6.24-5: the fame of the Aiakids spreads 'beyond the springs of Nile and among the Hyperboreans' (for the latter, see note on 3.59); also Pind. *Isth.* 2.41-2, where the Nile and Phasis (a Greek colony on the eastern shore of the Black Sea) represent the ends of the earth and constitute metaphorically the only limits to the generosity of Xenokrates. However , the reference to the Nile here, in spite of its brevity, may also be intended to suggest a specific mythic story involving a descendant of Asopos – most probably the encounter between Achilles and the Ethiopian king Memnon. This is supported by the fact that the 'Nile' is balanced, not by a simple geographical reference, as in the passages from Pindar quoted above, but by the specific story of the Amazons. See note on 46-7, below.

42 they who dwell i.e. the Amazons. The broad plain around the river Thermodon and the town of Themiskyra at its mouth, on the south shore of the Black Sea, was their legendary home (see Aisch. *Prom.* 723-5; Ap. Rhod. *Argonaut.* 2.995).

43 spear-skilled The spear was the Amazons' normal weapon, but they are sometimes armed also with the bow (cf. 'the host of archer women',

Pind. *Ol.* 13.89 and *sim. Nem.* 3.38) or the axe (Xenophon *Anabasis* 4.4.16).

daughters of Ares So described also by Ap. Rhod. *Argonaut.* 2.990. Their queen, Penthesilea, is likewise called daughter of Ares in the line of verse which was devised to attach the epic *Aithiopis* (see note on 46-7, below) to the end of the *Iliad*. The last line of the *Iliad* reads: 'so they attended to the burial of Hector, breaker of horses', but it was changed in antiquity to: 'so they attended to the burial of Hector. And the Amazon came, daughter of Ares, great-hearted, slayer of men' (see *schol.* T on *Iliad* 24.804).

45 much-envied The word (*poluzelotos*), used first by Bacch. and imitated by later writers (e.g. Eur. *Hipp.* 168), was usually applied by him to the victor (7.10, 10.48) or to the renown enjoyed by the victor (1.184). Its transference here to Asopos, envied for the renown of his descendants, equates the river with the victor, and underlines the fact that the whole myth is part of the programme of praise of Automedes and his home. See also notes on 7.10 and 5.53.

46-7 your descendants One of the daughters of Asopos was Aigina (see intro., above) whose union with Zeus produced Aiakos, father of Telamon and Peleus, and grandfather of Aias and Achilles (see genealogy in note on 57, below). Bacch. means that the fame of Asopos has spread even to the Amazons, and to Troy, for they learned of him through their encounters with these descendants. Prior to the Trojan War Telamon, with Iolaos, had sacked the city of Troy, then ruled by Laomedon, and had then attacked the Amazons (Pind. *Nem.* 3.36-9; according to the *schol.* on this passage, Telamon killed Melanippe, sister of the Amazon queen Penthesilea). Aias and Achilles were themselves central to the fighting against Troy as described in the *Iliad*, and when the Amazons came to assist the Trojans, Achilles killed their queen Penthesilea. This last episode was narrated in the epic *Aithiopis* (attributed to Arctinos, prob. seventh century BC) which purported to continue the story of the Trojan War, and was actually tacked on to the end of the Iliad (see note on 43, above). It may be that Bacch. had the *Aithiopis* particularly in mind here, rather than the *Iliad* or other sources, for the *Aithiopis* included also the story of the Ethiopian prince Memnon, killed by Achilles. If this is right, it would support the suggestion that the reference to the Nile in line 41 was specific rather than general. The Ethiopians, no less than the Amazons and Trojans, will have learned of the descendants of Asopos, when the report of the death of Memnon at the hands of Achilles was brought home to them (see note on 41, above). There is also a remarkable parallel in Pindar: 'their name' (i.e. of the sons of Aiakos) 'spreads afar over land and sea; it came even to the Ethiopians, when Memnon did not return ...' (*Nem.* 6.48-50).

47 lofty-gated A Homeric epithet for Troy, *Il.* 16.698 etc.

48 a broad pathway This is a variation of a common motif, normally used to indicate the breadth of opportunity for praise which the victor's achievements offer; cf. note on 'numberless pathways' at 5.33. By using it in reference to Asopos, Bacch. again equates the river-god and the victor, so that the praise of the latter is enhanced; see note on 45, above.

50 shining-girdled *liparozonos*) Probably coined by Bacch. – it is found only here and Eur. *Phoin.* 175 (prob. 412 BC) – as a variation of *kallizonos* ('lovely-girdled', 5.90) and *bathuzonos* ('deep-girdled', 5.11, etc.) Cf. also 'Charis of the shining veil' (*liparokrademnos*), *Il.* 18.382. For *liparos* = 'shining', see note on 1.158.

51 good fortune For the expression, suggesting the success of these foundations, cf. 5.52 and 11.116. It is common in Pindar also, e.g. *Nem.* 5.48, 10.25, etc.

52 cities The word used here literally means 'streets'; see note on 17, above.

never sacked The adjective is proleptic (cf. 65, below, and 11.41), looking forward to the impregnability which these cities would enjoy, and reinforcing the idea of their success and good fortune (see previous note). But see also note on 54, below.

53 For who does not know The rhetorical question, suggesting a negative answer, (i.e. there is no one who does not know) climaxes the foregoing assertion of the widespread renown of Asopos' daughters; cf. 4.18.

dark-haired (*kuanoplokamos*). See note on 11.83.

54 Thebe's well-built city Thebes was one of the most important cities of Greece in the Late Bronze Age, along with Mycenae, Tiryns, Pylos, Argos and Athens. Excavation has been hampered by the fact that much of the ancient city lies under the modern, but more than enough has come to light to attest its splendour. See e.g. E. Vermeule, *Greece in the Bronze Age*, p. 189f. Its importance is also borne out by the central position which it occupies in the mythology. Three epic poems are known to have dealt with Theban stories – *Oidipodea*, which included the marriage of Oedipus to his mother Jocasta; *Thebais*, which treated the ill-fated expedition of the 'Seven' (see also intro., above) and *Epigoni*, which dealt with the revenge attack on Thebes, and its destruction, by the children of the Seven, the 'Epigoni', or 'Successors' (mentioned already by Homer, *Il.* 4.406, and predicted by Teiresias in Soph. *Ant.* 1080f.). These myths provided rich material for the tragedians of the fifth century.

The historical city of Thebes did not remain, as Bacch. claimed, 'never sacked'; it was in fact destroyed in the mid-thirteenth century, in the upheavals which ultimately brought the mainland Bronze Age to a close, and this may well be the historical event behind the legend of the Epigoni. It may also be the reason why, in the 'Catalogue of Ships' (*Il.* 2.494f.), i.e. the list of the Greek allies who went to the Trojan War, only 'lower Thebes' is mentioned, not Thebes itself, which, as W. Leaf remarks in his commentary on *Iliad* 2.505: 'we are to regard as still lying waste after its destruction by the Epigoni'.

well-built A Homeric epithet (*eudmatos*), used of Troy (*Il.* 21.516) and its towers (*Il.* 16.700). Like the related 'god-built' (*theodmatos*, *Il.* 8.519), it may have arisen from the legend that the walls of Troy were built by Apollo and Poseidon (see note on 1.13-14), but it soon became a conventional honorific. Cf. 3.46, 5.149, 11.122 etc., where the same idea is expressed, albeit in different words.

57 gave birth to the hero Zeus carried Aigina off to the island in the Saronic Gulf which still bears her name; there she gave birth to Aiakos, ancestor of Aias and Achilles. The genealogy was as follows:

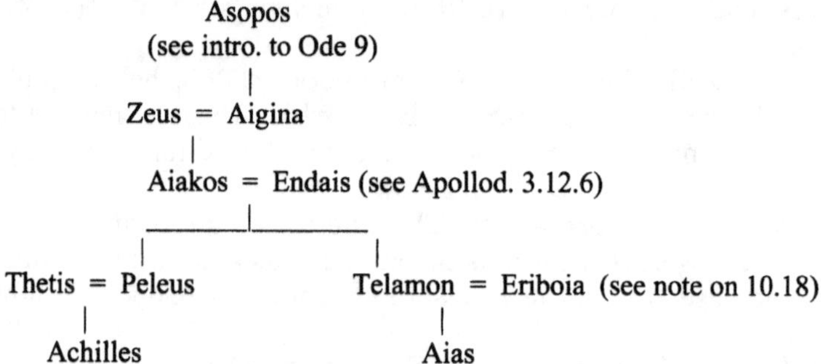

See also e.g. Pind. *Isth.* 8.23-6; also note on 46-7, above.

59-62 These broken and largely missing lines must have contained the names of two, and perhaps three, more of the daughters of Asopos. For line 61 Cleonai, Tanagra and Sinope are all possible; Jebb prefers the first of these on the ground that Bacch. would prefer a local reference (Cleonai is very close to Phleius in the northeastern Peloponnese); this is hardly a strong argument, given the prominence of Thebes. For line 62, Peirene, who gave her name to the sacred spring in Corinth, is almost certain, for metrical reasons.

62 with the braided crown (*helikostephanos*) The first part of the word (*heliko-*) means 'twisted', so here 'plaited' or 'braided'; it provides the first element of many compound adjectives, but this one occurs only here. Cf. Pindar's *helikampux* (*Paian* 3.15) = 'of the braided headband'.

63 and all the other The words form a summary conclusion to the mythic narrative, signalling the return to the victor and the celebration of his victory in 66-78.

64 the ... singing river A Homeric phrase (*Il.* 18.576; cf. 21.16). With this reference to Asopos the narrative returns to its departure point ('the dark swirling waters of Asopos', 39); the ring-composition also serves to mark the end of the myth and the transition to the victory celebration.

65 taken The notion of violence which often attaches to this word (here *e]damesan*) is certainly not present. See note on 1.116.

exalting The word (*arignotos*) literally means 'distinguished', 'renowned', but the usage is proleptic, i.e. it anticipates the result of the action described. Their union with gods confers honour on, and exalts, the daughters of Asopos. Cf. 52, above, and 11.41.

68 sound of pipes i.e. the *auloi* used in the celebration of the victory. See note on 2.12.

72 golden [Aphrodite] The name of the goddess does not appear on what survives of the papyrus here, but is certainly to be restored. She is called 'golden' also at 5.174. (The same adjective, however, is used of Artemis at 11.117, and of Io at 19.15.)

violet-haired Repeated at 3.71 (the Muses) and 17.37 (the Nereids). See note on 'violet-crowned', 3.3.

73 mother Aphrodite is described as 'mother of the Loves' (*Erotes*) also by Pindar (fr. 122.4); cf. Eur. *Med.* 844, where the *Erotes* escort the goddess.

unyielding Because Love is an irresistible power; cf. Hes. *Theog.* 120-2: 'Eros, who ... subdues the mind and shrewd counsel of gods and men'; also Soph. *Trach.* 441f.: 'whoever stands up against Eros ... is foolish, for he rules even the gods', and Soph. *Ant.* 781f.: 'Love unconquered in the fight ...'.

78 the song The description of the festivities at Phleius ends, appropriately, with reference to the present ode, so as to lead naturally into the generalization on the power of song to immortalize achievement. For a similarly elaborate treatment of this common theme cf. 13.59-66; also 1.181-4.

81 endless Bacch. uses this word (*atrutos*) also of the sky at 5.28; see the note there.

82 success The word used here is *kalon*, lit. = 'a good thing', 'a blessing', but the reference is, as usual, to athletic achievement. Cf. 101, below, and see notes on 1.146 and 3.96.

83 real praise With this subtle adjective Bacch. claims to be a genuine practitioner of the art of epinician poetry, and suggests that his poem will give to the victor and his victory the praise which is appropriate to them and which they deserve. For similar self-praise, see note on 5.9.

85 When men speak truly The emphasis on truth is a common motif in the poems, cf. 3.96, 5.188 and 8.19-21, with the notes there. These lines (85-7) repeat in general terms the idea that fame lives on in the poet's song, which had just before (79-82) been referred specifically to Automedes.

87 plaything The first appearance of this word (*athurma*) is *Il.* 15.363, where it describes a child's sandcastles at the beach. In the Homeric

Hymn to Hermes, it is used of the tortoise-shell, 'the delightful toy' from which the infant Hermes makes the lyre (Hom. Hymn 4.40), and the common element in subsequent usages seems to be 'that in which one takes delight', so Penelope gave 'delightful gifts' (*athurmata*) to the ungrateful Melantho (*Od.* 18.363), and at Bacch. 18.57 war and fighting are described as the *athurmata* of Ares, i.e. the things in which the War-god takes delight. Like the related verb *athurein* (= 'to play'; Hom. Hymn 4.485, Hom. Hymn 19.15, Pind. *Isth.* 4.43, etc.) the noun is commonly, but not exclusively, used in relation to music and song. Thus at Pind. *Pyth.* 5.23 the choir celebrating the victory is 'the delight (*athurma*) of Apollo', while Bacch. himself (Epigram 1.3) prays for success in the *athurmata* of the Muses, i.e. the contests of song and dance in which the Muses delight. So here 'the plaything of the Muses' can only mean the victory-song itself.

deep-girdled See note on 'lovely' at 1.116. The word is not on the surviving papyrus, but is a probable restoration.

88-96 These fragmentary lines seem to have contained a series of generalizations on the theme of the variety of human endeavour and the uncertainty of achievement, which stand as contrasting foil for the final praise, in concrete terms, of the victor, his homeland and his victory, in the last stanza of the ode. For the themes, cf. 10.36-47 and 14.8-18; see also Bundy's discussion of this common structure (which he calls 'the summary priamel'), Bundy, *Stud. Pind.*, p. 7f. There may also be an echo of the contrast between vain ambition and the worthy pursuit of honour, which was developed in the early part of the ode; see notes on 19, above, and 95-6, below.

89-90 God's will brings to light These two lines appear to be balanced by the contrasting couplet at the end of the antistrophe: only the gods know what is to come (89-90) – it is not given to men to see the future (95-6).

hidden in the dark of night For the thought cf. 10.45: 'the future brings to birth ends unforeseeable', and 16.33: 'the dark veil that covers things to come'.

95-6 to few men [is it given The papyrus is severely mutilated, but enough survives to secure the meaning. In saying 'few men', rather than the expected 'no man', Bacch. is perhaps allowing us to think of Amphiaraos, whose foreknowledge of the future has already been associated with foolish ambition. See intro., above, and notes on lines 12 and 18.

97-104 The punctuation, grammar and structure of this final Epode are woefully uncertain. There seems, however, to be a reference to the victory (97) and to the victor's home town of Phleius (98-9), followed by a twofold appeal to praise the victorious Automedes (101-2 and 103-4).

97 favour In such a context, the 'favour' (*charis*) of the god can only refer to victory in the Games. Cf. 3.97, where the same word is extended to the victory-ode itself, there described as a gift from the poet to the victor.

98 god-honoured Cf. 11.10 (of Metapontion). Here the town of Phleius is so called because the god has granted it the victory, through Automedes; perhaps also, however, the adjective is suggested by the town's traditional association with Dionysos.

city ... of Dionysos The connection between Phleius and the god of fertility and of wine must have been ancient, although this passage is the earliest evidence for it. In Ap. Rhod. *Argonaut.* 1.115f., Dionysos is father of Phleias, the hero who gave his name to the town; besides, Phleius depended on the production of wine for much of its economy and the god must have been central to its welfare. Paus. (2.13.6) tells us that the Phleiasians used to honour an image of a goat and adorn it with gold because they believed that the rising of the constellation 'Goat' could cause damage to the vines; and further (2.13.7) that there was an ancient sanctuary of Dionysos close to the 'Omphalos' (the centre, as they believed, of the Peloponnese). Perhaps also the distinction of Pratinas (see intro., above) as a writer of satyr-dramas (which were performed along with tragedies at the festivals of Dionysos) may point to the closeness of the association.

100 golden-sceptred (*chruseoskaptros*). Found only here. For adjectives compounded with 'gold-' see note on 4.1. In the *Iliad*, only Agamemnon (2.268) and the priest Chryses (1.15 = 1.374) carry sceptres of gold; here the reference is probably to a god, and it may belong to what follows in 101 – e.g. 'who wins success from golden-sceptred (?Zeus)'. This may be supported by the fact that the form of the adjective here echoes that used in line 1, above (*chrusalakatos* = 'of the golden distaff'), thus drawing attention to a significant ring-compositional parallel between the beginning and the end of the ode. As the Graces were invited to grant renown to the victor, so now he has enjoyed the favour of Zeus, manifested in his victory.

101 success The same word (*kalon*) as in 82 above; cf. note on 1.146.

ODE 10
FOR AN ATHENIAN
Stadion and Hippios, Isthmian Games

As is the case with Ode 9, nothing is known of the athlete celebrated in this ode, or of the occasion of his victory, other than the little that can be gathered from the poem itself. The victor's name, which must have stood somewhere in the sadly mutilated first strophe, does not survive; he was, however, from Athens (17) and belonged to the tribe Oineis in that city (18). The ode celebrates a double victory at the Isthmian Games (26-8) at which the victor won both the stadion (21-2) and the so-called 'hippios' (23-5). The ode does not in fact explicitly say that these two victories were

167

won at the same Isthmia, but this would be the natural assumption. It was not unusual for an athlete to win two, or even three, events at the same festival. Usually, and naturally, these victories would be in related disciplines, for example Pindar refers to Thessalos of Corinth who won both the stadion and the diaulos at the Pythian Games on the same day (Pind. *Ol.* 13.37). This was not always the case, however; Thessalos' son Xenophon, in whose honour the ode was written, had himself won both the stadion and the pentathlon (Pind. *Ol.* 13.30); cf. also Leonidas of Rhodes, who won twelve crowns at four Olympiads (Paus. 6.13.4).

The present ode was commissioned by the victor's brother-in-law (9), which may indicate that his father was dead and the victor himself still a boy. It is true that by the time of this ode he had achieved a total of ten victories in various Games (29-35) – which makes him the most successful athlete for whom Bacch. composed – but this need not undermine the suggestion that he was still competing in the 'boys' age class; a successful young athlete, aiming at a professional career, and travelling the circuit, as this one clearly did, could very soon accumulate so many wins. There is, however, nothing in the text which would confirm the athlete's age. Likewise, there is no evidence for the date of the Isthmian victories celebrated here.

A common organizational principle in the odes, as has often been remarked, is ring-composition, in which there is a balance, in theme and subject-matter, between the beginning and the end of the poem, and commonly also between the inner parts on either side of the central section. Here, unfortunately, the opening strophe is almost entirely missing, and the final epode is badly mutilated, so that it is impossible to discern what degree of balance, if any, may have existed between them. Apart from that, however, the structure of the poem appears to be straightforward and linear. It begins with an appeal to the personified 'Fame' to spread the renown of the victor around the world, and, perhaps, to give him rest from toil (1-8). This passes into a specific reference to the commission for the song which will declare the victor's excellence to the world (9-14); thus Bacch. represents himself and his song as the agent of 'Fame' in immortalizing the successful athlete. The general assertion that widespread fame will attend him is to be fulfilled by the particular activity of the poet. This in turn leads naturally to the celebration of the two Isthmian victories which are the main subject of the ode – first in general terms (15-20) and then in specific detail (21-8), with a vivid description of the moment of victory in each event – and this long victor-praise ends with the enumeration of earlier successes (29-35). A gnomic section follows, detailing various endeavours of men in the pursuit of renown (36-50); this is in the nature of a priamel (for this term see note on 3.86-92), the climax of which ('best is ... to be much-envied ...' 48-9) focuses attention once again on athletic success. This allows Bacch. to return at the end of the ode, via a transitional formula of a familiar type (51-2) to the festivities in

Athens and the victories which they celebrate. The complete ode included only two triads (56 lines) and there is no myth.

1 Fame Cf. 2.1, where Fame is urged to carry the news of Argeios' victory to Ceos. Similarly here, Fame is perhaps asked to spread the renown of the Athenian athlete throughout the world, as she visits 'the races of men' (1-2).

6 The name of the victor must have stood somewhere in this opening strophe. The most likely place for it seems to be here at the beginning of line 6, but the surviving traces of letters do not allow any plausible conjecture.

8 rest and ease It is impossible to discover the context of these words here, but for the idea that victory, and especially the song which celebrates it, can give respite from the cares and concerns of life, cf. 5.6f., where Bacch. urges Hieron to 'set aside your cares ... and direct your mind this way ...'. There is an interesting parallel also, in expression at least, at Ode 19.35-6 (the dithyramb for the Athenians): 'perhaps the Muses gave him rest from his cares'.

9 and now The structure of the opening of Ode 10 is very similar to that of Ode 11, and is found also in a number of Pindar's poems. It involves an invocation of a divinity, to which is attached a long explanatory description, which in turn is brought back to the present by the word 'now'. Thus in Ode 11 the invocation 'Goddess of Victory' (1) is followed by a long description of her role (2-9) and resumed by reference to the present victory 'now again' (9). Cf. Pind. *Ol.* 12. So here the words 'and now' mark what follows as the specific means and occasion whereby the general promise of universal renown for the victor contained in 1-8 will be made good.

your sister's husband The text is uncertain; perhaps 'his sister's husband' should be read (so Maehler, tentatively). In either case it must refer to the brother-in-law of the victor, who was presumably named somewhere in the preceding lines. The second person seems preferable, as it avoids what would otherwise be a very awkward shift; the whole of what follows in the antistrophe (11-20) is unquestionably in the second person.

10 sweet-voiced (*liguphthongos*) See note on 'screeching' at 5.22. The honey-bee is Bacch. himself, and the island is Ceos.

11-12 a deathless monument i.e. the victory song itself. For the song as a monument (*agalma*) which immortalizes the victor, cf. 1.184 and 5.4, with the notes there.

14 prowess Lit. = 'excellence' (*areta*); for the importance of *areta* see especially intro. to Ode 1, and note on 1.181-2.

who walk the earth The adjective used here (*epichthonios*) is one of the many Homeric epithets taken over by Bacch. and Pindar. See notes on 4.15-17 and 5.3. Cf. also Pind. *Ol.* 6.50, etc.

15 for the times when If this is right – there is a hole in the papyrus in line 15, which allows some uncertainty – it must be restricted to the two victories at this Isthmia which are the subject of the present ode (19). Maehler (vol. 2, p. 180), following an unpublished study by W.S. Barrett, finds this improbable, and consequently prefers a reference to the extent, rather than the frequency, of the honour, i.e. 'for the great glory which ... you brought to Athens ...' etc.

by the grace of See note on 6.9, where the same expression is used.

16 garlanding ... with flowers The reference is not to the victor's crown, which at this time at the Isthmia was made of wild celery, but to the ornamental wreaths of flowers worn by the victor and his friends at the celebration. See note on 1.158.

blond The epithet (*xanthos*) is surely literal here, rather than ornamental (cf. 9.24 and the note there); it would be very strange if Bacch. chose to describe his patron's hair as blond when it was not.

18 the sons of Oineus i.e. the members of the Athenian tribe Oineis, to which the victor evidently belonged. The ten tribes created in Athens by Cleisthenes as part of his democratic constitutional reforms (508 BC) were all named after local Attic heroes, except Aiantis, which took its name from the Salaminian Aias (Hdt. 5.66.2). But even Aias had a connection with Athens through his mother. Pindar (*Nem.* 5.14f.) relates how Peleus and Telamon, sons of Aiakos (cf. note on 9.57) were obliged to leave Aigina because of the murder of their half-brother Phokos. Peleus went to Phthia in Thessaly, and Telamon to Salamis, where he married Eriboia of Athens, Aias' mother (Diod. 4.72.6-7; cf. Ode 13.103). The Oineus named here was the son of Pandion, the legendary king of Athens (Paus. 1.5.2), but nothing further is known of him. He is not to be confused with Oineus of Calydon, father of Meleager and Deianeira by his first wife Althaia (see Ode 5), and of Tudeus, father of Diomedes, by his second, Periboia (see note on 11.62).

19 far-famed A common honorific epithet; cf. 5.119 (the palace of Meleager's father Oineus), 9.9 (the Labours of Herakles) and 11.80 (the heroes who dwelt in Tiryns).

21 the stadion's finishing line The *stadion* was originally a unit of length, a little under 200 metres, with minor local variations. The word then came to designate a race of that length, and finally the arena in which the race was held (hence the English word 'stadium'). Here, probably, the race is meant.

Lines 21-2 vividly depict the athlete's moment of glory at the end of the stadion race, while 23-5 show him crossing the line in the 'hippios' with such speed that the impetus takes him into the crowd of spectators behind the line. It is widely assumed that these two events were consecutive, but this is not actually stated. The exact order of events in the Isthmia is unknown. For Bacch.'s fondness for this kind of vivid detail, see esp. the notes on 3.9, 9.31 and 9.35.

23 **with oil** More exactly, no doubt, a mixture of oil, sweat and dust.

25 **the four-length course** i.e. the 'hippios', a middle-distance race of *c.* 800 m. which was part of the programme at the Isthmian and Nemean Games only (see Paus. 6.16.4; cf. also Plato *Laws* 833B and D, where it is called 'ephippios'). The race was run over four lengths of the stadium, with a 180-degree turn at each end. (cf. Eur. *El.* 824-5: 'more quickly than a "hippios" runner completed the double diaulos'; also Paus. 6.16.4). Bacch. is not strictly accurate here; he uses an expression which literally means 'the course with four turns', even though the 'hippios' involved only three turns; clearly he has in mind the four stadion-lengths of the race. For a similar inaccuracy cf. Pind. *Ol.* 3.33. The four-horse chariot-race was run over twelve lengths of the hippodrome (cf. *Ol.* 2.50 and *Pyth.* 5.33, see also the general introduction) but Pindar here speaks of 'the turning-post twelve times rounded' (*dodekagnampton terma*) when of course the race required only eleven turns. The name 'hippios' should have something to do with horses; according to E.N. Gardiner (*Athletics of the Ancient World*, p. 136 (Oxford, 1930) the race was so called because 'the length of the hippodrome' (i.e. the race-course for horses) 'was twice that of the stadium'. It is not clear to me, however, why this ratio should have any significance. (See further H.M. Lee, 'Pindar, *Ol.* 3,33-34: The Twelve-Turned Terma', *AJPh* 107 (1986), pp. 162-74, esp. 164 n. 6.) In any case, neither at the Isthmus nor at Nemea – the only two sanctuaries at which the hippios race was held, has the site, and therefore the length, of the hippodrome been identified. (See e.g. P. Valavanis, *Games and Sanctuaries in Ancient Greece*, pp. 293 and 312.)

26 **twice** i.e. after each of these two races.
   the heralds The word (*prophetes*) properly means 'one who interprets the will of the gods'; it is used (here only) in the sense of 'herald', appropriately, since the victory is seen as a gift of, and determined by, the gods.

29-35 These lines list the Athenian athlete's earlier victories, with the most important, at the panhellenic Nemean Games, heading the list. Many smaller city-states around Greece had their own religious festivals, and most of these included athletic competition. The places named are clustered in the northeastern corner of the Peloponnese (Nemea, Argos, Sicyon, Pellene) or otherwise within easy reach of Athens (Thebes, Aigina, Euboea). Perhaps this young athlete (see intro., above) had not yet competed so far from home as Delphi or Olympia. (See M. Golden, *Sport and Society in Ancient Greece*, pp. 107-8, on the preponderance of local athletes at many festivals, especially in 'boys' events.)

29 **by the altar of Zeus** The Nemean Games, like the Olympic, were dedicated to Zeus. The stadium at Nemea, in the Hellenistic period at

least, was at a considerable distance from the sanctuary, and, therefore, from the altar. The earlier stadium may have been closer, though it has not been found (see S.G. Miller, *Nemea: A Guide to the Site and Museum*, also D.G. Romano, 'The Early Stadium at Nemea', *Hesperia*, 46 (1977), pp. 27-31). In any case the phrase need not be taken to indicate that the race was run close to the altar; the reference is probably to the place where the victor was announced and received his crown.

30 Thebes There is a very similar list of victories in minor festivals in Pindar (*Ol.* 13.107f.) There Thebes is named after Argos, Pellene before Sicyon, and Euboea is at the end. If there was a ranking order for the minors, it was not rigidly observed. Cf. also Pind. *Ol.* 7.83f.

31 the dancing-grounds See note on 5.104.

32 by god's will The phrase (*kat' aisan*) is Homeric (*Il.* 10.445, etc.) and literally means 'in accordance with destiny', i.e. 'fitly', 'properly'. The athlete's prowess has won its proper reward in victory. The phrase belongs not to Sicyon alone, but to all the victories listed.

34 rich corn-lands The text is uncertain here, but this seems the likeliest restoration. The word (*poluleios*) is used by Homer (*Il.* 5.613, of Paisos) and by Hesiod (fr. 240.1, of Dodone).

35 the sacred island There was no special reason to call Aigina 'sacred', and the adjective is simply honorific and decorative (cf. 5.12 and 2.2, with the notes there). Here however, it picks up the 'holy altar' of line 29, thus providing a neat structural balance to this catalogue of minor victories. But see also note on 12.6.

36f. These lines represent the most elaborate expression in Bacch. of a motif which recurs at 9.88f. and 14.7f., where the phraseology is remarkably similar. They introduce the following priamel (see intro., above) and establish its point of reference. The various fields of human endeavour outlined in the following lines have as their common element the quest for renown (37). The priamel is suggested by, and arises directly out of, the preceding recital of victories whereby the Athenian athlete has won renown for himself and his city (16-20), and it returns to this theme in general terms at the end (48-9). There is thus a ring-compositional structure at work: the athlete has won renown by his victories; men seek renown in various ways; and the best of these is athletic success. The priamel, then, ends by focussing attention once again on the successful athlete, and is, as always, an elaborate device to enhance the victor's praise.

37 renown The relevance of the priamel to the athlete is made clear by the repetition of this word (*doxa*) from line 18.

clear The word (*arignotos*) recurs at 5.30; also 9.65, where however, the usage is different; see note on 'exalting' there.

38f. Bacch. is here once again drawing on Solon's discussion of the various lifestyles of mankind (Solon 13.43f.). Cf. 1.169f. and the note there. Solon lists six different activities whereby men seek to make a living, although as the poem progresses, the emphasis shifts from the profit-motif to the uncertainty of the outcome of any human endeavour. First in Solon's list is the merchant/seafarer (13.43-6), followed by the farmer (47-8), the craftsman (49-50), the poet (51-2), the prophet (53-6) and the doctor (57-62). Bacch. uses three of these as terms of his priamel; first is 'the clever man', combining Solon's poet and prophet (38-41); at the end is the farmer (43-4), while in the middle stands the lover (42), not represented in Solon's list. But in Bacch. the common element is not profit, as in Solon, but rather the quest for renown. Fame may be gained in any of men's chosen fields, but for Bacch. the ultimate is the renown to be won through success in the Games.

countless For the expression cf. 14.8.

39 the Graces' gift i.e. poetic skill; cf. 1.151, where the same words are used; see also note on 5.11.

40 skill in prophecy A slight variation of the Homeric 'well-skilled in prophecy' (*Il.* 6.438).

41 grows strong with ... hope Perhaps the idea is that such a person may bask in the knowledge that the gods are on his side, for poetry is the gift of the Muses (and the Graces), while prophecy is the gift of Apollo; cf. 13.220-2. Cf. also 1.163-5, where generosity to the gods gives 'hope of a greater glory'.

42 bends his ... bow at boys It is often claimed that in ancient Greece homosexual behaviour was widespread, open and accepted. Whatever may be the truth of this – Aristophanes cheerfully ridicules his entire Athenian audience as being 'wide-arsed' (*euruproktoi, Clouds*, 1088f.) – it seems likely that in practice it was largely confined to the upper classes of society. It is not likely that the ordinary farmer or artisan had the leisure or the financial resources required to engage in the sort of sophisticated erotic dilettantism to which Bacch. alludes here. On the other hand, the values of aristocratic society (see 14, above, and the intro. to Ode 1) found expression not only in the pursuit of *areta* (excellence) in the quasi-military competitiveness of the Games, but in more peaceful arts also, in music, dance, and the love of all things beautiful. Thus the gymnasium and the wrestling-school, where the young men trained, provided the leisured classes with a fertile field for the pursuit of these erotic encounters. (See K.J. Dover, *Greek Homosexuality*, London 1978; also W.K. Lacey, *The Family in Classical Greece*, London 1968, pp. 157-8.)

The image of the arrow of love piercing the heart of the beloved is now a worn-out cliché, but it was not in Bacch.'s time. Here the lover himself shoots the arrows, as in Pind. *Isth.* 2.1-4; sometimes Eros is the archer (Eur. *Troad.* 255, Eur. *Iph. Aul.* 548, etc.) or Aphrodite herself (Pind. *Pyth.* 4.213; cf. Eur. *Hipp.* 530-1, where Eros shoots the arrows of Aphrodite). Among the 'arrows' which the lover shoots to overcome his beloved, Bacch. would certainly include love-songs, a very popular genre since the time of Anacreon and Ibycos (both sixth century), alluded to by Pindar (*Isth.* 2.1f.): 'the men of old ... used to shoot ... their love-songs at young boys', and by Bacch. himself (fr. 4.80), where the joys of peace include 'banquets and love-songs for boys'.

bends his bow The phrase is Homeric, where it is used literally of warriors (*Il.* 5.97, 11.370, etc.).

artful The word (*poikilos*) literally means 'many-coloured' and is used frequently in Homer of arms and armour in the sense 'elaborately-' or 'cunningly-wrought' (*Il.* 4.432, etc.); the metaphor seems appropriate here in suggesting the wiliness required to overcome youthful resistance, whether real or pretended. Cf. 11.33.

43 the heart swells i.e. they take pride in their success in these areas. Cf. 1.162 (where the phrase is almost identical) and the note there.

ploughed lands The word here (*erga* = 'works') is more general in its literal meaning; it is, however, common in Homer in the sense 'tilled land' (*Il.* 12.283, 16.392, *Od.* 14.344, etc.) and occurs in this meaning also in the title of Hesiod's farming manual *Works and Days*. Here the business of farming is divided into its two major areas, tillage and herding.

45 ends unforeseeable Cf. 9.89-90. Here chance (*tucha*, 46) is the determining factor, rather than god's will (9.89). The *gnome* (also taken over from Solon, 13.65-6.; see note on 38f., above) marks the end of the priamel and introduces its climax: 'the future is unknown; success in any human endeavour is uncertain, but the surest way is ...'.

46 weighs down the scale For the image of the scale as a determinant of human fortunes, see note on 4.11-13.

48 much-envied (*poluzelotos*) One of Bacch.'s favourite adjectives. Apart from its use as an honorific for the legendary river-god Asopos (9.45; cf. the related word *poluzelos* used of Proitos, 11.61) the word is in Bacch. closely associated with athletic success, e.g. 7.10, where the victor is 'renowned among men and envied', and 1.184, where victory leaves 'an enviable monument of renown' (see notes on 1.181-2, 1.184, 7.10 and 9.45). These passages, together with the emphasis on 'renown' in this priamel (see notes on 36f. and 37, above) make it impossible, in my view, not to see a generalized reference to the victor's success in these lines. Maehler (vol. 2, pp. 191-2, in his note on 47-8) argues otherwise, but his interpretation ('men seek renown in various ways – the best thing is for a man, whatever his chosen field of endeavour, to be successful and so be envied') seems to me to be seriously anti-climactic. For the desirability of envy, cf. also 5.53.

49-50 wealth ... makes the useless useful A more succinct statement of themes presented at 1.161f. Wealth is no measure of a man's true worth, but may be used for good, even by the unworthy. See intro. to Ode 1.

51 **Why** ... **do I drive my song** For the metaphor cf. 5.176-7, and the notes there. The rhetorical question reflects the poet's 'sense of propriety in determining the content and proportions of the song' (Bundy, *Stud. Pind.*, p. 74) so as to avoid embarrassment to the victor or tedium in the audience. Knowing when to stop is as important as knowing what to say. The conventional device marks the end of the gnomic section, as at 5.176-7 it marks the end of the mythic narrative, and in both instances signals the return to the victor-praise.

52 **good cheer** (*euphrosuna*) i.e. the victory revel; cf. 11.11. For the use of this abstract word in the concrete sense, see Bundy, *Stud. Pind.*, p. 2.

54 **pipes** (*auloi*) The standard instrument used in the celebrations; cf. 2.12, with the note there, and 9.68.

ODE 11
FOR ALEXIDAMOS OF METAPONTION
Boys' Wrestling, Pythian Games

The background

In the latter part of the eighth century BC, there began what eventually became a huge shift of the Greek population from the mainland to new settlements around the Mediterranean. Encouraged by favourable reports from early adventurers, seafarers and traders, and driven by a variety of forces, such as the need to find new agricultural land for a growing population, the desire to establish new trading outposts, or to remove political dissidents, many Greek cities began to send out large contingents of their citizens to establish new settlements overseas. The movement gathered momentum rapidly, and the end of the seventh century saw Greek colonies established throughout the Mediterranean and beyond, as far afield as Massilia (Marseilles) in the south of France and Olbia and Trapezus (Trabzon) on the north and south shores, respectively, of the Black Sea. (See the useful map in Boardman, Griffin and Murray, *Greece and the Hellenistic World* (Oxford, 1986), pp. 18-19; also A.R. Burn, *The Lyric Age of Greece* (London, 1960) p. 69f., and A.G. Woodhead, *The Greeks in the West* (London, 1962) esp. p. 63.) The fertile lands of Sicily and the south of Italy were particularly attractive to the colonizers – Syracuse, founded by Corinth in 733 BC, was one of the earliest settlements in this region, and Sparta, after the Messenian War, established its only colony at Taras (Taranto) on the heel of Italy (*c.* 706 BC) The area of mainland Greece known as Achaia, in the north of the Peloponnese, sandwiched as it was between the Corinthian Gulf and the mountains of Arcadia to the south, and consequently without sufficient land to accommodate an expanding population, became a major player in the colonization movement, and the Achaians too turned their eyes to the south of Italy, founding a number of colonies along the coast of the Gulf of Taranto. One of these was Metapontion, home of the young athlete celebrated in Ode 11.

The term 'colony' is perhaps misleading, for these new settlements were from the beginning largely independent of their mother cities. Syracuse, for example, went on to become an important economic, political and military force in Sicily in its own right. Metapontion too prospered as a result of its location on the rich coastal plain of Lucania, although it remained an agricultural community – its later coinage featured an ear of corn – and did not play an important role in the history of the region. What these western colonies shared, however, was a keen sense of their Hellenic origins and culture, and they vigorously asserted their common Hellenism by taking part wherever possible in the religious life of the mainland, sending gifts and dedications to the great sanctuaries such as Olympia and Delphi, and competing in the panhellenic Games. Of the twelve 'Treasuries' which stood at Olympia between the temple of Hera and the stadium, five were dedicated by colonies in the west, including Syracuse and Metapontion, and only two by mainland Greek cities (Sicyon and Megara); see H-V. Herrmann, *Olympia – Heiligtum und Wettkampfstaette*, Munich 1972, esp. pp. 98-9. Bacch. himself in Ode 3 described the unsurpassed generosity of Hieron of Syracuse to Apollo's sanctuary at Delphi. Not all the westerners, however, were as rich and powerful as Hieron. The family of Alexidamos must have been reasonably well-to-do – they could after all afford to send the boy, with presumably at least a trainer and a guardian, all the way to Delphi – but they remain otherwise unknown. This must have created something of a problem for Bacch. – where could he find material with which to honour Alexidamos, scion of a prosperous but undistinguished family, from a prosperous but undistinguished city? Bacch. answered this problem in a unique way, by creative treatment of the myth.

The myth

The story which occupies the greater part of Ode 11 involves the daughters of Proitos, king of Argos, who in their youthful folly insulted the goddess Hera. In punishment Hera drove them from their home, to wander in madness for a year, until finally their father, after ritual purification, prayed to Artemis to intervene. Artemis persuaded Hera to release the girls from their madness, and in gratitude Proitos set up a sanctuary in her honour, instituting sacrifices and a festival, and so establishing the cult of Artemis at Lousoi in Arcadia.

There were essentially two versions of this story, each with some variation of detail. In one, the madness was inflicted upon the women of Argos generally (or the daughters of Proitos only – Hes. fr. 131, in Apollod. 2.2.2) by Dionysos, because they refused to accept his divinity. This is the version related at length in Hdt. 9.34; it is found also in Diod. (4.68.4),

Apollod. (1.9.11f.) and Paus. (2.18.4). In this version the girls are cured of their madness by the prophet and healer Melampous, whom, as Herodotos tells it, the Argives fetched from Pylos for the purpose, and the same story may underlie Hes. fr. 37, where Proitos, Melampous and his brother Bias, and 'healing through the arts of prophecy' are mentioned, although the context there is very uncertain.

At *Od.* 15.225f. Homer introduces a new character, Theoklymenos, who is descended from Melampous, and in a long digression obliquely relates how it came about that Melampous left his home in Pylos to live in Argos. Homer unfortunately does not allude to Proitos and his daughters at all, but the ancient commentator on this passage quotes at length from Pherekydes (fifth-century BC historian) who thus becomes our major source for the other version of the legend (Pherek. *FGH* 3 F114 = *schol.* MV on *Od.* 15.225). According to Pherekydes, the daughters of Proitos, king of Argos, were driven mad, not by Dionysos, but by Hera, as punishment for boasting that their father's house surpassed her temple in wealth. The girls were then eventually released from their madness after ten years, in Argos, again by Melampous. The same version appears in the fifth-century BC historian Akusilaos (quoted in Apollod. 2.2.2 = *FGH* 2 F28) who attributes the girls' madness to their disparaging the ancient image of Hera, without, however, mentioning the manner of their healing. This too is the version followed by Bacch. in Ode 11, with some mostly insignificant variations. For example, in Bacch. the daughters of Proitos are not merely driven mad by Hera, but must leave their home; their home is Tiryns, not Argos, and the madness lasts one year, not ten. But the one significant change which Bacch. has introduced is that the healing of the maddened girls is effected, not by Melampous, but by Artemis.

The Alexandrian poet Callimachos, writing some two hundred years after Bacch., also attributes the release of the daughters of Proitos from their madness to Artemis, and mentions the fact that Proitos, in gratitude, built a temple to the goddess at Lousoi in Arcadia, but provides no further detail (Call. Hymn 3.235-6). It is very unlikely that Callimachos was directly imitating Bacchylides; much more probable is that he was drawing on local legend, perhaps related in the *Phoronis*, a post-Homeric epic poem dealing with the history of the Argolid. (For the familiarity of the Alexandrians with obscure local legends, see intro. to Ode 1, and note on 1.127.) However that may be, Bacch. remains the first writer, in either the Dionysiac or the Heran version of the legend, to exclude Melampous from the story, and to put Artemis as healer in his place. The advantage of this change for Bacch.'s encomiastic purposes is clear.

Archaeology has revealed a substantial sanctuary of Artemis close to the ancient city of Metapontion, which was active from the seventh century to the end of the fourth century BC (see note on line 120). The large number of terracotta animal figurines found there testifies to the importance of Artemis to this rural and agricultural community. She was clearly central to the spiritual and cultural life of the town, and Bacch. makes her central to his poem. By substituting Artemis for Melampous in his narrative of the myth, Bacch. provides himself with an opportunity to trace the Metapontine cult of Artemis back to Lousoi in Arcadia, where it was established by Proitos in gratitude for the release of his daughters from their madness, and from where it was brought to Metapontion by the Achaians. (The sanctuary at Metapontion seems to have been used especially for rituals of purification and healing, which would connect it closely with the cult at Lousoi (see note on line 97), and confirm Bacch.'s version of events, that Artemis was brought from Lousoi to Metapontion.) In this way Bacch. is able to honour Metapontion through its direct association with the world of legend and the heroes.

This association is further reinforced by a kind of 'sleight-of-hand' on the part of Bacchylides. The cult of Artemis was no doubt brought to Metapontion by the historical Achaians from the Peloponnese who established the colony in the seventh century. But in Homer the term 'Achaians' is used collectively for all the Greeks who fought at Troy, and Bacch. (113f.) deliberately confuses the two meanings of the name, thus suggesting that the colony was founded by Homeric heroes in the course of their wanderings after the Trojan War (see notes on 114 and 122, below).

Finally, the use of Artemis in the myth allows Bacch. to draw a parallel between the daughters of Proitos and the victor Alexidamos, who two years earlier had been robbed of a victory at Olympia (see 24f.). Now Artemis has given him the victory at Delphi; she has cured his earlier disappointment, even as she cured the daughters of Proitos, so that Alexidamos himself is drawn into the world of the myth and honoured by this parallel. He too, like the daughters of Proitos, has enjoyed the special favour of Artemis.

The poem

Ode 11 falls into three major sections, the opening victor-praise (1-39), the myth (40-112) and the conclusion (113-26). Each of these sections is delimited and separated from the next by clear verbal echoes, while at the same time the transitions between the sections are easy and natural, creating a fluid continuity for the poem as a whole. Ring-composition is, again, the major structural principle.

The poem opens with the invocation of the personified goddess of victory, Nika, who is responsible for the celebrations which the young victor is presently enjoying (1-12). This leads naturally into the more specific victor-praise, in which Bacch. mentions the victor's family, the place of victory (Delphi) and its god (Apollo), the celebration and finally, the victor himself, Alexidamos (13-23), thus fulfilling all the requirements of the commission. The glory of the present victory is then further enhanced by comparison with a previous occasion, at Olympia two years earlier, when Alexidamos failed to achieve a victory which should have been his (24-36). There are, again, several verbal echoes which place these two occasions in close relation (for details see note on 25f., below), so that the earlier failure – perhaps due to some god (34) – heightens by contrast the value of the present success – the gift of Artemis (37-9).

The mention of the goddess leads naturally into the mythic narrative (40-112), describing the foundation of her cult at Lousoi. The story begins at its end, with the building of the altar by Proitos and his daughters (40-1) and it returns to this point at the end (110-12). Within this frame Bacch. recounts the story of the girls' insolence and punishment, the year-long wandering and their final release from their suffering, while at the centre of this narrative, and interrupting it, stands a seemingly unconnected episode – the quarrel between the brothers Proitos and Akrisios, which was the occasion for Proitos and his daughters to leave Argos to live in Tiryns. But although this episode may seem irrelevant, it is in the poem for a purpose. The sequence of events – crisis / prayer / divine intervention / release (64-76) – exactly parallels the fortunes of the daughters of Proitos (85-109), and so draws attention to the importance of this motif, which in turn illuminates the fortune of the victor also (see above). There is in fact throughout the mythic narrative a complex pattern of parallels and verbal echoes which illuminates both the structure and the themes of the ode.

The final section of the ode (113-26) describes how the cult of Artemis was brought to Metapontion by the Achaians. In this way Bacch. ties the myth to the victor's city, thus resuming his encomiastic programme and honouring Metapontion through this association with Homer's Achaians (see above), while Alexidamos himself is honoured once more, at the end, by the oblique suggestion that the prowess of his victory continues the tradition of valour established by these heroic ancestors.

1 **Goddess of Victory** For the personification cf. 3.6, 5.35, and 6.9, with the notes there, and for a similar opening invocation cf. 'Fame, giver of proud gifts', 2.1.
   whose gifts are sweet The adjective (*glukudoros*) recurs at 3.1 (of Klio) and at 5.5 (of the Muses' gift); see the notes there.
3 **high-throned** (*hupsizugos*) A common Homeric epithet for Zeus, literally = 'high-benched', a nautical metaphor from the helmsman of a ship. See note on 1.155, where, uniquely, the word is used of Poseidon. The fragmentary lines 2-3 seem to have described in general terms the function allotted to Victory by Zeus, which is then detailed more specifically in lines 4f.
4 **standing at the side of Zeus** Nika (Victory) was the child of Styx and Pallas; her siblings were Zelos (Emulation), Kratos (Strength) and Bia (Force). In gratitude for their assistance in his battle against the Titans, Zeus honoured and rewarded the children by ordaining that they should live forever at his side (Hes. *Theog.* 383f.). Their mother however, although she was differently honoured (see on 9, below),

became 'the hateful river', who dwelt far apart from the gods (Hes. *Theog.* 775-7).

5 rich in gold A typical decorative adjective (*poluchrusos*), applied to Mycenae (*Il.* 11.16) and to Delphi (Soph. *OT* 151, Pind. *Pyth.* 6.8) where it is literally suitable. Jebb (p. 321, note on 4f.) objects that the word is too material for Olympus, but is well answered by Maehler (vol. 2, p. 207) who points to several passages (including *Il.* 4.1-2, Pind. *Nem.* 10.88 and *Isth.* 4.67) which describe the palace of the gods as golden.

6 the end of excellence For the importance of 'excellence' (*areta*) in the value-system of the aristocratic society for which Bacch. wrote, see intro. to Ode 1. For Bacch. *areta* especially means prowess in athletic pursuits, and the proper 'end of excellence' is success in the Games (see note on 1.181-2). This is what Nika determines, both for gods and men (line 7). In the divine sphere this is not appropriate at all, for the gods do not, ordinarily, take part in athletic contests; hence the phrase must mean something more general, such as 'the outcome of endeavour', and may refer to the assistance given in the battle against the Titans. (Alternatively, 'for immortals' may have been added simply for the sake of a rhetorical balance with 'for men'; cf. note on 34, below.) In the human sphere, however, the 'end of excellence' is exactly what Nika determines, and the expression thus anticipates her role in overseeing the victory of Alexidamos as the outcome of his prowess (8f.).

8 long-haired Although the image is common-place, the word (*bathuplokamos*) is new; evidently coined by Bacch., it is not found elsewhere until the Hellenistic period, when it is imitated by Ap. Rhod. (*Argonaut.* 1.742).

9 Styx, who judges straight For her help against the Titans (see note on 4, above), Styx too was honoured by Zeus, who appointed her to be 'the great oath of the gods' (Hes. *Theog.* 400). Henceforth, in disputes between the gods, they were obliged to swear by the water of Styx, and she would punish the perjurer (Hes. *Theog.* 782f.). Cf. *Il.* 15.37f., where Hera swears by 'the water of Styx, which is the greatest and most fearsome oath for the blessed gods', and the oath of Leto to Delos (Hom. Hymn 3.85-86) where exactly the same words are used. Bacch. here slightly extends the Hesiodic role of Styx from punisher to judge; further, while the adjective used here ('straight-judging', *orthodikos*) is actually applied to the mother, Styx, the meaning seems to flow on to the daughter Nika, so as to suggest that the present victory represents the right and proper decision, in contrast to the faulty decision at Olympia two years before. See note on 27, below.

now again The phrase brings the generality of the opening invocation back to the specifics of the immediate occasion. See note on 10.9 for this common stylistic device.

10 by your favour The preposition used here (*hekati*) expresses the goodwill, grace and favour of a divinity, especially, in Bacch., Victory. See notes on 1.118 and 6.9.

god-honoured A typically general honorific adjective in praise of the victor's city, cf. 9.98. Here, however, it is picked up by the more fully developed city-praise at the end of the ode (115f.) and so anticipates the role of Artemis in the city's, and the victor's, fortunes.

11 **festal cheer** Cf. 10.53, where the same word (*euphrosuna*) is used. For Bacch.'s fondness for vivid detail in presenting the celebration of the victory, cf. 18-20, below; also 3.15-16.

12 **strong-limbed** (*euguios*) One of several adjectives compounded from *guia* (= limbs) and coined by Bacch. See note on 9.38. Pindar too uses similar epithets (*Ol.* 9.111, *Nem.* 9.24, *Pyth.* 8.37, etc.) but usually metaphorically; in Bacch. the literal usage points to his admiration of physical perfection.

14 **admirable** i.e. much-admired (*thaetos*); the word recurs at 13.115 (of Ilion).

15 From the celebrations in Metapontion, Bacch. turns to the celebration in Delphi after the victory, and finally to the victory itself.
lovely The word (*bathuzonos*) literally means 'deep-girdled', and is merely a conventional descriptor for female beauty, whether human or divine. See 5.11 and note on 1.116.
Leto's son i.e. Apollo, cf. 3.39; the birth of Apollo and Artemis to Leto is briefly noted in Hes. *Theog.* 918-20.

16 **god born on Delos** Cf. 3.58, with the note there; for the full story of the birth of Apollo to Leto on the rocky and inhospitable island of Delos, see Hom. Hymn 3 (to Delian Apollo).
welcomed The same verb (*dekto*) is used in the list of victories at 10.31f. ('Thebes welcomed him ...'). So here 'Apollo welcomed him with gracious glance' means that the god favoured him with victory in his Games.

17 **with gracious glance** The adjective echoes 'be gracious' (8, above), thus connecting the invocation of Nika to the narrative of the victory.

18 **crowns of flowers fell** The reference is to the *phullobolia*, the custom of throwing garlands of flowers at the feet of the victorious athlete. Cf. Pind. *Pyth.* 9.123-4, and see note on 1.158. At 4.10 Bacch. uses the image metaphorically, of his scattering songs before the victor, as does Pindar, *Pyth.* 8.57.

19 **the plain of Kirrha** i.e. the coastal plain below Delphi. See note on 4.16.

20 **Alexidamos** The victor-praise finally arrives at its climax with the victor's name and a brief description of his prowess. Cf. 9.26, and the note there.

22 **at least** The restriction probably anticipates the contrast with the failure at Olympia, which Bacch. is about to relate; i.e. 'success may have eluded him at Olympia, but at Delphi at least he was victorious'.

the sun did not see him The sentence combines two conventional stylistic devices: the witnessing-motif (cf. 5.38 and the note there) and a negative form of expression, which provides variety to, and invigorates, the assertion of prowess. Cf. 5.13 5: 'never yet was he (Pherenikos) stained by the dust of horses in front'.

24 I will say this The use of the first person future of verbs meaning 'to assert', 'to claim', 'to boast', etc., is a common stylistic device of epinician poetry. Cf. 8.20: 'I shall make this boast'; Pind. *Ol.* 6.21: 'I will bear witness'; *Ol.* 11.14: 'I will sing', etc.; for additional examples and discussion see Bundy, *Stud. Pind.*, p. 21f. The device is designed to emphasize the assertion which follows, to underscore its veracity and to forestall scepticism from the audience. It is therefore commonly used to introduce particularly bold assertions, as at 8.20: 'no one has won more victories than Liparion ...'. So here, it introduces the claim that Alexidamos should have been declared the winner at Olympia, and would have been, if justice had been done. See also note on 8.19-21.

25f.   The description of the earlier failure at Olympia is framed by balanced references to the occasion of the present success at Delphi: 'That day ...' (23) is picked up by 'But now ...' (37). This structure places the two events in close relation, and this is highlighted by several close verbal parallels: 'many crowns of flowers fell' (18) is recalled by 'he would ... have crowned his hair' (27-8); there is emphasis in each case on the place of the event: 'on the plain of Kirrha' (19) balances 'on the soil of holy Pelops' (25), and on the prowess of the athlete: at Delphi he was not 'thrown to the ground' (23), while at Olympia 'many a boy he brought to the ground' (32, although the text is conjectural there). In the end these similarities serve only to highlight the fundamental difference between the two events: one led to failure, while the other ended in success. The missed victory serves the victor-praise in two ways; to come close to a victory at Olympia is praiseworthy in itself, but more importantly it stands as foil for the present victory, enhancing its glory by contrast. The Pythian Games were held in the third year of each Olympiad, by Greek inclusive counting (see note on 9.23), or, as we would say, two years after the Olympic Games. Alexidamos' failure presumably occurred at the immediately preceding Olympics, two years earlier.

25 on the ... soil of ... Pelops i.e. at Olympia. For the connection of Pelops with Olympia, see notes on 7.3-5 and 8.32. Cf. also 5.181.
hallowed Because Olympia was home to a major sanctuary of Zeus. See note on 5.12.

26 by Alpheos' ... stream Another standard periphrasis for Olympia; see note on 6.3.

27 had not ... straight justice been diverted The words 'straight justice' (*ortha dika*) here are a clear echo of 'Styx who judges straight' (*orthodikos*) in line 9, so that this too becomes part of the pattern of contrast between the earlier failure and the present success. The expression also recalls the only other reference to a victory missed in Bacch., when Hieron was robbed of success at the Pythia. See intro. to Ode 4 and note on 4.11-13. In discussing that passage I have argued (*LCM* 19 (1994), pp. 20-1) that divine responsibility for the wrong decision must be excluded, and that is certainly the case here also, in spite of line 34. Bacch. in fact says: 'if someone had not diverted the pathway of ... justice', which indicates human frailty, whether error or corruption, even more directly than my translation would suggest. See also note on 34, below.

29 **the silvery olive** The wreath which was the victor's prize at Olympia. For a very similar expression cf. 8.31 and the note there; for the prizes at the other panhellenic Games, see the general introduction.
that welcomes all i.e. the prize is open to all competitors; so Jebb, rightly (p. 323, note on 28f.). Jebb compares similar expressions in Pindar (*Ol.* 6.63 and 3.18) and in Soph. (fr. 328).

30 **and come** The triumphant return of the athlete to his home is the climax to his achievement; cf. 5.184 and 9.39.
calf-rearing Perhaps suggested by the fact that Metapontion was surrounded by, and depended on, rich farmland (see intro, above).

31 **of the lovely dance** The same word (*kallichoros*) is used of Calydon at 5.104; see the note there. Here too it suggests a community at peace, able to turn its attention to religious and cultural pursuits. Cf. also 10.31: 'the broad dancing-grounds of Argos'.

32 **he brought [to the ground]** The text is very uncertain here, but this restoration is at least supported by 9.37-8: 'throwing strong-limbed bodies to the ground', where the same verb (*pelazein*) is used.

33 **subtle** The word (*poikilos*), lit. = 'many-coloured', 'variegated', is commonly metaphorical. See note on 'artful' at 10.42.

34 **either a god was to blame** This is not to be taken at face value. The motif of divine intervention in human competition goes back as a literary device (as most things do) to Homer. In the chariot-race held as part of the Funeral Games in honour of Patroklos (*Il.* 23.362f.) Athena allowed her favourite Diomedes to win by smashing the yoke of the chariot of Eumelos, the front-runner (23.392f.). Bacch. may be glancing at this tradition; at all events the suggestion of divine interference is designed simply for rhetorical balance with the following line; cf. note on 6, above. But there is a greater appropriateness here as well, in that it provides a balance and contrast with the reference to Artemis which follows: a god may have robbed him of success at Olympia, but a god (Artemis) has now given him the victory at Delphi. See also note on 25f., above.

35 **the wandering judgments of men** Pindar, on the two occasions when he alludes to a missed opportunity for victory, attributes the failure to bad luck in the draw (Pind. *Nem.* 6.62-3) or to the reluctance

of the parents to allow their son to compete at the highest level (*Nem.* 11.22f.) Bacch., on the other hand, has no qualms about imputing either incompetence or corruption to the judges, both here and at 4.11f. Jebb (p. 324, note on 31-6) goes to great lengths to deny this, but his argument, which goes hand in hand with his restoration of the missing line 32, has nothing to support it.

36 goddess of the wild More exactly = 'the huntress' (*agrotera*, from *agra* = 'the hunt'); it describes Artemis' association with wild animals and the hunt, as goddess of wild nature. It is used again of Artemis at 5.123.

37 of the golden distaff This is the adjective (*chrusalakatos*) used at 9.1 of the Graces; see the note there. Homer however, uses the word only of Artemis (*Il.* 16.183, 20.70, *Od.* 4.122, etc.) and the ancient *scholia* on these Homeric passages paraphrase the word as 'with lovely bow' (*kallitoxos*), evidently extending the meaning of *alakata* from 'distaff' to 'arrows', because of the similarity of shape. For Homer, this is probably right, and some scholars would take this to be the sense here also, claiming that Artemis had nothing to do with the distaff (so Jebb, p. 325, note on 37-9; cf. also Jebb's note on Soph. *Trach.* 636 and W. Leaf's note on *Il.*16.183). Certainly Artemis was very early characterized as huntress, goddess of the wild, and in this role her association with archery was ancient, natural and firmly established (cf. also Hom. Hymn 5.16-18, Hom. Hymn 27.1-2). So 'goddess of the golden arrows' may be right here, and this view is perhaps supported by 'famed for archery' in the next line, which could be taken as simply reinforcing the description. (Cf. the accumulation of adjectives at *Il.* 20.70-1, where Artemis is goddess 'of the clamour of the hunt, of the golden bow, of the showering arrows'.) But Pindar and Bacch. use the word of other divine females who had nothing to do with arrows (see note on 9.1), and besides, Artemis was quintessentially a woman's goddess also; she watched over women in childbirth and looked after new-born and growing children. So it is at least possible, surely, that Artemis' involvement in the life of women might be extended to the realm of women's work, to spinning, allowing her to be called 'goddess of the golden distaff'. I prefer to think, then, that although Bacch. took over the Homeric formulaic epithet for Artemis, he gave it back its original meaning. This allows a nice balance in the description in these lines. Unusually, Artemis is given four epithets; two, expressing her connection with the world of nature and the wild, frame the other two which express her femininity and gentleness, thus encompassing the whole nature of the goddess. (See W.F. Otto, *The Homeric Gods*, p. 80f., for a sensitive discussion of the nature of Artemis and its apparent contradictions.)

38 gentle Artemis The adjective (*hemera*) was the cult title of Artemis at Lousoi in Arcadia (*IG* V 2, 403; Call. Hymn 3.235-6; cf. Paus. 8.18.8).

The use of the word here thus looks forward to the foundation of that cult in consequence of the healing of the daughters of Proitos (107f.) and establishes the link between the myth and the victor. See intro., above.
famed for archery (*toxoklutos*) A variation of the more usual *klutotoxos*, used of her brother Apollo; see note on 1.147; also note on 37, above.

39 has given … victory There is a clear echo of line 1 ('Victory, whose gifts are sweet'), which signals the end of the opening section of the poem and the transition to the myth; see intro., above and note on 9.39.
shining See note on 1.158.

40 the son of Abas i.e. Proitos. Abas, father of both Akrisios and Proitos (cf. 64-5), was the twelfth king of Argos (see Paus. 2.16.1-2 and Apollod. 2.2.1).

41 set up an altar This is the climax of the story; from this point Bacch. takes us back in time to the starting-point – the quarrel between Proitos and Akrisios – and then forward again, with typical ring-composition, to this conclusion at 110: 'at once they built an altar'.
rich in prayer Proleptic, looking forward to the popularity and importance which the sanctuary would acquire. Cf. 9.65.

42 his daughters Hesiod (fr. 129) gives their names as Lusippe, Iphinoe and Iphianassa; so also Apollod. 2.2.2.

44 lovely This word (*eratos*) occurs only once in Homer (*Il.* 3.64); nevertheless it seems to have a conventional ring (cf. 17.109 and fr. 4.79). It may however be intended to heighten the pathos by contrasting the girls' earlier life with their present suffering. Cf. notes on 47 and 61, below.

46 madness The notion of 'madness' here is conveyed by the word *paraplex*, derived from a verb meaning 'to knock sideways', and used here (for the first time) metaphorically. There is a remarkable parallel to this passage in Euripides. In the prologue to the *Bacchae* Dionysos describes how he punished the daughters of Kadmos for their claim that he was not the son of Zeus: 'therefore I drove them in madness from their homes, and they dwell on the mountain-side, deranged' (Eur. *Bacch.* 32-3). 'Deranged' translates a word (*parakopoi*) which, like *paraplex* in Bacch., also comes from a verb meaning 'to knock sideways'.

47 in youthful spirit Bacch. minimizes and excuses the sin of hybris in these foolish young girls, in order to increase sympathy for their plight.

48 precinct of the goddess The ancient sanctuary of Hera at Argos, commonly known as the Argive Heraion, lay at some distance from the city, about 8 km to the northeast across the Argive plain. The foundations of the Doric temple of Hera, as well as other remains from the sanctuary, are still visible at the site. It was the scene of the Heraia, the festival in honour of the goddess, in which young unmarried girls seem to have taken part; this may be what Euripides has in mind in *Electra*, when the Chorus comes to invite Electra to the festival 'with all the other Argive maidens' (Eur. *El.* 171-4), and it may be what Bacch. also has in mind here as the occasion for the visit of the daughters of Proitos to the Heraion. It is true that Proitos was now king

Fig. 10. The Argive Heraion, looking south-west towards the city of Argos. See note on 11.48.

of Tiryns, not Argos (57f.), but he and his daughters would have continued to worship at the Heraion, which remained within his territory (Paus. 2.16.2). The antiquity and the closeness of Hera's association with Argos is already attested in Homer (*Il.* 4.8, 4.50-2, 5.908); cf. also Soph. *El.* 8, where the landmarks of Argos described to Orestes by the Paidagogos include 'Hera's famous temple'.

49 the purple girdle The compound (*porphurozonos*) occurs only here, and was no doubt coined by Bacch. It is one of the many vivid colour words in Bacch.'s vocabulary (cf. *porphureos*, 'purple', 17.112 and 18.52, and see esp. note on 'blood-red' at 9.10). But see also the note on *porphurodinas* (9.39), where colour is not prominent in the meaning. Hera's girdle was given to her by Aphrodite (*Il.* 14.214f.) where it is described as 'variegated' (*poikilos*; see note on 'artful' at 10.42).

50 claimed This is the version given by Pherekydes; Akusilaos says that the girls belittled the simple, old-fashioned wooden image of the goddess, which is not essentially different in its assertion of superior wealth. See intro., above.

51 fair-haired (*xanthos*) See notes on 5.38 and 5.91.

52 wide-ranging power This translates an adjective (*eurubias*) which is also used of the Calydonian boar; see 5.105 and the note there. A similar adjective (*euruanax*, 'wide-ruling') is used of Zeus at 5.18.

54 wandering confusion This is essentially a re-statement of 45-6. The girls were no longer able to think straight or rationally; they were deranged by Hera.

55 shivering A Homeric word (*smerdaleos*) used to describe fearsome sounds, e.g. the wild yell of aggressive ferocity uttered by Aineias in defence of Pandaros (*Il.* 5.302) or the cry with which Diomedes tried (in vain) to stop the fleeing Odysseus in his tracks (*Il.* 8.92). There is often an element of the uncanny (the thunder of Zeus, *Il.* 7.479) and the effect is similar here, suggesting an unearthly cry like the wailing of the banshee, the kind of wild scream that makes your skin crawl and your toes open and shut.

56 they ran Echoes line 43, so as to frame and highlight the cause of the girls' madness and suffering – their own hybris. The motif of flight recurs at intervals throughout the narrative (also 82-4 and 92-3), punctuating it and framing its major episodes.

to the mountain Bacch.'s phraseology suggests an immediate shift from home to mountain, whereas the mountains of Arcadia, where Proitos and his daughters eventually fetched up (92-4), are a considerable distance from Tiryns. The Maenads (the frenzied devotees of Dionysos) were especially associated with mountains, e.g. Hom. Hymn 2.386: '(she rushed) like a Maenad down a forested mountain-side' and Eur. *Bacch.* 217-9: 'the women have left their homes and dash about on the forested mountain', which suggests the same kind of rapid shift from city to mountain as does Bacch; cf. also Eur. *Bacch.* 32-3, quoted in the note on 46, above. Bacchylides may have been thinking of the girls as Maenads here, and there may be a faint echo of the other version of the legend in which the daughters of Proitos were driven mad, not by Hera, but by Dionysos. See intro., above.

slender-leaved The word is used several times in the Odyssey (*Od.* 13.102, etc.), always of olive trees, for which it is obviously more suitable; see note on 93, below.

57 the city of Tiryns One of the most important cities of Bronze Age Greece, Tiryns lay only a few km south-east of Argos, on the ancient coastline (now a short distance inland) near the modern town of Nafplion. The surviving remains confirm the importance of Tiryns in the palace culture of the late Mycenean era, although the city is mentioned only once in Homer, in the 'Catalogue' (*Il.* 2.559). Destroyed at the end of the Bronze Age (*c.* 1200 BC, i.e. shortly after the supposed date of the Trojan War), Tiryns was subsequently re-occupied, but never again attained the same prominence, and its earlier splendour was gradually forgotten. Even Homer's only memory of it is in the phrase 'Tiryns of the huge walls' (*Il.* 2.559); see note on 78, below.

58 god-built See note on 1.13-14, where the same word (*theodmatos*) is used of Corinth; here the epithet anticipates the story of the building of the walls by the Cyclopes (77f., below).

59 fearless warriors i.e. Proitos and his followers; the word so translated occurs only here and at 5.157; see the note there.

60 bronze-armoured A fairly common epithet in the lyric poets (cf. Pind. *Ol.* 9.54) and one naturally used of the Bronze Age heroes.

demigods According to Hesiod, the fourth generation of mortals created by Zeus was: 'a god-like race of hero-men called demigods' (Hes. *Works and Days* 159-60). The word (*hemitheos* = 'half-divine') then came to be applied by the poets to the heroes of legend (cf. 0.11, 13.155; also Pind. *Pyth.* 4.184).

61 **envied** See notes on 9.44 and 10.48. Here the word points the contrast between their peaceful, happy life at Tiryns and the ensuing disaster.

62 **Argos** The city of Argos lay (lies) toward the southern end of the rich Argive plain, below the citadel hill called Larisa. From there it looks south to the Gulf of Argos and north to Mycenae, with which it was always, in legend at least, closely linked. (Indeed it is difficult to be certain which of the two, Mycenae or Argos, was the principal seat of the family of Atreus and Agamemnon; see G.S. Kirk, *The Iliad, A Commentary* (Cambridge, 1985), vol. 1, p. 180.) In Homer, Diomedes is king of both Argos and Tiryns (*Il.* 2.559-68); his father Tudeus had taken part in the unsuccessful expedition of the 'Seven against Thebes' (see intro. to Ode 9) and Diomedes himself was one of the Epigoni ('Successors') who avenged their fathers' defeat (see note on 9.54). After the destruction of Thebes Diomedes returned to Argos, married the daughter of Adrastos, and inherited the kingship. The story of Proitos and Akrisios agreeing to share Tiryns and Argos between them belongs to an earlier period.

66 **raging** An Epic adjective (e.g. *Il.* 6.179, of the monster Chimaira, killed by Bellerophon); sometimes used also of fire (Hes. *Theog.* 319, Soph. *OT* 177). Here it seems designed to point the contrast between the ferocity of the quarrel and the triviality of its cause.

slight cause Bacch. does not trouble to tell us the reason for the quarrel. According to Apollod. (2.4.1) Proitos had seduced Danae, Akrisios' daughter – hardly a 'slight cause' – but if Bacch. knew of this he has suppressed it, in order to avoid the imputation of any blame or responsibility to Proitos (cf. note on 47, above). Other versions of the quarrel which caused Proitos to leave Argos for Tiryns appear in Paus. 2.25.7 and Apollod. 2.2.1.

67 **passing justice** Lit. = 'not within the bounds of justice'; the adjective was evidently coined by Bacch., as it occurs only here. For its formation, see note on 5.157.

69 **sons of Abas** i.e. Proitos and Akrisios themselves; see note on 40, above.

70 **rich barley-land** The epithet here (*polukrithos*) is another of Bacch.'s coinages; it is a simple variation of the Homeric *poluleios* ('rich corn-land', *Il.* 5.613); see note on 10.34. The expression anticipates the nature of the settlement; the land was more than adequate to support both of the brothers, and they need only divide it between them.

72 **some grim necessity** An oblique allusion to armed conflict; the quarrel was resolved by the intervention of the people, before it came to that point. Bacch.'s pacifism is evident throughout this passage (see also note on 5.200).

74 the race of Danaos Danaos, Lynkeus and Abas were successively kings of Argos. Danaos had fifty daughters (the Danaids) who, compelled to marry their cousins, the fifty sons of Aigyptos, swore to kill their husbands on their wedding night. One daughter, Hypermnestra, broke this oath; her husband Lynkeus thus survived to inherit the kingdom of Argos and to become the father of Abas (and ancestor of Herakles, according to Hes. *Shield*, 327). For the earlier part of the Danaid story, see Aisch. *Suppliant Maidens*.

77 Cyclopes For Homer the Cyclopes are primitive (and not very bright) herdsmen, living in a pastoral backwater (*Od.* 9.105f.). In Hesiod (*Theog.* 139f.) they are the offspring of Earth, giants who make the thunderbolt for Zeus, 'and strength and craft were in their works' (Hes. *Theog.* 146). Later writers too portray them as workmen assisting the god Hephaistos in his smithy (e.g. Call. Hymn 3.46f., Verg. *Aen.* 8.424).
mighty This is the same word (*huperphialos*) as used by Homer of the Cyclopes (*Od.* 9.106), where it seems to have its more usual sense 'arrogant', 'overbearing'. But even the ancient authorities disputed the meaning, and 'arrogant' does not seem appropriate here.
came From Lycia, according to Strabo, 8.6.11; from Thrace, according to *schol.* Eur. Or. 965. Thucydides records a popular belief that the home of the Cyclopes was Sicily (Thuc. 6.2.1).

Fig. 11. A corridor within the Cyclopean walls of Tiryns. See notes on 11.57 and 11.78.

78 built a splendid wall The massive walls which defended the citadel and palace of Tiryns are still referred to as the Cyclopean walls (as are those of Mycenae). Built of huge blocks of rough-hewn stone, the walls are on average 6 m. thick, and the largest individual blocks are estimated to weigh more than 14 tonnes. It is easy to see how the legend arose that these walls were built by the Cyclopes, giants in service of the gods; cf. Pind. fr.152 (of Tiryns); Eur. *Herakles* 15 and 944 (of Mycenae), and see also Paus. 2.25.8 and Apollod. 2.2.1.

80-1 These two lines echo, with very close verbal parallels, the departure from Argos to Tiryns described in 59-62. The repetition forms part of the ring-compositional structure of the ode, framing the central episode – the quarrel – and marking its close.

81 horse-rearing A common Homeric epithet for Argos (*Il.* 2.287 etc.); the wide fertile plains of the Argolid were especially suitable for horses. Cf. 19.17.

82 from there i.e. from Tiryns. The narrative of the flight from Tiryns is resumed, after the digression, from 56-7, again with close verbal echoes. See notes on 56 and 84.
virgin Again Bacch. draws attention to the youth of the girls, in order to excuse their folly. See 47, above, and the note there. The adjective (*admatos*, lit. = 'unsubdued') recurs at 5.167, of Deianeira; see the note there, and note on 1.116.

83 hair shining black The word used here (*kuanoplokamos*) is compounded from *kuaneos*, which properly means 'dark-blue' (cf. Eng. cyan), but which seems to have passed into the more general meaning 'dark', without, however, altogether losing its original colour reference. Bacch. is fond of the word and its compounds; he uses the simple *kuaneos* at 13.64 ('the dark cloud of death') and compounds are used of night (25.15), the sea (13.124), the prow of ships (in reference to the practice of painting the prows dark-blue; 13.161 and 17.1) and finally hair (5.35, see note there; also 9.53 and here). In regard to the last three passages, the expression 'with dark-blue hair' is intended to suggest, I think, the sheen of hair so deeply black that it appears almost blue. (Cf. 'violet-haired', 3.71, and see also the note on 'violet-crowned' at 3.3.) In the *Iliad*, the mourning Thetis wears a veil described as *kuaneon*, 'than which there was no garment more black (*melanteron*)', *Il.* 24.94.

84 rushed off in flight Picks up 'they ran' at 56, and in turn is picked up by 'wandered in flight', 92. In all three places the same word is used in Greek (*pheugon*), so as to make the echo unmistakeable. See note on 56, above.

86 a strange thought Explained in the following lines. The thought, that he should kill himself, was 'strange' in the sense that he would not normally have thought of such a thing. It was, as Jebb says (p. 330, note on 85f.) 'foreign to his saner moods'.

88 he had a mind Not 'he considered' killing himself; rather the meaning is that he determined to do it. Bacch. may be thinking of *Il.* 1.188f., where Achilles, insulted by Agamemnon, is about to draw his sword to kill him and is restrained by Athena. There are, however, major differences. Achilles' motive is anger, not sorrow, and he wants to kill not himself, but Agamemnon. See also the following note.

90 with soothing words The same expression is used at *Od.* 10.442; Odysseus considers drawing his sword to kill the rebellious Eurylochos, and is restrained by his companions. This too may have served as a model for Bacch. here.

92 twelve-month Bacch. actually says 'thirteen months', but a single year is clearly intended. The reason for the expression is quite uncertain; perhaps some form of inclusive counting is involved (see notes on 9.23 and 1.125).

wandered in flight See note on 84, above.

93 thick-shaded forest The adjective here (*daskios*) suggests the darkness of dense virgin forest on the mountains. Interestingly, the same word is used in the passages describing the behaviour of the Maenads (Hom. Hymn 2.386 and Eur. *Bacch.* 219) quoted in note on 56, above. It is clearly more appropriate than the elegant 'slender-leaved' used in 56 (see the note there).

94 sheep-pastures The open parts of the Arcadian uplands, suitable for summer pasture. Cf. Pind. *Ol.* 6.100: 'Arcadia rich in sheep'.

96 Lousos The name of the spring near Lousoi, in Arcadia, where the daughters of Proitos were finally released from their madness. The historical town of Lousoi lay, according to Pausanias, on the borders of Cleitor (i.e. just to the south of the modern Kalavrita), and was once prosperous enough to have produced a victor in the horse-race at the Pythian Games, but already when Pausanias visited, no material remains were visible (Paus. 8.18.7-8). Archaeology in the sanctuary, however, has brought to light material dating back to the eighth century, as well as a number of inscriptions recording dedications to Artemis (see *IG* V 2, 397-409).

97 he cleansed Ritual purification preceded the prayer. Popular etymology connected Lousoi with the verb *louesthai* (= 'to bathe'), as if the place took its name from this performance.

98 raising his hands For the gesture, in prayer, cf. 3.36.

99 the sun The prayer is not directly addressed to the sun, but the sun-god is invoked as witness to the promise that Proitos is about to make. Cf. *Il.* 3.277 and 19.259, where the sun is called upon to witness the solemn oaths sworn by Agamemnon. On both of these occasions Agamemnon too raises his hands to the sky (*Il.* 3.275 and 19.254).

swift chariot The idea that the sun-god traversed the sky in a horse-drawn chariot appears already in Hom. Hymn 2.88-9, and is suggested in Hom. *Od.* 23.244-5 (Athena holds back the horses of Dawn, to prolong the night of the reunion of Odysseus and Penelope).

100 daughter of Leto i.e. Artemis; cf. 15, above, with the note there; also 5.122.

soft-eyed This is the standard Homeric epithet for Hera (*Il.* 1.551 etc.), used of Artemis only here. Bacch. uses it also of Amphitrite (17.111).

101 the crimson veil (*phoinikokrademnos*) The word recurs at 13.222, of the Muses. On Bacch.'s fondness for vivid colour words, especially compounds of *phoinikos*, see note on 9.10. The word in the second half of the compound (*krademnon*) indicated a type of women's headdress. In the plural it is used metaphorically to mean 'battlements', so that the *krademnon* may have stood up from the forehead, but at all events it must have included a veil (see Hom. *Od.* 1.334, 6.100, etc.). See also H.L. Lorimer, *Homer and the Monuments*, London 1950, p. 385.

103 wandering frenzy Not a literal reference to their actual wanderings, but to their wandering in mind; cf. 54, above, and the note there.

105 blood-red Lit. = 'red-haired' (*phoinikothrix*), cf. 'red-backed' (*phoinikonotos*) at 5.99, also of cattle for sacrifice, and see note on 101, above. Maehler, in his note here (vol. 2, p. 237), strangely remarks that in Homer also, red cattle were preferred for sacrifice, but none of the Homeric passages which he cites there relate to sacrifice. Certainly in Bacch. these words were purely decorative.

106 whose father is supreme The translation represents a single compound adjective (*aristopatra*), perhaps coined by Bacch., although it appears as the name of the daughter of the famous boxer, Diagoras of Rhodes, according to the ancient *Hypothesis* to Pind. *Ol.* 7 (464 BC). See also note on 7.7.

107 huntress of wild beasts (*theroskopos*) The same word is used of Artemis at Hom. Hymn 27.11; cf. also 36, above, and the note there).

108-9 and gave The subject is Artemis; it was of course Hera who released the girls from their madness, but Bacch. structures the sentence in such a way as to give Artemis the credit.

flower-crowned Cf. 5.102, where Artemis herself is 'flower-crowned' (*kalukostephanos*). Here the adjective is proleptic (cf. 41, above; also 9.65) – in the festival in honour of Artemis established to celebrate their release (cf. 112), the girls would wear garlands of flowers in their hair.

gave ... rest from their godless madness The expression closely echoes that used at 76 above (including the same verb) which brings to an end the quarrel between Proitos and Akrisios. There is a close parallel between that episode and the fortunes of the daughters of Proitos (see intro., above), and the verbal echo here makes the parallel unmistakeable.

110 at once they built The story is brought to its end by returning to the point from which it began; see 40-2 above, and note on 41. The festival of Artemis established here represents the legendary foundation of the historical cult of Artemis Hemera (Artemis the Healer) at Lousoi; cf. note on 38, above.

113 you followed The subject is Artemis. The apostrophe enhances the closeness of the connection between the goddess and the city of Metapontion.

114 lovers of war A common Homeric epithet for the heroes (*Il.* 2.778, etc.). The use of the adjective here begins the deliberate confusion between Homer's 'Achaians' and the historical Achaians who founded Metapontion (see intro., above). The latter, like the Metapontines themselves, were not 'lovers of war', and remained neutral as far as possible in local conflicts.

115 horse-rearing See note on 81, above. The rich coastal plains of Metapontion were no less suitable for horses than those of Argos.

116 with good fortune Cf. 9.51, where the same expression is used of the foundation of new cities.

118 Kasas The name is not found elsewhere, but this is almost certainly the river Casuentus mentioned by Pliny, *Nat. Hist.* 3.15.3 – the modern Basiento, which flows into the Gulf of Taranto, close to Metapontion.

120 a lovely … sanctuary For the sanctuary of Artemis at Metapontion – which has been identified at the site of the sanctuary of San Biagio, 2 km to the west of Metapontion (G. Olbrich, *PP* 31 (1976), pp. 376-408) – see intro., above.

121 the will of the … gods See *Il.* 15.69-71; also 2.324f., where Kalchas interprets the omen of the snake and the sparrows at Aulis: 'and in the tenth year we shall take the city of the wide ways'. Cf. also e.g. Soph. *Phil.* 1409f.: Herakles tells Philoktetes that Troy is fated to fall to him (1428), and announces this as 'the will of Zeus' (1415).

122 they sacked The ambiguity of 'Achaians' in 114 (see note above) is here abandoned, as Bacch. now speaks explicitly of Homer's heroes. There was in fact a legend (Strabo, 6.1.15) that Metapontion had been founded specifically by heroes from Pylos, under the leadership of Nestor, during their homeward journey from Troy. Bacch. suppresses this detail, preferring a more general association with Homer's heroic Achaians.

well-built Cf. 5.149, and the note there.

123 bronze-armoured A Homeric epithet, e.g. *Il.* 4.448, 8.62; cf. line 60, above, and the note there. A different word is in fact used in 60, but the sense is essentially the same.

124-6 whose mind is straight There is an echo here of 'Styx who judges straight' (9, above), where it is suggested that the present victory is the victor's proper reward. Thus Bacch. returns at the end, via praise of the victor's city, to praise of the victor himself. These last three lines are an example of the 'envy-motif', cf. 3.67-8, 5.188-90 and 13.199-202, and the meaning here is the same as in those passages; the general sense is: 'the man whose mind is not warped by envy will be able to give the required and proper praise to the victor's prowess and success'. See esp. notes on 3.67 and 5.189.

126 Achaians The repetition from 113 demarcates this final section of the poem. At the same time it continues the fusion of the historical Achaians, and their Metapontine descendants, with Homer's Achaians, so that Alexidamos himself and the prowess of his victory are drawn into the renown of the legendary heroes.

ODE 12
FOR TEISIAS OF AIGINA
Wrestling, Nemean Games

Nothing is known of the circumstances of the victory celebrated in Ode 12, or of the athlete himself, beyond the few details which can be gathered from the title appended to the ode in the papyrus, or from the fragmentary remains of the poem itself. It celebrates a victory in the wrestling at the Nemean Games by Teisias of Aigina, but the age-class in which Teisias competed and the date of his success are both unknown. This is one of only two odes which Bacchylides composed for athletes from Aigina; the other, Ode 13, celebrates a victory in the pankration by Pytheas. Indeed, Aigina seems to have specialized in producing experts in what one might call the more vigorous (brutal?) body-contact sports. Of the eleven odes written by Pindar for Aiginetans, no fewer than nine are for victories in wrestling or the pankration, and one of the other two (*Nem.* 7) celebrates a victory in the pentathlon, which included wrestling. Pindar seems to have enjoyed particularly close relations with the aristocratic society of Aigina – his eleven odes for Aiginetans represent a quarter of his total output – but as Maehler points out (vol. 2, p. 243) he certainly had no monopoly on commissions from that island. It is true that Pindar and Bacchylides were both engaged to write for the victory of Pytheas (Bacch. 13, Pind. *Nem.* 5), but on this occasion the family of Teisias, which could boast of thirty victories at the panhellenic Games (12.36f.), and must have been distinguished in sporting circles on Aigina, preferred to commission Bacchylides alone.

The papyrus is broken vertically to the right of Column 26, which ends at 12.8, and the next continuous text begins somewhere within Ode 13. The obvious question then is – how much is missing from the end of Ode 12 and the beginning of Ode 13? We are fortunately in a position to answer this seemingly intractable question. Two fragments of the main papyrus were discovered in 1938 by Medea Norsa, and published by her soon after (*ASNP* 10 (1941), pp. 155-63; now = *PSI* XII 1278). One of these, *PSI* XII 1278 B, was identified by its metre as belonging to Ode 12, and it has been installed at the bottom of the next column, i.e. Column 27 – the only place where it could, sensibly, have stood. It contains the last five lines of an antistrophe and the first five lines of an epode, and this has allowed the length of the triad (strophe, antistrophe and epode) in Ode 12 to be calculated. In order to fill out Column 27 above the new fragment, given the average column length of 34/35 lines, 24, or at most 25, lines are required, which in turn, given the known length of the strophe/antistrophe of 7 lines, requires an epode of 9 (or perhaps 10) verses. (From here on, the lower figure will be used, for a reason to be indicated shortly). Thus the triad in Ode 12 contains 23 lines (7 + 7 + 9) and Column 27 will have contained the last six lines of Antistrophe 1 (6), Epode 1 (9), Strophe 2 (7), Antistrophe 2 (7), and the first five lines of Epode 2 (5), a total of 34 lines, taking us down to 12.42. Now Ode 13 begins at the eleventh line of a 12-line strophe; that is, there are at least 10 lines missing from the beginning of this poem, and the triads in Ode 13 are of 33 lines (12 + 12 + 9). Bearing in mind that the missing text after Column 27 is most likely to contain a multiple of 34 or 35 lines, we find that if we suppose that the missing columns contained the last 4 verses of Epode 2 of Ode 12, and a third complete triad (23 lines), followed by a complete triad of Ode 13 (33) and the first 10 verses of its second strophe, the total of missing lines comes to 70, which is exactly right for two columns. (A ten-line epode in Ode 12 (see above) would give a total of 72 lines missing, which is not impossible, but is very unlikely. In the entire papyrus, as far as can be determined, only one other column (Column 31) reaches 36 lines.)

Ode 12, then, consisted of three triads, a total of 69 lines. Unfortunately only 18 verses survive, in two disjunct pieces, and from these meagre remains very little can be discerned of the content or structure of the ode. It begins with the typical appeal to the Muse to inspire the song, and passes at once into the 'programme', mentioning the victor's homeland (6) and the contest and the place of victory (8). No doubt the victor-praise was developed more fully in the following lines. The other surviving section of the poem (34f.) contains a reference to successes at local festivals, followed by a summary catalogue of victories won at the panhellenic Games, presumably by other members of the family of Teisias. There is room, in the lost final portion of the ode, for a short mythic narrative, but there is no trace of it.

1 **Klio** One of the nine Muses; see note on 3.1. She reappears in Ode 13, in the invocation (13.9) and again in its conclusion (13.228). For the conventional appeal to the Muse(s), see note on 1.1; cf. also 4.8, 5.10, 6.10, etc.
   queen of song Cf. 6.10, where the same attribute is given to Urania, although a different Greek word (*humnoanassa*) is used for it here. This was presumably coined by Bacch., as it is found nowhere else. For the connection of the Muses with song, see note on 1.3.
2 **if ever before** The prayer for help now or in the future relies on the fact that favour has been shown in the past. Cf. the appeal of Chryses to Apollo: 'if once before you listened to my prayers ... so one more time bring to pass ...' (*Il.* 1.453-5); also Sappho 1.5.
   guided my mind Cf. 13.229, where Klio has 'filled my mind with song'.
4 **skilled helmsman** Maehler (vol. 2, p. 246) cites a number of passages which testify to the high regard in which such a person was held,

especially among the coastal Ionians, who depended heavily on the sea. Some of these passages (Archil. fr. 211W; Aisch. *Supp.* 770) use the same words as Bacch. here.

5 **Victory** A common personification in Bacch.; cf. 6.9 and the note there, also 3.6, 5.35, 10.15, and 11.1.
august (*potnia*) A common epithet in Homer, usually of Hera (*Il.* 1.551, etc.). In Bacch. it occurs only here and in Epigram 1.1 (= *Anth. Pal.* VI 313), where it is also used of the personified Victory.

6 **Aigina's blessed island** For Aigina, 'daughter' of the river-god Asopos, and eponymous heroine of the island, see intro. to Ode 9 and the notes on 9.45-6 and 9.57. The adjective 'blessed' may be regarded as appropriate, because of the island's mythic connections with the divine, or it may be simply honorific (see note on 10.35).

7 **god-built** (*theodmatos*) See note on 1.13-14, where the same adjective is used of Corinth. Here the word is purely decorative and honorific.
for guest-friends See esp. note on 5 9. Bacch. must have established relations of 'guest-friendship' with the family of Teisias in Aigina, just as he claims in Ode 5 to have done with Hieron of Syracuse. The qualities of respect, friendship and hospitality involved in such a relationship are often alluded to in the odes, and often become an element in the praise of the victor or his family, e.g. 3.16 (see note there), 5.49, 13.224-6; see also note on 1.150.

8 **strong-limbed** The same adjective (*guialkes*) is used at 9.38 (also of wrestling). This is one of several compounds in Bacch. based on *guia* (= limbs); all of them seem to be his own creations. See notes on 9.38 and 11.12.

34 **guest-friend** The same word (*xeinos*) as used at 7, above, but the ode is too fragmentary to discover whether there is any ring-compositional structure involved here.

35 **the Games of neighbouring peoples** This presumably concludes a list of, or is a passing reference to, victories won at various local festivals. There is, however, nothing to indicate how much detail Bacch. gave here; at 1.158 victories at minor festivals are alluded to briefly as 'other shining crowns', whereas in Ode 10 each success is mentioned separately (see 10.30f., and the note there).

37 **they were celebrated** This must refer to the same athletes as those who were successful at the local Games just mentioned. Who were they? The only possibilities are (1) Aiginetans generally, and (2) members of the family of Teisias. In Ode 2 Bacch. claims that athletes from Ceos had (by the mid-fifth century) won seventy victories at the Isthmian Games alone (2.7-10), so that thirty victories for Aiginetan athletes, at the Nemean, Pythian and Isthmian Games together, seems much too few, even if Ode 12 is relatively early (see esp. note on 2.7). We should assume, therefore, that Bacch. is here praising previous successes by other members of the family of Teisias.

Pytho i.e. at Delphi, at the Pythian Games. The name does not survive on the papyrus, but since the other panhellenic festivals are all mentioned (Isthmia, 38-9; Nemea, 40-1; Olympia, 42f.) there can be no doubt that a reference to the Pythia should be restored here. For the name Pytho, see note on 8.17.

38 at the throat of Pelops' ... **island** i.e. at the Isthmian Games. A similar metaphor for the Isthmus occurs at 2.10; see note there. For Pelops' island (the Peloponnese) see note on 1.13-14.

39 holy Not especially appropriate to the Peloponnese as a whole, the adjective may have been suggested by the reference to the Isthmian Games held in honour of Poseidon. But it may also be simply a general honorific (see note on 5.12; also 2.2 and 2.8).

41 the crimson lightning (*phoinikosteropas*) Bacch.'s fondness for vivid colour words (especially red) has often been noted. For adjectives compounded with *phoiniko-* see esp. notes on 9.10 and 5.99. This one occurs only here and at Pind. *Ol.* 9.6.

42 [Alpheos] The name of the river does not in fact survive on the papyrus here, but is certainly to be restored from 8.28, where the same phrase, 'silver-swirling Alpheos', is used. Besides, Bacch. is presenting a catalogue of victories at the panhellenic festivals. The Pythian, Isthmian and Nemean Games have all been mentioned; the list must surely climax with the most important of them all – the Olympic. It is possible that this is not a reference to a victory already won, but rather a prayer for an Olympic victory in the future (cf. 8.26f.). For expressions involving the Alpheos as a periphrasis for Olympia, see note on 6.3.
silver-swirling for Bacch.'s fondness for river-adjectives compounded from *-din-* (= 'swirl', 'eddy') see note on 5.40. All of them, except 'gold-swirling' (3.44) are purely conventional and decorative.

ODE 13
FOR PYTHEAS OF AIGINA
Pankration, Nemean Games, before 481 BC

The background

Ode 13 celebrates the victory of Pytheas, son of Lampon, of Aigina, in the pankration at Nemea. Pindar too was commissioned to write for this victory (*Nem.* 5), as he did also for two subsequent Isthmian victories won by Pytheas' younger brother Phylakidas (*Isth.* 5 and 6), and it is from these three odes that we derive most of our knowledge of the family. Pytheas belonged to the clan Psaluchidai (Pind. *Isth.* 6.62), one of those ancient and distinguished aristocratic sporting families in Aigina which brought such great renown to that island through their prowess in boxing, wrestling and the pankration (see also intro. to Ode 12). His father Lampon, while not known as a victor himself, encouraged his sons' athletic endeavours with good advice (Pind. *Isth*. 6.66-9) and, no doubt more usefully, by employing the successful Athenian trainer Menandros (Bacch. 13.191-8; Pind. *Nem*. 5.48-9). His uncle Euthumenes had won twice in the local Games in Aigina (*Nem*. 5.41f.) and was later successful at Nemea also (*Isth*. 6.57f.). His maternal grandfather Themistios, who had won twice at Epidauros, in the boxing and the pankration, was honoured with a statue in the vestibule of the Aiakeion, adorned with victory garlands (*Nem*. 5.50f.) and the younger brother Phylakidas not only won the two Isthmian victories referred to above, but was successful at Nemea as well (*Isth*. 5.18-19). Pytheas himself, in addition to the Nemean victory celebrated here, seems to have won also in the local Games in Aigina, as well as at Megara (*Nem*. 5.45-6), although the text there and its interpretation are not universally agreed. Bacch. does not mention these victories, but a reference to them may have formed part of the victor-praise in the lost opening section of the ode.

The date of Pytheas' Nemean success cannot be exactly determined, but some indications can be gathered, again from Pindar's odes, to suggest an approximate date. *Isth*. 6, celebrating an Isthmian victory by Phylakidas, refers (2-3) to Pytheas' victory at Nemea, so that this ode must be later than *Nem*. 5/Bacch. 13; also, at *Isth*. 5.17-19, Pindar credits Phylakidas with *two* victories at the Isthmus, so that *Isth*. 5 must be in celebration of the second of these, and *Isth*. 6 the first. Further, at *Isth*. 6.57 Pindar mentions a victory at Nemea won by the uncle Euthumenes, but this does not appear at *Nem*. 5.41f., where Euthumenes (at least on the most natural and probable reading of the words there) is credited only with victories in the minor local festival. Euthumenes must therefore have won at Nemea after Pytheas, and before Phylakidas won at the Isthmus. The relative order of these victories is therefore fairly clear: (1) Pytheas at Nemea (Bacch. 13/*Nem*. 5); (2) Euthumenes at Nemea (mentioned *Isth*. 6.57f.); (3) Phylakidas at the Isthmia (*Isth*. 6) and (4) Phylakidas again at the Isthmia (*Isth*. 5). Absolute dating is less certain, but again Pindar provides a clue. In praising the victor's homeland in *Isth*. 5, Pindar refers to the important role played by Aigina in the battle of Salamis against the Persian invaders (*Isth*. 5.48-50), and the expression is such as to suggest that the event was very recent. The battle of Salamis took place in late 480 BC; the first Isthmian festival after that was in April 478, so that this is the probable date of *Isth*. 5 and Phylakidas' second victory. Working back from there, Phylakidas may have won his first Isthmian victory at the preceding festival of 480; Euthumenes cannot therefore have won his Nemean victory later than 481, which leaves 483 or shortly before for Pytheas.

Pytheas was competing either in the 'boys' or the 'youths' age-class. Pindar describes him as 'not yet showing on his cheeks that summer ripeness, mother of the tender bloom' (*Nem*. 5.5-6), which appears to mean that his facial hair had not yet begun to grow. This may suggest that he was still young enough to compete as a boy (probably under 17), but in fact the word for 'youth' (*ageneios*) actually means 'beardless', so that this may be what Pindar had in mind. Maehler (vol. 2, p. 250) and Jebb (p. 214) both take the latter view.

The myths

Herakles and the Nemean Lion

There are two distinct mythic narratives in Ode 13. The first of these, of which only the last fourteen lines remain (44-57), deals with one of the Twelve Labours of Herakles – the killing of the Nemean lion. There is a passing reference in Ode 9 to this same exploit (9.7-9), where it serves a twofold purpose; first, it honours Nemea, home of the Games, through its association with Herakles as the scene of the 'first of his far-famed Labours' (9.9), and second, it glorifies the victors in the Games by creating a parallel between their prowess and that of the great hero himself (see note on 9.7). (For the Labours of Herakles in general, see intro. to Ode 5; for the Nemean lion in particular see notes on 9.7 and 9.9.) Here in Ode 13 the story is told in a much more expansive and dramatic manner, but its function within the ode is essentially the same. The fight between Herakles and the lion is described by an excited eye-witness (whose name does not survive on the papyrus – perhaps Athena, perhaps the nymph Nemea; see note on 44f., below), and the speaker concludes the account by predicting that one day Games will be held on this spot: 'I declare that here one day the sweat will run ...' (54-5). Thus Nemea and its Games are once again honoured by a simple geographical association with Herakles, as the scene of his first Labour. Further, the narrator draws particular attention to the fact that the lion could not be killed by the sword (50-3), so that Herakles was obliged to wrestle with the beast, very much in the manner of the pankration (46-9). The ensuing prophecy, therefore, that one day the Greeks will contest the pankration at Nemea, creates an unmistakeable parallel between the struggles of Herakles and those of the later athletes, so that the pankratiasts in general, and Pytheas in particular, are seen to emulate the exploit of the hero, and can bask in the reflection of his glory.

It is worth noting that Bacch. does not claim that the Games were founded to commemorate the killing of the lion, and the standard foundation legend involving the Seven against Thebes (see intro. to Ode 9) is not contradicted here. Having said that, it is hard not to feel that the juxtaposition of the two events implies some kind of direct connection, and it is possible that the Alexandrian Callimachos drew this inference from Bacch.'s narrative. In the third book of the *Aitia*, Callimachos relates how Herakles, on his way to Nemea to deal with the lion, stopped at Cleonai, where he was entertained by Molorchos. While there he told his host of a prophecy given to him by Athena concerning the institution of the Nemean Games and its prizes, which would seem to suggest that the Games were established as a direct consequence of the killing of the lion (see Call. *Aitia*

3, frr. 55-9; similarly, *schol.* Pind. *Nem.* 6.71b (Drachmann III, p. 110) claims that Herakles, having killed the lion, established the use of celery for the crown at Nemea). The *Hypothesis* to Pindar's Nemean Odes (Drachmann III, p.1) takes the story a step further, claiming that 'some say' that the Games were founded by Herakles himself.

Aias and Achilles at Troy

The second mythic narrative in Ode 13 concerns two of the greatest and most familiar heroes of Greek legend, Aias and Achilles, who claimed descent, through their grandfather Aiakos, from Zeus and the nymph Aigina, daughter of the river-god Asopos (see the intro. to Ode 9 and note on 9.57). It would be difficult to imagine an ode in praise of an athlete from Aigina which did not include at least some mention of that island's most glorious sons. All of Pindar's eleven odes for Aiginetans contain such a reference, albeit brief in many cases. Even in Ode 9, in which Bacch. praises the victor's hometown of Phleius on the basis of its close association with Asopos and his daughters, the Aiakid heroes are again prominent, although their connection with Phleius, through their descent from Asopos and Aigina, is quite indirect and remote (see esp. note on 9.46-7). Ode 12, for Teisias of Aigina, is very fragmentary, and its myth, if there was one, does not survive, but here in Ode 13 Bacch. takes full advantage of his opportunity.

The episode which Bacch. chooses to relate here is taken directly from the *Iliad* – indeed it could be regarded as the turning point in the entire action of that poem. Bacch. highlights the moment when the Greeks, in the absence of the great Achilles, have been driven back to the shore and their ships by Hektor and the Trojans; Hektor stands poised to fire the Achaian ships, and only valiant defence by the mighty Aias holds him and the Trojans at bay (*Il.* 15.592f.). This is the climax to which the whole of the antecedent action has been building – it is the wrath of Achilles, his withdrawal from the fighting in anger at the dishonour done him by Agamemnon, which has brought the Greeks to this pass and allowed the Trojans, urged on by Apollo, to drive them back upon their ships – and it is the point from which the epic's tragic consequences flow. For it is the desperate plight of the Greeks which spurs Patroklos to return to the fighting in Achilles' place, a foolhardy venture which leads to his death at the hands of Hektor, and so to the revenge killing of Hektor by Achilles. The crucial importance of this pivotal moment in the epic is marked by the fact that it is the occasion for what is in effect a summary of the entire poem (*Il.* 15.59-77), in which Zeus foreshadows the intervention and death of Patroklos, the death of Hektor, and the ultimate capture of Troy, all in fulfilment of his promise to Achilles' mother Thetis that he would grant honour to her son (*Il.* 1.503f.).

All of this is encapsulated in Bacch.'s poem. But although the scene is drawn from the *Iliad*, and Bacch. devotes no less than 75 lines to it, the manner of its telling is far from Homeric, in spite of the elaborate and quasi-Homeric simile at its centre (124-33). In contrast with, for example, the narrative of the meeting between Herakles and Meleager in the Underworld (5.56-175), which unfolds in the leisurely, conversational style typical of the epic, Bacch. here selects a single dramatic moment – Aias on the deck holding off the furious onslaught of Hektor and the Trojans (13.103-9). He returns to this point later (149-63), so that the heroism of Aias forms a ring-compositional frame, within which is highlighted the greatness of Achilles. The remarkable thing, however, is that Achilles is not actually there. Three times Bacch. clearly and specifically draws attention to the fact that he has withdrawn from the fighting (110f., 121-3 and 134-7). Achilles is, so to speak, conspicuous by his absence. But this is no criticism. On the contrary, whereas the heroism of Aias can be seen in his valiant defence of the Greek ships, the heroic greatness of Achilles is to be understood precisely from the effect of his withdrawal. It is only the absence of Achilles from the battle-field which has emboldened the Trojans to the point where they now threaten the ships; it is his absence which has created the opportunity for, and indeed necessitated, the heroism of Aias. The function of the myth within the ode is to praise the victor's homeland, and so indirectly the victor himself, and by adopting this structure, which Maehler (vol. 2, p. 253) rightly calls a 'master-stroke of composition', Bacch. is able to praise both of Aigina's great heroes, equally and on the same level, thus circumventing any difficulty which may have arisen from the acknowledged superiority of Achilles to Aias as warrior and hero (see esp. *Il.* 768-9).

The poem

The first 43 lines of Ode 13 are missing (see intro. to Ode 12). All that survives of this long opening section is a tiny fragment from the top of the previous column (Col. 29), on which nothing can be read with certainty except the name of the Muse Klio (line 9). The opening stanzas may therefore have contained the typical invocation and appeal to the Muses for inspiration and help in creating the song (cf. Odes 1, 3 and 12). Bacch. returns to the Muses at the end of the ode (222), and to Klio in particular (228f.), which suggests that there was an overriding ring-compositional structure, although it is now impossible to discover its nature or extent. It is likewise impossible to discover how the transition from the opening invocation to the first myth was managed. The surviving text begins in the middle of the narrative of Herakles and the Nemean Lion, and from there at least the ode flows smoothly, with easy and seemingly natural transitions from one section to the next, while at the same time there is, once again, the typical ring-composition. At the centre stands the major myth of the ode, the story of Achilles and Aias at Troy (100-67); on either side of this stands praise of the victor's homeland Aigina (77-99 and 182-9) and of the victor Pytheas himself (67-76 and 190-8), while all of this is framed by gnomic sections of similar content, reflecting on the close connection between success and fame (58-66 and 199-220).

The victory of Herakles over the lion is the occasion for the first of these gnomic passages: 'victory brings renown which lives on beyond death' (58f.). This serves as transition to the first victor-praise. The success of Pytheas and the renown which he has won (67-8) are the specific example which illustrates the general truth of the *gnome*. Further, Pytheas has returned victorious to celebrations at home, on 'the island of his fathers' (72), and so the victor-praise passes easily into praise of the victor's island home. Bacch. imagines choruses of young women, dancing and singing the praises of Aigina, which inevitably include her glorious descendants – Aiakos, Peleus and Telamon, and their sons Achilles and Aias. Thus Bacch. arrives at the subject of his myth, and the transitions between victor-praise, city-praise and myth are so natural as to be virtually unnoticeable.

The myth too has a ring-compositional structure of its own. The defence of the ships by Aias is the frame for the heroism of Achilles (see above); within this frame the terror which the presence of Achilles on the battlefield inspired in the Trojans (114-20) is itself framed by, and contrasted with, the relief and confidence which they draw from his absence. The emphasis on this effect of Achilles' absence is interrupted by, and resumed after, the delaying device of the long simile (124-32), which vividly illustrates the eagerness of the newly confident Trojans. And so Bacch. returns to the point from which he began – the furious fighting by the ships (149f.). But the confidence of the Trojans is misplaced, and Bacch. looks forward to the day when Achilles will return to the fighting, and he and Aias together will fill Scamander with Trojan blood (164-7). This brief and oblique reference to the glorious exploits of the Aiakids in the future not only picks up the announcement of the theme of the myth (100-4), thus completing the ring-compositional structure; it also signals the end of the myth and the transition into the following gnomic section.

The papyrus is broken and the text partly missing at this point (168f.), but from the surviving fragments it seems inescapable that these lines contained the confident asserton: 'the fame of Aias and Achilles will live on beyond their death', which not only provides a fitting conclusion to the narrative of their heroic exploits, but echoes the theme of the first gnomic passage (58-66; see above) and leads naturally into the second (175f.), reflecting once again on the enduring renown to be won through *areta* ('excellence'). There is a close parallel in thought and function between these two passages, and just as the first led into specific praise of the victor (67-76) and his city (77-99), so too does the second, but this time in reverse order, continuing the circular ring-compositional structure of the ode. The renown of *areta* spreads its light over Aigina, the victor's homeland (182f.), which leads in turn to renewed praise of Pytheas himself (190f.), and

Bacch. then concludes the ode with a final gnomic section, in which the themes are once again the same: 'truth will prevail against the carping and the envy of lesser mortals, and success nobly won will confer undying fame' (199f.), but this time he includes, typically, a reference to his own role in the creation of this immortality (221-31).

9 Klio One of the nine Muses. On the role of the Muses in epinician poetry, and of Klio in particular, whose name may be related to the verb *kleiein* (= 'to make famous') see esp. notes on 3.1 and 1.1.

44f. The surviving text begins in the middle of an excited and vivid account of the fight between Herakles and the Nemean Lion, spoken, clearly, by someone watching the event. The name of the speaker does not appear; the two most likely candidates are Athena, who frequently appears on vase paintings at the side of Herakles as his friend and protector (see esp. note on 5.91), and the nymph Nemea, daughter of Asopos (see intro. to Ode 9) and eponymous heroine of the place where the fight took place and where the Games would later be held.

44 violence The word used here is *hubris*, which often, but not always, includes the suggestion of physical violence. The fundamental meaning of the word is arrogant or outrageous behaviour, based on a misplaced sense of superiority, and always with the sense of overstepping the mark, whether in one's relations with one's fellows or with the gods.

45 exacting ... their punishment This more or less paraphrases and explains the preceding line; by punishing the sinners Herakles will prevent them from further acts of hubris (and perhaps discourage others who might be so inclined). For this aspect of Herakles' role, cf. Pind. *Nem.* 1.61f., where Teiresias predicts that the infant Herakles will one day kill not only beasts and monsters, but 'any man that walks in crooked insolence ...'.

46 Perseus' son Not literally. Patronymic adjectives (see notes on 5.69 and 6.12) such as that found here are often used to mean 'descendant of ...' rather than 'son of ...'; cf. 166, below. The genealogy was as follows:

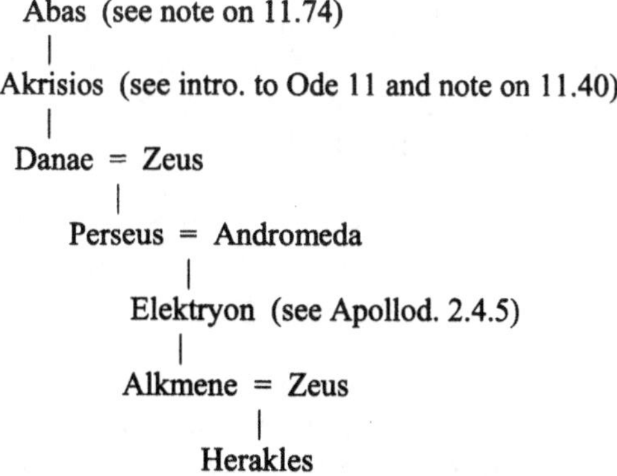

48 raw flesh eater Cf. 9.8, where the lion is called 'slayer of sheep'.

49 with wrestling skills (*technais*) The same word is used at 11.32-3, describing the wrestling contests of Alexidamos at Olympia: 'many a boy he brought to the ground with subtle skills' (*poikilais technais*). The use of the word here thus contributes to the creation of a parallel between the fight against the lion and the pankration contest of the Games (see intro., above). The following lines (50-3) give the reason why Herakles was obliged to wrestle with the beast in this way.

50 flashing (*aithon*) Properly = 'fiery', 'blazing', but often used of metal objects and weapons (*Il.* 9.123, etc.), perhaps suggesting the colour of burnished bronze (although it is used of iron also, *Il.* 4.485, etc.) As a colour word, it reappears at 5.126, describing the hide of the Calydonian boar.

51 will not pass through The invulnerability of the lion seems to have been part of the legend from the beginning; it appears already on a black-figure amphora of the late sixth century BC (Beazley, *ABV* 291) and Pindar alludes to it (*Isth.* 6.47). Cf. Apollod. 2.5.1, where he specifically describes the lion as 'invulnerable' (*atroton*). In the long poem *Herakles the Lion-killer*, generally attributed to Theocritos, the hero, having tried in vain to shoot the beast with his bow, is obliged to batter its head with his club and then wrestle and strangle it from behind (Theocrit. 25.255f.).

52 fearsome Lit. = 'unapproachable'. Sophocles uses the same word (*aplaton*) of the Nemean Lion at *Trach.* 1093.

53 the blade bent back The past tense describes the moment just past when Herakles tried unsuccessfully to kill the lion with his sword, whereas the future in 51 ('will not pass through ...') expresses the conclusion – that the lion's hide is impenetrable – which the speaker draws from having observed this failure.

58 by the altar of Zeus Presumably the place where the victor was proclaimed and crowned (see note on 10.29) and thus the starting-point, so to speak, of his undying renown.
whose rule is supreme This translates an unusual epithet (*aristarkhos*), found elsewhere only in Simonides, 614. Bacch. is fond of such compounds; cf. *aristokarpos* (3.2) of Sicily 'where the best grain grows', and *aristopatra* (11.106) of Artemis, 'whose father is supreme'. Both of these seem to have been coined by Bacch.

59 the flowers of Victory A metaphor for the victory itself, rather than a literal reference to the victor's crown, which at Nemea was made, not from flowers, but from dried wild celery (Paus. 8.48.2-3). The metaphor is perhaps assisted by the fact that the victor and his friends would commonly wear garlands of flowers in their hair during the celebrations; cf. 69-70, below, and see notes on 1.158 and 10.16. Further, Bacch. several times uses the same metaphor in reference to his own poems ('garlands of paians', 16.8-9; 'flowers of song', fr. 4.62-3; 'a lovely garland of the Muses for Hieron', fr. 20C 3-4; see also 5.187 and note there), and it is very likely that he intended to include this sense here also. It is not only the victory itself, but Bacch.'s song in celebration of it, which brings renown. Cf. 9.1, where Bacch. invokes the Graces to grant renown (*doxa*) through his song.

bringer of glory See note on 183, below, where the same word (*pherekudes*) is used, forming part of the complex texture of echoes and repetitions throughout the ode.

62 that shines afar The translation represents an adjective (*poluphantos*) which occurs only here. Observe the contrast with line 60: the renown of the victor is visible to many, but few can achieve such glory. Cf. also 'far-shining', 175, below.

63-4 the dark cloud of death The phrase is Homeric: 'and the black cloud of death covered him over' (*Il.* 16.350; also *Od.* 4.180). For the adjective 'dark' (*kuaneos*, lit. = 'dark-blue'), see note on 11.83. The idea that victory brings renown which will live on after death – something of a natural commonplace in the epinician poems – finds one of its fullest and most elaborate expressions here; cf. esp. 1.181-4 and 9.78-87; the latter passage also makes quite explicit the relation between fame and the poet's song (see notes on 59, above, and 228-31, below).

65 a destiny unshakeable (*sun aisai*) See note on 10.32, where a very similar phrase (*kat' aisan*) is used.

unshakeable The undying fame of the victorious athlete will stand firm against the carping envy of lesser mortals. Thus the phrase suggests the so-called 'envy-motif', a common rhetorical device in the poems (see Bundy, *Stud. Pind.*, p. 57f.; see also 3.67, 5.188f. and 11.124-6, with the notes there). The oblique suggestion of the motif here points forward to, and is picked up at, 199f., where it is fully developed.

66 the … fame of success The idea returns (in a very similar expression) at 205-7, below.

69 and come The return of the victor to his home marks the climax of his achievement, and is often highlighted; see esp. 9.39 and the note there. Here, as there, it creates an easy transition from the victor-praise (here much abbreviated) to praise of the victor's homeland.

69-70 garlands of flowers See note on 59, above. There is a remarkable parallel to the expression here in Sappho. Consoling her daughter Kleis for the lack of a fashionable purple headband, Sappho passes on her mother's advice that it really is better for blondes (as presumably Kleis was) to adorn their hair 'with garlands of flowers in full bloom' (Sappho, fr. 98a 8-9).

all in bloom (*panthales*) The word occurs only here and in 228, below, and was clearly coined by Bacch. (Sappho – see previous note – uses a slightly different form, *erithales*). On the significance of the repetition see note on 'rich in flowers', 228, below. (Cf. also 9.5, and 14B.7, where a related word (*euthales*, 'verdant', 'fertile') is used, with, probably, an underlying reference to the victor's crown.)

71-3 The papyrus is badly damaged at this point and much of the text is uncertain. I follow Maehler's restorations.

71 high-built streets (*hupsiaguian*) Lit. = 'the city of high streets'; not to be understood literally, since the city of Aigina lay, not in the hills, but on the west coast of the island. Maehler (vol. 2, p. 264) suggests that Bacch. may be thinking of streets flanked by high buildings; this may be right, but Bacch. is very fond of adjectives compounded with *hupsi-* ('high') – he uses ten such words – and not all of them are literal; cf. 'vaunting', 44, above (*hupsinoos*, lit. = 'high-minded', but certainly in a pejorative sense here) and 'high pride', 84, below (*hupsauches*). Perhaps the metaphor in 'lofty' is used here as a vaguely general term of praise.
[Aiakos'] city i.e. Aigina. The name does not survive, but the restoration is virtually certain. For Aiakos, see intro., above, and note on 9.57.

73 swells] Lit. = 'teems with', 'is full of'; this conjectural restoration is supported by the use of the same word in a similar context at 3.15 and 16. Cf. fr. 4.79: 'the streets are filled with lovely banquets'.
the sweet voice (*habrothroon*) Very little of this word survives, but this conjecture seems most likely. For the meaning of adjectives compounded with *habro-* ('graceful', 'delicate') see note on 3.49; here there would certainly not be any suggestion of the effeminacy which sometimes attaches to the word.

75-6 you displayed ... A periphrasis for 'you won', cf. 9.31 and the note on 2.8-9. Bacch. often gives us a vivid description of the physical aspects of the contest (including, sometimes, reference to the presence of spectators, here only implied); see esp. notes on 9.31 and 9.35. But in this ode these two lines are all that we get. No doubt the reason is that the fight between Herakles and the Nemean lion, presented in such a way as to suggest a pankration contest (see intro., above, and note on 49), is substituted for a description of the actual event.

78 the swirling river i.e. Asopos; for Aigina as the daughter of Asopos, see intro. to Ode 9.
swirling (*dinantos*) Cf. 'the dark swirling waters' (*porphurodinan*) 'of Asopos' (9.39), and 'Scamander's swirling waters' (*dinanta*, 165, below). For Bacch.'s fondness for this root (*din-* 'eddy') and its compounds in words applied to rivers, see note on 5.40. Often these adjectives are purely conventional and decorative.

80 has given you great honour Echoed at 182-3, below; there Aigina is honoured by the renown which is won through *areta* ('excellence'), i.e. victory in the Games, and that victory is, here as always, the gift of the god (Zeus, son of Kronos, 79).

81 displaying Picks up the same word (*phainon*) from 75. Pytheas has displayed his prowess, and Zeus 'displays' his victory, making it known to all the Greeks, so as to honour Aigina.

82 the blaze Bacch.'s words literally mean displaying the victory 'like a beacon'. Thus the phrase echoes 'renown that shines afar' (61-2) and is in turn picked up by 'far-shining excellence' (175).

84 a girl ... **sings** Pindar similarly imagines a young girl singing the praises of Hieron 'at her door' (Pind. *Pyth.* 2.18). This is perhaps a variation of the 'witnessing-motif', whereby the praise is put into the mouth of a third party, so as to suggest that it does not depend on the sole authority of the poet; see note on 5.191-4. Bacch.'s description here of young girls dancing and singing in honour of Aigina may be coloured to some degree by images of Maenads ranging over the hillsides in their worship of Dionysos, (but here without any suggestion of frenzy or madness); see following note and note on 11.56. For choruses of girls, see esp. 11.112; also notes on 11.48 and 11.108-9.

in high pride (*hupsauches*) Found only here; see note on 71, above.

86 like a fawn The fawn-simile goes back to Homer (*Il.* 4.243, 21.29 and 22.1) but there it is used only to express fear or bewilderment, rather than *joie de vivre*, as in the later poets. Euripides has an interesting parallel (given the suggestion in the previous note) at *Bacch.* 862f. There the Chorus of captive Bacchant women, or Maenads, look forward to their release, when they can dance once more, 'like a fawn at play in the green joy of the meadow'. Cf also Eur. *El.* 860: the Chorus urges Electra to 'dance now like a fawn that leaps for joy ...'.

90 famed Famed for what? Jebb suggests either beauty or noble birth, or both, but surely the epithet is purely decorative; cf. 2.10, 8.32, etc.

91-2 crowned with flowers See note on 59, above.

crimson Restoration of this word is probable, but not certain. See note on 9.10.

93 their native ornament The word translated 'ornament' (*athursin*) occurs only here. It is clearly related to *athurein* ('to play') and *athurma* ('plaything', 'source of delight'), see note on 9.87. Bacch. alludes to what was evidently the local custom of combining rushes with flowers in festive and decorative garlands. Cf. the garlands adorning the statue of the victor's grandfather Themistios (see intro., above) which Pindar describes as 'crowns of flowers entwined with grasses' (Pind. *Nem.* 5.54).

94 sing of your child i.e. Aiakos. The girls, extolling the glories of Aigina, sing of the first two generations of her descendants – Aiakos, Peleus and Telamon (see genealogy in note on 9.57). Bacch. then takes up the story himself (100f.) so that the praise of the victor's homeland provides an easy transition into the myth.

95 queen of the land i.e. Aigina herself. The direct address picks up the similar vocative in 77, above, thus framing the city-praise and signalling its end.

that welcomes all The same word (*panxenos*) is used at 11.29, of the olive wreath, the prize at Olympia (see note there). Here the meaning is more literal, referring, as part of the homeland-praise, to the hospitality for which Aigina was renowned. Cf. Pind. *Ol.* 8.21: 'there' (viz. in Aigina) 'they worship Themis, consort of Zeus, god of hospitality'.

96 Endaïs Daughter of the Megarian hero Sciron and wife of Aiakos (Apollod. 3.12.6; Plut. *Thes.* 10); see note on 9.57. Pindar similarly refers to Peleus and Telamon simply as 'the renowned sons of Endais' (Pind. *Nem.* 5.12).

rose-armed Women were more commonly given the decorative epithet 'white-armed' (see notes on 5.173 and 9.7), but 'rose-armed' (*rhodopachus*) is used also by Hesiod, of two of the daughters of Nereus and Doris (*Theog.* 247 and 251), by Sappho, of the Graces (Sappho, fr. 69) and again by Bacch. himself, of Deianeira (fr. 64.10).

102 swift The typical description of Achilles in the *Iliad* ('swift of foot' *Il.* 1.58, 'swift-footed' 2.860 etc., and cf. 13.325), although Bacch. uses a different word from those used in Homer.

103 Eriboia Cf. Soph. *Aias* 569; Pindar too mentions Eriboia as the mother of Aias (*Isth.* 6.45). According to Apollodoros she was the daughter of Alkathoos of Megara (Apollod. 3.12.7); see also note on 10.18.

104 hero of the mighty shield This represents the single word *sakesphoron* (lit. = 'shield-carrier'), used of Aias by Sophocles also (*Aias* 19). It appears to echo the Homeric formula 'carrying a shield like a tower' (*pheron sakos eute purgon*) used three times of Aias (*Il.* 7.219, 11.485 and 17.128) and of no other hero. The great shield, which was unique to Aias and for which he became so renowned, was built of seven layers of oxhide, with an outer facing of bronze (*Il.* 7.220-3); it may be an epic reminiscence (certainly exaggerated) of the tower-shield depicted on artefacts of the Late Helladic I period of the Bronze Age. See Lorimer, *Homer and the Monuments*, pp. 181-2. Note that Aias and Hektor each are given two epithets, one relating to temperament and the other to physical appearance; 'high-couraged' (103) corresponds to 'bold-hearted' (106), and 'hero of the mighty shield' (104) to 'bronze-helmeted' (107). This is no doubt designed, as Maehler notes (vol. 2, p. 270) to present Aias and Hektor as evenly matched heroes.

105 stood upon the stern There are two slight variations from the Homeric account here. In Homer, Aias leaps from ship to ship to fend off the Trojans as need requires; here he stands firm upon a single ship. Bacch. may have had the ship of Protesilaos in mind; at *Il.* 15.704f. Hektor grasps the sternpost of this ship and calls for fire. In Homer too, Aias is eventually obliged to give ground (15.727f.); Bacch. naturally suppresses this detail.

107 bronze-helmeted Most of this word is missing from the papyrus, but it is a common Homeric formulaic adjective (*Il.* 6.199, etc.) and is used at *Il.* 5.699 of Hektor.

109 fire inhuman The adjective (*thespesios*) perhaps echoes, and varies, the word used by Homer (*thespidaes*) at *Il.* 15.597: 'throw on the curved ships the inhuman ... strength of fire'.

110 nursed the tearing anger These two lines suggest the whole of the antecedent action: the quarrel between Agamemnon and Achilles, the seizure of Achilles' prize, Briseis, his anger and withdrawal from the fighting for the insult to his honour – all of this would have been familiar to Bacch.'s audience from the *Iliad*, and there was no need for him to elaborate. Cf. note on 164-5, below.

tearing The word (*trachus*) literally means 'rough', 'jagged', and this is its only sense in Homer; cf. Bacch. 5.82, where it is used of an arrow. Non-literal usages are, however, common in post-Homeric writers; cf. Eur. *Med.* 447, where it is again used of 'anger' (*tracheian orgen*).

113 destruction The word so translated here is *ate*, a crucial concept in archaic Greek thought. In Homer it means 'delusion', almost always of divine origin; as Dodds defines it (*The Greeks and the Irrational*, (Berkeley, 1964), p. 5): '*Ate* is a state of mind – a temporary clouding or bewilderment of the normal consciousness', and in Homer it is always used to explain irrational or otherwise unaccountable behaviour, without any moral overtones. But in the post-Homeric world the word was moralized (Dodds, p. 38f.), and the meaning was extended to include not only the delusion, but the punishment which attended deluded, and therefore sinful or hybristic, behaviour. Sometimes too, the gods were still regarded as visiting *ate* upon the individual, and the concept, together with that of *miasma* ('pollution') became an important part of attempts to explain and interpret the notion of inherited guilt (see Dodds, p. 33f., and note on 14.3-6). See also Soph. *Ant.* 582-625, where these ideas are developed at length, and note esp. the last four lines: 'evil seems good to him whose mind god leads to sin' (*ate*); 'such a one is only briefly free of doom' (*ate*) (Soph. *Ant.* 622-5). Here is the whole range of meaning: heaven-sent delusion, sinful behaviour, and consequent ruin. Thus the meaning of *ate* passes into 'disaster', 'destruction', 'ruin', and this must be the sense here in Bacch. (but without any very prominent moral overtone). It cannot mean 'delusion' here, for the Trojans are not deluded; they are, as Bacch. describes it, cowering behind the walls of Troy for fear of being slaughtered by Achilles – a very sensible response. Nor can it mean, as Maehler seems to suggest (vol. 2, p. 271), 'bewilderment', or 'the paralysis of fear' (Erstarrung). As a state of mind, *ate* does not mean ordinary fear, bewilderment or uncertainty; it only means that clouding of the mind which leads to unaccountable behaviour, and there is nothing irrational or unaccountable about the Trojans' behaviour. Bacch. can only mean, then, that the withdrawal of Achilles has freed the Trojans from the death and destruction which would otherwise be visited upon them, whether soon or in the future.

116 many-towered The word does not survive on the papyrus, but is a reasonable restoration; it suggests the strength and security of the walls behind which the Trojans take refuge. The adjective occurs elsewhere only at Hom. Hymn 3.242.

117 the painful fighting Homer uses the same adjective (*oxus*, lit. ̄ 'sharp') of the war-god Ares himself (*Il.* 7.330).

120 murderous Cf. 'the bronze that lays men low' (50, above), of the sword of Herakles. Affective epithets such as this are not usually attached to weapons in Homer, but they become common in the lyric poets. Cf. e.g. Pind. *Ol.* 9.79 and 13.2.

121 But when This sentence is not completed, being interrupted by the long simile expressing the new-found hope and confidence of the Trojans (124f.). The sense is then resumed in the apodosis of the simile: 'so the Trojans ...' (133f.).

122 the Nereid i.e. Thetis, one of the fifty daughters of Nereus, and mother of Achilles. For Nereus, see note on 1.7-8; cf. also 17.101f., where Theseus, having descended to the palace of Poseidon under the sea, finds the daughters of Nereus dancing, with gold-braided ribbons in their hair.

violet-crowned (*iostephanos*) See note on 3.3. A similar adjective (*ioplokos*) is used of the Nereids at 17.37.

124 as the wind Not only does Bacch. derive his myth in Ode 13 from Homer's narrative of Hektor's assault on the Greek ships (*Il.* 15.592f., see intro., above) but he even includes a variation of the simile which Homer uses there (*Il.* 15.624f.). Bacch. has, however, changed the focus of the simile from Greeks to Trojans, and has incorporated also elements from another Homeric sea-simile (*Il.* 7.4f.). In *Il.* 15 the terror of the Greeks in the face of Hektor's onslaught is compared to the terror of storm-driven sailors; *Il.* 7.4f., on the other hand, compares the relief felt by the Trojans when Hektor and Alexandros rejoin the fighting to the relief which a following wind brings to sailors wearied from rowing. Bacch. combines these two images, in such a way as to make the simile his own. The terror felt by the Trojans, hard pressed by the storm of Achilles' fury, is relieved by his withdrawal.

from the North Storm winds in the Mediterranean blow mostly from the North (see note on 5.46). They are often described in the literature as originating in Thrace, that wild, inhospitable and little-known region to the north of Greece. Cf. the magnificent simile in *Antigone*: *ate* strikes the whole family 'like the wave that comes when the winds of Thrace run over the dark of the sea. The black sand of the bottom is brought from the depth; the beaten capes sound back with a hollow cry' (Soph. *Ant.* 586f.; trans. Elizabeth Wyckoff). Cf. also *Il.* 9.4f. and 23.230.

125 dark swell This represents an adjective (*kuananthes*) which occurs only here. For the meaning of the first part of the word (*kuan-* = 'dark') see note on 11.83. The second half of the compound is related to *anthos* ('flower'), and the whole word should mean something like 'darkly

210

blooming', but the origin and point of the metaphor remain obscure. Note however that Pindar uses a similar compound (*leukanthes*, 'pale-blossoming') of the smoke of funeral pyres (Pind. *Nem.* 9.23).

127 sunders the hearts The words are borrowed directly from Homer's simile, *Il.* 15.629.

129 it leaves off The same verb is used of Achilles at 123, above, pointing the closeness of the comparison between Achilles and the storm wind.

132 unhoped-for Used again at 3.29, of the day of one's death.

134 spear-fighter Agamemnon so describes Achilles at *Il.* 1.290.

135-6 was staying ... Picks up 110-11 and 121-3; Bacch. punctuates the narrative with repeated references to Achilles' absence. At the same time there is almost certainly a conscious echo (and variation) of Homer: (the followers of Achilles took no thought for the fighting) 'since ... brilliant Achilles lay where the ships were, angered over the girl of the lovely hair, Briseis' (*Il.* 2.688-9).
fair-haired (*xanthos*) A common decorative adjective; see notes on 5.91 and 5.38.

137 desire in her lovely limbs The translation represents a single adjective (*himeroguios*), made from the words for 'desire (*himeros*) and 'limbs' (*guia*). It occurs only here, and is one of Bacch.'s most striking creations. For Bacch.'s fondness for such adjectives, expressing his admiration for physical beauty, see notes on 9.38 and 11.12. Cf. also 17.9, where Bacch. uses a similar creation (*himerampux*) to describe Aphrodite: 'she whose headband is desire'.

139-40 seeing the sunlight The metaphor resumes and reinforces the terms of the simile (128-9); the withdrawal of Achilles represents the dawn of a new day of hope for the Trojans.

141 headlong The word may mean 'with all their forces', as it regularly does in fifth-century writers, but in Homer the meaning is always 'with all speed' (*Il.* 2.12, etc.), and an expression of haste or eagerness seems more appropriate here.

142 Laomedon's walls The walls of Troy were built for the king Laomedon, Priam's father, by Poseidon and Apollo (see e.g. *Il.* 7.452-3); hence the adjective 'god-built' (163, below). See also note on 1.13-14.

144 the strong encounter The phrase (*krateran husminan*) is a Homeric formula (*Il.* 5.84, etc.) for general fighting, and would certainly have been familiar as such to Bacch.'s audience. In the hope of producing a similar *frisson* of recognition, I have taken the liberty of borrowing Lattimore's fine translation.

145 the Danaans Originally the subjects of Danaos, king of Argos (see note on 11.74), then extended to mean the Greeks as a whole (*Il.* 1.42, etc.).

146-7 Ares ... and Apollo Ares plays no part in Homer's account. Zeus has forbidden the gods to intervene (*Il.* 8.10f.), and when Ares seeks to defy him and enter the fighting to avenge his slain son Askalaphos, he is forcibly detained on Olympos by Athena (*Il.* 15.113-42). Apollo, on the other hand, plays a major role; on Zeus' orders he goes to the wounded Hektor (*Il.* 15.231-3), revives and encourages him (15.253-70) and provides practical help by kicking down the embankment protecting the Greek ships (15.355-66).

147 **Loxias** For the meaning of this title of Apollo, see note on 3.66.
lord of Lycians The association of Apollo with Lycia in Asia Minor was early and close, although not usually expressed as emphatically as here. It may have originated in a confusion of the god's title *Lukeios* with the adjective *Lukios* (= Lycian). The meaning of the title *Lukeios* is still uncertain; it is perhaps derived from the root *luk-* (= 'light', cf. Latin 'lux') and attached to Apollo as 'god of light'. Similarly, the adjective *lukegenes* (*Il.* 4.101), anciently interpreted as 'born in Lycia', may rather mean 'born of light'. This derivation, however, is no longer widely accepted. Others, involving wolves (*lukos* = 'wolf'), have been proposed, or there may yet be some underlying geographical association. See G.S. Kirk, *The Iliad: A Commentary*, vol. 1, p. 340, note on 4.101. The Lycians are prominent in Homer's description of the fighting by the ships; cf. *Il.* 15.424-5 and 15.485-6.

149f. **they fought by the ... sterns** So the narrative returns to its starting point, the last-ditch defence of the ships by Aias (see intro., above). The ring-compositional structure is emphasized by verbal echoes: 'splendid sterns' (150) picks up 104, where Aias 'stood upon the stern', while the reference to Hektor (154) echoes 106.

151-2 **the dark earth ran red** Borrowed directly from Homer: 'and the dark earth ran with blood' (*Il.* 15.715).

155-6 **the heroes** The papyrus is broken here; the text and the exact meaning of these two lines are not recoverable. However, since 'the onrush of the godlike' must surely refer to the charge of the attacking Trojans, 'the heroes' (155) will presumably refer to the defending Greeks, so that the lines may be describing generalized fighting, as an extension of, and in parallel to, the individual combat suggested by the reference to Hektor (154). For 'heroes' (*hemitheoi*, lit. = 'half-divine') see note on 11.60. In the next line Bacch. uses the almost identical word 'godlike' (*isotheoi*) simply, no doubt, for the sake of variation.

157f. Again, the papyrus is badly damaged here, and the text is very uncertain, especially at the beginning of the lines. The general sense, however, seems fairly clear. The description of the eager assault on the ships is developed, and concluded, with a reference to the hopes of the Trojans for imminent victory. They thought that they would burn the ships, drive out the Greeks, and celebrate with victory banquets in their city. This leads, through a brief mention of the future disappointment of these hopes (164-5) to renewed praise of the Aiakid heroes (Achilles is now included, 166f.), and so the mythic narrative comes back finally to where it began (100f.).

157 proud hopes Cf. *Il.* 15.701: 'the spirit within the breast of every Trojan hoped to burn the ships'.

160 Trojan horsemen 'Trojan' is missing from the papyrus, but is certainly to be restored; cf. the description 'horse-breakers' (*hippodamoi*) often applied to them in Homer (*Il.* 4.352, etc.).

161 dark-eyed (*kuanopis*) For adjectives compounded from *kuaneos*, 'dark-blue', 'dark', see note on 11.83). Before Bacch. the word was used only of dark-eyed women (e.g. Hom. *Od.* 12.60, of Amphitrite; Hes. *Shield* 356, of Themistonoe, daughter of Ceyx, king of Trachis). Bacch. transfers it to ships here as a simple variation of Homer's 'dark-prowed' (*kuanoproros, Il.* 15.693), suggested no doubt by the contemporary practice of painting eyes on the bows of ships. See Morrison and Williams, *Greek Oared Ships* (Cambridge, 1968), plate 21e; also Morrison and Coates, *The Athenian Trireme* (Cambridge, 1986) p. 150 n. 21. (Cf. also Aisch. *Supp.* 716: '(the ship's) prow, scanning the way before it with its eyes'.) The reference is probably not literally to the 'eye' of the ship itself, which would not have been 'dark', but painted in bright colours against the dark-blue background. Aisch. also uses 'dark-eyed' of ships, at *Pers.* 559 and *Supp.* 743; *Persai* was produced in 472 BC, and *Supp.* is now generally thought to be after 470, so that Bacch. was probably the first to use the word in this way.

162 banquets The word (*eilapinai*) refers particularly to festive banquets on special occasions, such as marriages (*Il.* 18.491, etc.) It is thus appropriate for the victory celebrations which the Trojans thought they would soon enjoy.

163 god-built See note on 142, above.

164-5 But see, before that Expressions of this kind, embodying the poet's own comment on the action, are very frequent in Homer; see M. Edwards, *The Iliad: A Commentary* (Cambridge, 1991), vol. 5, p. 5. They are often used, as here, to highlight the folly of misplaced confidence, e.g. *Il.* 12.113f.: 'poor fool, he was not going to escape destruction and return again to windy Ilion', and *Il.* 17.497f.: 'poor fools, they were not going to come back ... without the shedding of blood'. Here the reversal, the contrast between the high hopes of the Trojans and their ultimate failure, is emphasized by the close echo of 150-1; it was not after all Greek blood shed that would bring the conflict to its climax. Bacch. is looking forward to *Iliad* 21, the fight between Achilles and Scamander, and perhaps especially to 21.212f., where the voice of Scamander rises up out of the 'deep-eddying' river and complains that his waters are choked with the corpses slain by Achilles. Again (see note on 110-11, above), Bacch.'s audience would certainly have been familiar with this episode; there was no need to go into detail, and the expression gains greatly in dramatic impact from the brevity of the allusion.

would stain blood-red Scamander's swirling waters Exactly the same words are used at 27.36-7, in a prophecy regarding Achilles' future. Cf. also 3.44-5: 'the swirling waters of Paktolos ... run red with blood'.

swirling (*dinanta*) For this adjective and its compounds, applied to rivers, see notes on 5.40 and 3.44.

166 sons of Aiakos The patronymic 'Aiakids' is used here; Achilles and Aias were actually grandsons of Aiakos, but see note on 46, above. Bacch. is clearly thinking primarily of Achilles (see previous note), but Aias is included to pick up the reference at 102-4 and complete the ring-composition.

169-74 Only two half-lines survive from this passage, but even this small fragment is sufficient to make the general sense clear: 'even if their bodies perish and disappear, whether in the grave or on the funeral pyre, their fame will live on for ever', an assertion which leads into the following *gnomes* on the enduring value of *areta*. On the structure and sequence of thought in this section of the ode, see intro., above.

175-81 far-shining excellence This gnomic passage closely echoes that at 59-66, and is in turn echoed by 199f. The repetition punctuates and provides structure to the ode, emphasizing the important themes. For the thought, see esp. 1.181-4, 3.90f., and 9.85-7, with the notes there; cf. also Pind. *Isth*. 6.10f. On the importance of 'excellence' (*areta*) to Bacch. and his patrons, see intro. to Ode 1.

far-shining This word (*pasiphanes*) occurs only here. It echoes the adjective used at 62, above, (*poluphantos*, also unique to Bacch.), as well as the phrase at 82 (see the notes there), thus reinforcing the structural patterning of the ode. For the expression, cf. 'shining excellence' (*phaennai aretai*), Pind. *Nem*. 7.51.

177 the lightless veil of night A striking metaphor for darkness and obscurity. Given the close parallel between the gnomic passages in this ode, however, there may also be a suggestion of the idea that *areta* will live on beyond the grave; cf. 63, above.

178-9 renown enduring Perhaps a variation of the Homeric 'undying fame' (*Il*. 9.413). The adjective used by Bacch. here (*akamatos*) literally means 'untiring'; the idea is more appropriate to the act of spreading than to the renown itself, but it seems intended to suggest that the renown will not weaken or fade. The same epithet is used, more appropriately, at 5.26, where it indicates the ceaseless swell and movement of the sea (see the note there).

179 she spreads Although the idea is not explicit at this point, Bacch. is surely thinking of the role of his own song in spreading the fame of success throughout the world. It becomes explicit at the end (13.228-31), and is a common theme in the odes; cf. e.g. 3.94-98. For the motif of fame spreading over land and sea, also common in the victory-poems, cf. 9.40f., also Pind. *Isth*. 4.46 and *Nem*. 6.48.

181 restless (*poluplanktos*) Lit. = 'wandering', cf. 'the wandering judgements of men' (11.35). Homer uses the word of a storm-wind at sea (*Il*.

11.308), suggesting the sudden veering of the wind from one quarter to another; Bacch. may have taken the word from there, and transferred it to the sea itself.

182 she honours Bacch. passes now into praise of the victor's homeland, which stands as a concrete example illustrating the truth of the preceding *gnome*. Excellence (*areta*) and good repute (*eukleia*) – here both personified – go hand in hand. Aigina wins honour not only through the *areta* of her citizens, but through the renown won by those who display this quality, and for Bacch. that means especially her successful athletes.

183 glorious Properly 'bringing glory', cf. 59, above (and see note on 1.128). So here the meaning is that the island of Aigina confers glory on her people by association with the heroic exploits of their Aiakid ancestors (especially Achilles and Aias).

185 Eukleia The word means 'fame', 'good repute', and is here personified (see note on 182, above).
lover of the crown The choice of adjective (*philostephanos*) makes it clear that Bacch. is thinking especially of the fame to be gained from success in the Games.

186 Eunomia Aigina is praised also for her stability and good order (*eunomia*, also personified here), which allow her to flourish in peace and to enjoy the benefits of that peace, such as religious festivals and revelry. Cf. fr. 4.61f.: 'peace brings to men wealth ... and garlands of song ... thighs of oxen burn to the gods ... young men turn their minds to exercise ... and revelry'. In Hesiod (*Theog.* 901-2), Eunomia was one of the three *Horai* (Hours), daughters of Zeus and Themis ('Law') and her sisters were Dike ('Justice') and Eirene ('Peace'). Cf. Pind. *Ol.* 9.15-16: 'Themis , and her daughter of great renown, Eunomia', and Bacch. 15.55-6, where he speaks of 'Justice, attendant of holy Eunomia and wise Themis'. Pindar also describes Aigina as 'well-ordered' (*eunomon*) at *Isth.* 5.22.

187 allotted At *Il.*15.190-2 Poseidon relates how he, Zeus and Hades drew lots to divide control of the world between them; Poseidon won the sea, Zeus the sky and Hades the underworld. Later poets also sometimes use expressions indicating that the other gods too received their individual spheres of influence by lot; cf. e.g. Pind. *Nem.* 11.1; *Ol.* 9.15.

190 Sing, boys A direct address to the young men of the chorus who are singing this ode. For choruses of young men singing the *komos*, cf. 6.5-6 and 9.102 (the text in this latter passage, however, is partly conjectural); also Pind. *Isth.* 8.2f. The words echo the image at 83-4, above: 'to praise your power a girl in high pride sings ...', as part of the parallel between the first and second victor- and city-praise.

192 Menandros' care and help This is the only passage in Bacch. in which the athlete's trainer is singled out for special praise. The Athenian (Pind. *Nem.* 5.49) Menandros must have been one of the most successful professional trainers of his time; as Bacch. tells us, his protégés had already won many victories at Olympia (193-5), as well as 'countless' crowns at the other panhellenic Games (196-8), and he is praised by Pindar too in his ode for this same victory (*Nem.* 5.48-9). It is a measure of the importance placed by Lampon, the victor's father, on the physical and athletic development of his children, that he was prepared to employ a trainer of such distinction for them.

care and help In the first of his two odes for Pytheas' younger brother Phylakidas (*Isth.* 6; see intro., above) Pindar alludes to the dictum of Hesiod: 'care profits the work' (Hes. *Works and Days* 412) and praises Lampon for impressing this good advice on his sons (*Isth.* 6.66-8). Bacch. here uses language which closely echoes that of Hesiod, and it is clear that he too had the Hesiodic passage in mind. See also note on 3.60.

193 holy Athena The adjective (*semnos*) appears for the first time in the Homeric Hymn to Demeter (Hom. Hymn 2.1) and is widely used thereafter of various gods. Bacch. applies it to Artemis at 5.101. For a similar accumulation of epithets, cf. 5.101-2; also 11.37-9, where four are used, again of Artemis.

great-hearted Bacch. may have borrowed this expression from the *Odyssey*, where the word, common enough in the *Iliad* as an epithet for the heroes, is used twice of Athena (*Od.* 8.520 and 13.121).

194 of the golden chariot The word so translated (*chrusarmatos*) is especially favoured by Pindar (*Ol.* 3.19, *Pyth.* 5.9 and *Isth.* 6.19; he does not, however, apply it to Athena). It is not found elsewhere, unless it is to be restored at 3.27; see the note there.

195 by the waters of Alpheos i.e. at Olympia; see note on 6.3. Maehler suggests (vol. 2, p. 285) that the reference to Olympic victories achieved by other protégés of Menandros represents a wish for similar success for Pytheas in the future. For such a wish cf. 8.26-32 and note on 8.27.

196 and crowning The grammatical structure of this sentence changes in mid-stream, but the meaning is clear. Reference to victories won by pupils of Menandros must continue; not only has Athena rewarded the trainer's care and dedication with victories at Olympia, but she has done the same at other festivals as well.

197 victors' garlands The words echo 69-70, which describe the homecoming of Pytheas, 'hair crowned with garlands', thus continuing the parallel between the first and second sections of victor-praise. See note on 190, above.

198 the panhellenic Games After the reference to victories won by Menandros' charges at Olympia, this must mean 'the other' panhellenic Games, i.e. the Pythian, Nemean and Isthmian, where they have also been successful. Bacch. actually says: 'at the Games of the panhellenes'; Maehler (vol. 2, p. 286) understands this to mean: 'Games in which all Greeks could take part', and would include minor local festivals as well as the four 'majors', but this seems unlikely. Pindar draws a clear distinction between minor festivals such as those at Athens and Sikyon on the one hand, and 'the common festivals of the panhellenes' on the other (*Isth.* 4.27-32) and this was almost certainly the normal usage. At 11.29 the crown at Olympia is 'the silvery olive that welcomes all', and there are similar expressions in Pindar (*Ol.* 3.18 and 6.63).

199f. The praise of the trainer Menandros passes into the final gnomic section of the ode. The transition is effected smoothly by the fact that 'the man of skill' (202) might initially be thought to continue the praise of Menandros, but the reference is certainly widened in this generalized gnomic section to include all men of skill, and in particular, successful athletes. The second half of this long passage (210-19) is missing, but it is clear from what survives that the themes of the first two gnomic passages (59-66 and 175-81) are here continued and developed, and there are many parallels and echoes. The themes are, principally, the need to give praise where praise is deserved, unconstrained by malice or envy, and the connection between success and undying fame.

199-202 overmastered by envy These lines pick up and develop the oblique suggestion of the motif at 65, above; see the note there. For other significant expressions of the 'envy-motif', see esp. 3.67 and 11.124-6, with the notes there.

203 mortal men find fault Something of a commonplace in early poetry; cf. Pind. *Ol.* 6.74: 'reproach from others who are envious hangs over ... (those who win)'; cf. *Pyth.* 1.81f., *Theog.* 799f. and 1183.

204 truth will prevail i.e. sooner or later the truth will out, and success and *areta* will win the renown which is their due. For the idea, cf. 175f., above.

205 time that overcomes all things The same phrase is used by Simonides in his epigram for the fallen at Thermopylai (*PMG* 531.5) written a few years after Ode 13; Simonides may have been imitating his nephew.

207 success nobly won Recalls 66, above, where the wording is very similar. See also 14.18 and the note there.

209 unseen Note the synaethesia (the blending of the visual and the auditory) in the metaphor; cf. Pind. *Nem.* 7.61: 'keeping away dark blame'. The adjective 'unseen' is proleptic, i.e. it anticipates the result of the action; the criticism will fade away, so that it is then 'invisible'.

220 warms ... with hope For very similar expressions see 1.164-5 and 10.41, with the notes there. This line is the conclusion and climax of the whole long gnomic section ('I too' (221) clearly turns to a new topic) and as such it may represent a hope, and a wish, for future (presumably Olympian) success for Pytheas. Cf. note on 195, above.

221-2 in this i.e. (presumably), in the hope for future success just mentioned (220).

and in the Muses Bacch. concludes the ode with a final statement of this important theme: the athlete's prowess and the poet's song will combine to create undying fame. He thanks his host and patron Lampon, the victor's father, for his hospitality, for which the present ode, honouring Pytheas, is not only grateful recompense, but the source also of widespread renown (230-1). For similar statements of the poet's role in the creation of immortality, see esp. 3.90f., with notes on 3.92 and 96; cf. also note on 5.4.

222 crimson-veiled The word is used at 11.101 of Leto, mother of Artemis; see the note there, and for Bacch.'s fondness for such colour words see note on 9.10.

223 I display The same verb (*phainein*) is used at 75 and 81, above. Just as Pytheas 'displayed' his strength in the pankration, and Zeus 'displayed' the victory to all the Greeks, so Bacch. 'displays' his poem of praise. The repetition underscores the close relation between success and the fame which the poet's song will bring to it.

225 hospitality One of the central values of ancient (as indeed it still is of modern) Greek society; see note on 1.150.

228 Klio This reference to the Muse responsible for Bacch.'s song picks up the reference at 9, above (see the note there) and thus completes the ring-compositional structure; cf. note on 3.97.
rich in flowers Cf. 70, above, where the same epithet (*panthales*) is used of the garlands adorning the victor's head on his return home. This is yet another of the many significant echoes which unite the victory and the song as bringing fame. Cf. also 59, above.

229 filled my mind Cf. 12.1-2, where a similar expression is used (again of Klio).

230 shall herald The word is more appropriate to the official announcement of the victory at the Games.

231 to all the people Just as Zeus displayed the victory 'before all the Greeks' (81), so too will Bacch. with his song. The echo serves once more to point the connection between the victory and the song. The conclusion of Ode 13 is remarkably similar to that of Ode 3; see esp. 3.96-8, and note on 221-2, above.

ODE 14
FOR KLEOPTOLEMOS OF THESSALY
Chariot-Race, Petraian Games

The background

It appears from the title, and from the remaining part of the poem, that Ode 14 was written to celebrate a victory by the Thessalian Kleoptolemos in the chariot-race at the Petraia, a minor local competition held somewhere in Thessaly, in honour of Poseidon. 'Petraios' (which means 'of the rock') was a cult name of Poseidon in Thessaly, but evidence for the cult, and for the Petraian Games associated with it, is very scant indeed, and depends on late sources. Pindar (*Pyth.* 4.138) calls Pelias, the legendary king of Iolkos in Thessaly, 'son of Poseidon Petraios', and one of the *scholia* on this passage (*schol.* 246b) tells us that 'Games were organized in honour of Poseidon 'Petraios' at the place where the first horse sprang forth from the rock (*petra*); for this reason he is also called *hippios*' (i.e. 'god of horses'). The same story lies behind other late sources, such as *Et. Mag.* 473, 42-5: 'Poseidon is called 'god of horses' because he produced the first horse, in Thessaly, by striking the rock (*petra*) with his trident; whence the sanctuary of Poseidon Petraios was established in Thessaly.'

Ap. Rhod. (*Argonaut.* 3.1244) refers to a place called Petra, and the *schol.* (a) explains this as ' a town in Thessaly where Games of Poseidon are held, taking the name Petraion, from the place'. It is, however, impossible to determine where Petra lay, or in what part of Thessaly the Petraia was held; the other *schol.* on Pindar *Pyth.* 4.138 (i.e. *schol.* 246a; see above) relates that Poseidon was honoured as 'Petraios' among the Thessalians because 'he cut through the mountains' (i.e. the rocks, *petrai*) 'and allowed the river to flow through'. If there is anything behind this story, perhaps Petra and the Petraia should be sought somewhere in the Tempe valley in northeastern Thessaly, through which the river Peneios flows to the sea, but this is only a guess.

Finally, Vergil (*Georg.* 1.11-12) also alludes to the legend that Poseidon produced the first horse by striking the earth, and Servius, the fourth-century AD commentator on Vergil says, on this passage: 'for this reason equestrian contests were established for Poseidon by the Thessalians'. The fact that Servius explicitly refers to 'equestrian contests' may suggest that the Petraian Games were confined to this type of event, but there is no other evidence either for or against this.

The poem

Ode 14 opens with a long and elaborate sequence of *gnomes*, which for Bacchylides is an unprecedented structure. Individually, each of these *gnomes* expresses what is in effect a commonplace of archaic and early classical thought, and parallels can easily be found in other writers, especially the earlier elegiac poets Solon and Theognis, as well as in other poems of Bacch. himself. Collectively, however, the sequence is unique, and Bacch. has carefully structured this opening gnomic section so as to lead from the broadest generalization of lines 1-2, into the specific victor-praise which begins at line 19. The whole section might be paraphrased as follows: 'The best you can hope for is that the gods have got you marked down for good fortune (1-2), because we mortals have no control over our own destinies (3-6); all you can do is behave with as much decency and honour as you can, whatever your chosen pathway in life – and there are many (7-11). Every human activity has its proper time and place, whether it be war with its suffering and grief, or the joyful pursuits of peace – music, dancing and festivities (12-18), and now is the time to celebrate the victory … (19).' Thus Bacch. brings his ode around to the immediate subject and embarks upon his 'programme' – the praise of the victor Kleoptolemos (19f.) – referring briefly to the victor himself, the Games, the event, and the victor's father. It is probable, given the elaborate nature of the introduction, that the victor-praise was developed here at some length; indeed, it is likely that the whole ode was similarly and proportionately extensive. Unfortunately the papyrus is broken to the right of Column 35, which ends at 14.23, and this is the last surviving column of the roll. All that we have of Ode 14, then, is the introduction and the first few lines of the victor-praise, and there is nothing to indicate how much of the ode is missing, nor how many odes may have followed it on this roll, (but see the introduction to Ode 14 B).

1 **fate-favoured of god** i.e. to enjoy good fortune is best, whether it comes from fate (*moira*) or from the gods. There was in Homer and in early Greek thought no essential difference between fate and the gods; both are seen as the 'cause of events which man is powerless to alter' (W.C. Greene, *Moira* (Harper Torchbooks, 1963) p. 14), and sometimes both are named together, e.g. *Il.* 18.82-4: 'cursed destiny has put me in your hands; and I think I must be hated by Zeus the father who has given me once more to you'; cf. Solon, 13.63-4: 'Moira brings good and evil to mortals, and the gifts of the … gods are inescapable'. For the thought expressed here cf. 5.50-3: 'blessed is he to whom god has given his share of good and a life to live of wealth and coveted good fortune', and 4.19-21: 'what better than to be loved by gods and win one's share of blessings of every kind?' In Ode 5 Hieron is described as 'fate-favoured' (5.1), and the good fortune that the gods have bestowed on him is there understood especially in terms of his success in the Games (as it is also in Ode 4; see notes on 5.51 and 4.19-21). So here the *gnome* looks forward to the introduction of the victor in line 19 as one who has enjoyed the special favour of the gods. In Odes 4 and 5 the victor's success expands into the generalization; in Ode 14, however, the opposite is true – the focus narrows, from the opening *gnome*, to concentrate attention finally upon the victor.

3-6 These lines explain the opening *gnome*. We mortals can only hope that the gods are on our side, because we cannot foresee what will happen to us (a familiar theme, cf. Bacch. 10.45: 'the future brings to birth ends unforeseeable', and 9.89-90: 'God's will brings to light what is hidden in the dark of night'; similarly, e.g. Theog. 135-6 and Solon 13.65-6); we certainly have no control over what happens to us, and worst of all, our fortunes clearly bear no relation to our behaviour.

Here Bacch. is giving expression to what was the central moral dilemma of Archaic Greek thought, and not only of Greek, but of another major contemporary culture as well, for there are, as will become evident, astonishing parallels between the mentality and the thought patterns of Archaic Greece and those of the early Hebrews as revealed in the Old Testament. The dilemma in question is the age-old problem of undeserved, irrational suffering. For it is evident that the good do not always prosper, nor the wicked always suffer, and complaints about the unfairness of the world ring loud and clear in the ancient literature: 'How, Zeus, can your mind venture to hold the sinful and the just in equal fortune?' (Theog. 377-8); compare with this the lament of Job: 'wherefore do the wicked live, become old, yea, are mighty in power? ... their houses are safe from fear, neither is the rod of God upon them' (Job 21:7-9), and the plaintive cry of the psalmist: 'Lord, how long shall the wicked triumph?' (Psalm 94:3); cf. Jeremiah 12:1.

The doctrine that all human fortune, whether good or ill, comes from the gods, was virtually universal in the Archaic Age: 'Zeus holds the ends of all things that are, and disposes as he will' (Semon. 1.1-2); 'no man is the cause of ruin or gain; the gods are givers of them both' (Theog. 133-4); 'Moira brings evil and good to mortals, and the gifts of the immortal gods are inescapable' (Solon 13.63-4; note incidentally the fusion of Moira (Fate) and the gods; see note on 1, above). So it was in Homer too; at *Iliad* 24.527f. Achilles describes to Priam the twin urns, one of good, one of evil, from which Zeus dispenses to mortal men their destiny. Homer is fully aware that suffering is the normal condition of mankind; no one receives exclusively from the urn of good fortune. But in the *Iliad* this is never a moral issue; it is simply described and accepted as the way the world is: 'such is the way the gods spun life for unfortunate mortals, that we live in unhappiness, but the gods themselves have no sorrows' (*Il.* 24.525-6); compare again the words of Job: 'man that is born of a woman is of few days and full of sorrow' (Job 14:1). So what changed between the Bronze Age as described in the *Iliad* and the Archaic Age as reflected in the poetry of Solon, Theognis, Bacchylides and others? Why did the suffering of the innocent become a moral problem?

Two books are of crucial importance in understanding this issue: E.R. Dodds, *The Greeks and the Irrational* (Berkeley 1964), and Julian Jaynes, *The Origin of Consciousness in the Breakdown of the Bicameral Mind* (Penguin Books, 1976). Dodds outlines the rise of morality, with brilliant insight, in what he describes as the shift from 'shame-culture' to 'guilt-culture', but he is unable to explain why or how this happened. For that we must turn to Jaynes, who, with equally brilliant insight, shows how this new morality, this new consciousness of right and wrong, which did not exist in Homer, and had never existed before, was able to emerge from the ruins of bicamerality.

Jaynes points out that there are in the *Iliad* no words for good and evil, right and wrong, for conscience, will, or morality, and that the words do not exist because the notions did not exist at that time. Human choice, human action, was not driven from within; it did not depend on a person's inner consciousness of right and wrong, but was imposed as it were from without – it was god-driven, and the mechanism was what we would call hallucination. All the important actions in the *Iliad*, all the important decisions, are initiated by gods. Especially at moments of great stress, in unprecedented situations which could not be dealt with on the basis of habit, the individual heard (hallucinated) the voice of his god, which told him what to do. So Achilles saw and heard Athena telling him not to kill Agamemnon (*Il.* 1.197f.), so Thetis appeared to him to remind him of his destiny (18.94f.) and Iris urged him back to the fighting (18.169f.). So too did Moses hear the voice of God from the burning bush commanding him to deliver the Israelites from Egypt (Exodus 3:4f.) and Abraham was commanded by God to kill his son (Genesis 22:2f.). But the intervention of the gods in this way is not to be understood as a poetic fiction, either in the Old Testament or in the *Iliad*; it is in fact an actual description of a type of event which could, and did, take place in real life. (Just so do schizophrenics even today hear inescapable voices commanding them to do sometimes bizarre and self-destructive things.) 'The gods were what we now call hallucinations' (Jaynes, p. 74); they 'took the place of consciousness' (id., p. 72).

But in the enormous turmoil, upheaval and movement of populations which accompanied the end of the Bronze Age, social cohesion broke down, traditional authority structures broke down, and the voices were heard more and more erratically, and finally not at all. 'And Saul asked counsel of God ... but He answered him not that day' (I Samuel 14:37); 'O my God, I cry in the daytime, but Thou hearest not' (Psalm 22:2); cf. *Il.* 22.226f., where Hektor is deluded by the disappearance of Athena. And when the voices fail, only morality, based on a consciousness of the consequences of action, can tell men what to do (Jaynes, p. 286). And only then, when men base their actions and choices on this inner sense of right and wrong, newly emergent in human mentality, could the disparity between behaviour and reward become apparent. Thus there arose, in the Archaic Age for the first time, the problem of undeserved suffering.

The answer to this dilemma (at least the answer which became standard in Archaic Greece) was to suppose that the sinner would pay for his sins through his descendants, and thus was born the doctrine of inherited guilt – 'they who escape themselves ... the innocent pay for their deeds, either the children or the generation thereafter' (Solon 13.29-32); 'he who ... does wicked deeds without regard for the gods should himself pay ... and the sins of the father should not become a misfortune for the children' (Theog. 733-6); cf. 'when once a house is shaken by the gods, the curse does not fail ... and no generation can free the next' (Soph. *Ant.* 584f.); and 'for I the Lord thy God am a jealous God, visiting the iniquity of the fathers upon the children unto the third and fourth generation' (Exodus 20:5).

The concept of inherited guilt, mythologized into the hereditary curse, provided material for some of the most powerful ancient Greek tragedies. But Bacch. is not writing as a tragedian; he is not concerned here with moral issues, and merely states the dilemma as a fact of life – the common disparity between behaviour and reward is presented here as foil for the deserved success of the athlete, whose victory is a mark of god's favour.

7 **each has a different ... honour** For the expression cf. 10.36-7 and the note there.

8 **men win success in countless ways** Lit. = 'countless are the *aretai* of men'; for the expression cf. 10.38 (also fr. 20 C 19: 'countless are the skills of men'). For *areta* ('excellence'), which in Bacch. is always, if sometimes only implicitly, associated with athletic success, see intro. to Ode 1, and note on 1.181-2. So here the *gnome* with its summary climax ('there are all kinds of *aretai*, but the best is ...') anticipates the imminent focus on the athlete himself, which emerges in line 19. It is, in other words, the victor who has 'justly handled the task at hand' (i.e. the contest). See also note on 18, below.

13 **sweet song** The adjective used here (*liguklanges*) occurs only in this passage and at 5.73 (see note there). For the meaning of compounds based on *ligu-* see note on 5.22.

14 **heavy with grief** This adjective (*barupenthes*) is another of Bacch.'s many coinages; it occurs here for the first time, and is borrowed by later writers. For adjectives compounded with *baru-* see note on 7.3, and cf. 'a heavy burden', 3, above (*barutlatos*).

17-18 **the [right time] is best** i.e. actions must be appropriate to the circumstances and the situation. The restoration can be regarded as certain; cf. Hes. *Works and Days* 694 and Theog. 401-2, in both of which the wording is virtually identical. This positive proposition stands as conclusion to the two preceding negative statements; it suggests that now is the right time for song and celebration, and thus leads directly into the specific victor-praise which follows (19f.).

18 **god also [...]** The missing verb will have meant something like 'extols', 'supports', 'causes to prosper'. This is not a version of the common assertion that the victory itself is the gift of god; rather the meaning is that the athlete, by virtue of his success, will enjoy god's continuing favour and support.

him who succeeds The words used here (*eu erdein*) are in fact fairly general in meaning; the sense is 'to do good' (5.36), or, with an object, 'to behave well towards' (1.163). But at 13.66 and 207 (and in a similar phrase at 3.94) the words carry an unmistakeably specific reference to success in the Games, and this is certainly the meaning here also. The sentence echoes 1-2, providing a ring-compositional structure for the opening section of the ode, while at the same time the reference to the victorious athlete confirms that the whole of this gnomic sequence reflects upon the victor: it is he who has dealt justly with the task at hand (10-11); it is he who has displayed his *areta* (8); it is he who is 'fate-favoured' (1). Thus this final climactic *gnome* forms the natural transition to the following victor-praise.

19 Now Marks, as often, the return from the generalities of the opening section to the present occasion of celebration. Cf. 10.9 and 11.9, with the notes there.

a gift (*charin*) The word stands in apposition to the sentence. The celebration itself (and the poet's song) are the gift to the victorious Kleoptolemos. For the usage cf. 3.97; see also 9.97 and the note there.

20 the sanctuary i.e. the place where the victory was won. For Petraios as a cult title of Poseidon, see intro., above.

23 who Refers, no doubt, to the victor himself, Kleoptolemos, while the following adjectives form part of the praise of the victor's father or of his family.

hospitable A common element in the victor-praise; cf. 3.16 and 5.49 (both in reference to Hieron); also 13.224-6.

right-judging (*orthodikos*) Used at 11.9 of the river Styx, in the Underworld; see the note there. Cf. also 'straight-judging' (*euthudikos*, 5.6).

ODE 14B
FOR ARISTOTELES OF LARISA

The two poems, or rather fragments of poems, designated 14A and 14B, survive on a piece of papyrus found at Oxyrhynchus in Egypt, published by E. Lobel as Pap. Oxy. 23.2363, and referred to in discussion of the text of Bacchylides as Pap. L. It contains traces of letters and a few words from the last six lines of one poem, followed by the first eleven lines of another. Faint traces of the title of the second ode are visible at the broken left edge.

It was at once obvious that this new papyrus fragment came from another copy of the victory odes of Bacchylides, for the text of two unplaced fragments of the main papyrus (Pap. A, frr. 22 and 11) reappears in Pap. L. But there is no room, even in the longer gaps in Pap. A, for these two newly discovered poems; they must therefore have stood after Ode 14, and, probably, represented the last two poems on the roll of victory odes. The fragment has therefore been inserted between the victory odes and the dithyrambs, but in order not to disrupt the established numbering of the dithyrambs, which begin at Ode 15, they have been numbered as Odes 14A and 14B.

Nothing can be discovered of the occasion or content of 14A, and the surviving eleven lines of 14B are only marginally more informative. It was

224

written to honour Aristoteles (line 8) of Larisa in Thessaly (6 and 10), and the fact that Aristoteles is praised as a winner twice at Delphi (7-9) led Lobel to the view that the ode was written for a Pythian victory, perhaps in the horse- or chariot-race (see note on 10, below). But this is very unlikely. It is true that the rationale behind the ordering of the victory odes of Bacch. is not entirely clear, but the principle of diminishing importance seems to have been at least partly at work, and it is improbable that a victory at Delphi would have been consigned to the end of the book, especially if it was won in an equestrian event, for these carried the greatest prestige. Besides, the scant remains of the title of the ode (see above) do not, apparently, support the restoration 'Pythia'.

Ode 14 celebrates a victory at the Petraia in Thessaly, and it might be thought that 14A and 14B were likewise written for victories in minor local Games. (Cf. Pind. *Nem.* 9 and 10, which are not 'Nemean' odes at all, being written to celebrate victories at Sicyon and Argos respectively). But Maehler (vol. 2, pp. 302-3) argues persuasively against this also. First, the poem begins with a long and elaborate invocation of Hestia, goddess of the hearth and home; although there were indeed altars of Hestia at both Olympia and Delphi (cf. e.g. Hom. Hymn 24.1-2), she seems to have had no real involvement with athletic competition. Second, it is a rule in epinician poetry that the victory which is the occasion of the ode is always mentioned first (cf. e.g. Ode 10.28f.) even if earlier victories were more important and prestigious. We should expect then, unless this rule is uniquely broken in Ode 14B, that the minor victory which it celebrates would be mentioned before the reference to the twofold success at Delphi in lines 7-9.

It seems likely therefore, that the occasion of the ode is not athletic at all, but is connected in some way with the goddess Hestia who is the subject of its opening lines. There is an interesting parallel in Pindar. *Nem.* 11, the last in Pindar's book of Nemean odes, is neither Nemean nor a victory ode, but was written to celebrate the installation of a certain Aristagoras into the civic office of *prutanis* in the island of Tenedos; this ode too begins with a long invocation of, and prayer to Hestia, and Maehler, not least on the strength of this parallel, suggests that the occasion of Ode 14B was similar, celebrating the installation of Aristoteles into a civic office in Larisa, perhaps the office of *hipparch* (commander of the cavalry).

1 **Hestia** In the mythology Hestia, whose name means 'hearth', is the daughter of Kronos and Rhea, and the sister of Demeter, Hera, Hades, Poseidon and Zeus (Hes. *Theog.* 453f.). Apart from this, however, there is very little of mythological interest attached to her name. She does not appear as a goddess in Homer, but even there the hearth is already central to the life and sanctity of the home (*Od.* 6.52), a place of refuge for suppliants (*Od.* 7.153) and the basis of a solemn oath (*Od.* 14.157).

As the personification of the 'hearth', Hestia thus becomes the goddess who represents the centre and focal point of home and family life, and in the civic sphere likewise, she protects and watches over the hearth/altar/sacred fire of the city, and is thus a major focus of the religious and political life of the community. The invocation of Hestia therefore, is appropriate to an important civic occasion, and supports Maehler's suggestion regarding the occasion of the ode (see intro., above).

gold-enthroned (*chrusothronos*). If there was indeed a statue of Hestia by the city's central hearth, it is not likely to have been of gold, and the adjective is better regarded as conventional and decorative, as it is in Homer, who uses it of several goddesses (e.g. *Il.* 1.611, of Hera). For such adjectives compounded with *chruso-* ('gold') see note on 4.1.

2 **seated in mid-city** The expression literally means: 'seated in the middle of the streets', but Bacch. has used 'streets' elsewhere by metonymy for 'city' (9.17, 9.52, and fr. 4.79; see note on 9.17) and this is surely the meaning here also. The reference is probably not literally to a seated statue of the goddess (see previous note), but metaphorical, simply indicating the position of the hearth in the city centre, in the building known as the *prutaneion* ('town-hall' is perhaps the closest equivalent). Pindar, in his similar invocation of Hestia (*Nem.* 11, see intro., above) specifically locates her in the *prutaneion* (11.1-3).

4 **Agathokleadai** Presumably the name of the family or clan in Larisa to which Aristoteles belonged. The form is 'patronymic', meaning 'children of …' or 'descendants of …' (cf. note on 13.46); the name on which it is based (Agathokleas) is fairly common, and is found in inscriptions from various parts of Thessaly, including Larisa, as well as from other parts of Greece. For a similar patronymic clan name cf. the Euxantidai, honoured in Ode 1, and see esp. note on 1.127.

5 **Peneios** The most important river in Thessaly, flowing eastward through the fertile plains of central Greece. The city of Larisa (one of the longest continuously inhabited towns in Greece) stands on the right bank of the river, at the point where it turns northwards, to flow eventually through the lush but narrow valley of Tempe, between Mt Olympos and Mt Ossa, and finally into the northern Aegean. There was a legend that Tempe had been cut through the mountains by Poseidon, to allow the river to flow through (see intro. to Ode 14).

sweet-smelling As Maehler points out (vol. 2, p. 306, following Lobel) Bacch. several times enhances his description of rivers with adjectives referring to flowers: 'on the flowered banks of Hebros' (16.5); 'amid the roses on Lycormas' bank' (16.34); 'the flowery Nile' (19.39-40). The usage here represents a bold transference of the image of fragrance from the flowers which grow along the river-bank to the river itself. The same word (*euodes*) is used by Simonides to describe 'the sweet-smelling water of the Muses' spring' (*PMG* 577b).

6 the valleys The word (*guala*) hardly seems appropriate to the open plains of Thessaly. Aischylos uses similar language (*Supp.* 546f., probably after 470 BC) in describing the wanderings of poor maddened Io: 'through lands of Asia fast she went, and across Phrygia grazing sheep ... and Lydian vales (*guala*)' (Bernadete's translation), and expressions of this kind seem to have become something of a poetic cliché.

sheep-rearing At 11.94 this adjective (*melotrophos*) is used in reference to the mountain pastures of Arcadia.

7 Kirrha The coastal town on the plain below Delphi, where the equestrian events were held. But the name is often used to refer generally to Delphi itself and its Pythian Games (cf. 4.16 and the note there; also 11.19) so that this reference need not be taken to support the view that Ode 14B celebrates an equestrian victory (see intro., above).

fertile Used also of Nemea (9.5); perhaps a conventional honorific, rather than a specific description.

8 Aristoteles also Presumably others of his family had competed at Delphi before Aristoteles himself.

10 a grace Here the word (*charis*) seems to mean that Aristoteles' victories have brought glory and renown to Larisa; elsewhere it refers to the victory itself (9.97), or to the poet's song which celebrates that victory (3.98 and 14.19).

horse-mastering The fertile plains of Thessaly were especially suited to horse breeding, and the word is best regarded as a general honorific; cf. the similar words used at 11.81 (of Argos) and 11.115 (of Metapontion). It could, but need not, be taken to support the view that the ode celebrates an equestrian victory. The word itself (*anaxippos*) is one of six adjectives in Bacch. compounded with *anax-*; all but one of these occur only in Bacchylides and were probably all coined by him (cf. note on 6.10).

Index

Hieron of Syracuse, 1, 16, 17, 81, Odes
    3, 4, 5 comm. *passim*, 196
Himera, 88, 95, 97, 98, 126
Hippias (of Elis), 19
hippios-race, 9, 12, 171
Hippodameia, 7, 139
Hippolochos, 6
Homer, vii, 2, 4, 6, 7, 74, 75, 78, 79,
    81, 96, 100, 111, 112, 116, 117,
    127, 128, 130, 132, 133, 137, 138,
    158, 177, 183, 192, 208, 209, 221
  Homeric narrative style, 120, 201
Homeric Hymn
  to Apollo (= Hom. Hymn 3), 10, 81,
    103, 123, 130, 149, 180, 181
  to Demeter (=Hom. Hymn 2), 94-5,
    123-4, 129, 187
homosexuality, 173
Hyperboreans, 103, 151, 161

Ibycos, 15
inclusive counting, 80, 159, 182, 191
Ino, 12
Isthmus (of Corinth), 9, 12, 15, 19, 69,
    75, 171
Italy, 175-6

Jaynes, J., 137, 221f.
Jebb, R.C., 21, 71, 72, 80, 84, 85, 86,
    87, 90, 100, 103, 104, 106, 117,
    121, 124, 128, 132, 133, 142, 146,
    150, 180, 184, 199

Kalliope, *see* Muses
Kalypso, 111
Kastalia, 99
Kenyon, F.G., 21
Kirk, G.S., 212
Kirrha, 113, 181, 182, 227
kithara, 4, 10, 13
Klio, *see* Muses
Knossos, 4, 6, 70, 78
Kore (= Persephone), 93, 94, 95, 123,
    129
Koressia (Ceos), 77, 78, 80
Kouretes, 116, 134, 135
Krisa, 9
Kronos, 81

Lachon of Ceos, 1, 2, 3
Laomedon, 162, 211

Larisa (Thessaly), 225, 226
Leaf, W., 79, 164
Lee, H.M., 19
Lefkowitz, M., 83, 142
Leto, 101, 135, 156, 180, 181, 218
Lorimer, H.L., 192, 208
Lousoi (Arcadia), Ode 11 comm.
    passim
Loxias, *see* Apollo
love-songs, 174
Lucian, 20
Lucretius, vii

Maehler, H., vii, 21, 77, 78, 87, 95, 97,
    100, 106, 108, 111, 112, 121, 123,
    124, 126, 134, 146, 150, 160, 169,
    170, 174, 180, 192, 194, 195, 199.
    201, 209, 216, 225, 226
Maenads, 187, 191, 207
mares, 95, 111
Meleager, 101, Ode 5 comm. *passim*,
    201
Melikertes, 12
Memnon, 162
Menandros, 20, 215, 216, 217
Menelaos, 103
Metapontion, 16, Ode 11 comm. *passim*
Miller, S., 8, 19, 20
Minoans, 4, 6
  Minoan dress, 78, 79
Minos, 6, Ode 1 comm. *passim*
Minotaur, 6
Moira (pl. Moirai = the Fates), 104,
    119, 134, 135, 136, 220, 221
Muses, 2, 16, 73, 74, 75, 78, 84, 87, 91,
    92, 94, 104, 107, 112, 122, 123,
    147, 156, 166, 169, 173, 192, 195,
    203, 217
  Kalliope, 94, 138
  Klio, 94, 107, 123, 143, 179, 195,
    201, 203, 218
  Urania, 112, 123, 141, 143, 195
Mycenae, 75, 163, 188, 190
Myceneans, 4, 6
Myson (vase-painter), 93, 102

name-cap, 106, 138, 147, 160
Nemea, 1, 7, 9, 13, 15, 154, 157, 204
Nemesis, 145
Nereus, 75, 209, 210
Nestor, 7, 135, 193

Theocritos, 204
Theognis, 137, 219, 220, 221, 222
Theseus, 6, 78, 102, 210
Thetis, 100, 200, 209
tholos tombs, 100
Thucydides, 9, 75, 189
Tiryns, 76, 116, 163, Ode 11 comm.
    passim
trainers, 20, 198, 215, 216, 217
Troy, 76, 90, 130, 162, 164, 178

Underworld, 79, 82, 116, 130, 131

Vergil, 101, 131, 219
Vermeule, E., 78, 79, 163
victor-lists, 69-70, 87, 89, 114, 140,
    142, 144, 148

Webster, T.B.L., 154
West, M.L., 75, 88
willingness-motif, 112, 123, 140, 157
witnessing-motif, 127, 140, 150, 182,
    207

Xenophon, 126

Young, D.C., 72,

Zeus, 1, 8, 13, 19, Odes 1, 3 comm.
    passim, 112, 116, 124, 130, 131,
    179, 204, 211, 215
Zuntz, G., 95